D1522121

Refocusing Chaplin

A Screen Icon through Critical Lenses

Edited by Lawrence Howe,
James E. Caron, and Benjamin Click

THE SCARECROW PRESS, INC.
Lanham • Toronto • Plymouth, UK
2013

Published by Scarecrow Press, Inc.
A wholly owned subsidiary of The Rowman & Littlefield Publishing Group, Inc.
4501 Forbes Boulevard, Suite 200, Lanham, Maryland 20706
www.rowman.com

10 Thornbury Road, Plymouth PL6 7PP, United Kingdom

British Library Cataloguing in Publication Information Available

Library of Congress Cataloging-in-Publication Data

Refocusing Chaplin : a screen icon through critical lenses / edited by Lawrence Howe, James E.
Caron, and Benjamin Click.
pages cm
Includes bibliographical references and index.
ISBN 978-0-8108-9225-5 (cloth : alk. paper) — ISBN 978-0-8108-9226-2 (ebook)
1. Chaplin, Charlie, 1889–1977—Criticism and interpretation. I. Howe, Lawrence, 1952–, editor of
compilation. II. Caron, James Edward, 1952–, editor of compilation. III. Click, Benjamin, 1958–,
editor of compilation.
PN2287.C5R46 2013
791.4302'8092—dc23
2013018734

♾ ™ The paper used in this publication meets the minimum requirements of American
National Standard for Information Sciences Permanence of Paper for Printed Library
Materials, ANSI/NISO Z39.48-1992.

Printed in the United States of America

Contents

Preface

Why Refocus Chaplin?

Charlie Chaplin holds a rather remarkable place in film history. Widely recognized in his persona of the Tramp, Chaplin's image has entered popular culture through numerous parodies and impersonations, as well as advertising. Within the industry, he transcended the role of actor to become screenwriter, director, composer, producer, and finally studio head. A cinematic life this capacious has led to an outpouring of biographical study in both professional and personal terms. As with another iconic American artist, Mark Twain, the biographical projects will certainly continue to add to our appreciation of the relationship between the artist and the man and between his art and the culture. This collection of essays both assumes axiomatically the value of the biographical treatments that have helped to delineate and distinguish the myth and the man called Charlie Chaplin and embraces a critical opportunity that the concentration of life-writing has laid open to the contributors.

Much has changed in the last half-century of academic criticism. Film studies, in particular, has adapted critical strategies of modernism and postmodernism to cinematic texts or advanced interpretive theories of its own, all of which have provided provocative angles of inquiry and new depths of understanding. Indeed, many of the notable intellectuals in this evolving field—such as Theodor Adorno, Alfred Bazin, Walter Benjamin, Gilles Deleuze, Laura Mulvey, and Slavoj Žižek, among others—make mention of Chaplin in some regard; however, all too frequently theorists reference this diminutive giant of cinema only incidentally to exemplify a specific conceptual nuance. The collaborators in this volume take these tangential references as a cue to systematically apply a wide range of theoretical perspectives in their interpretations of Chaplin's persona and films. The collection approximates a kind of laboratory experiment in which the richness of Chaplin's work, on the one hand, and the virtues and vicissitudes of interpretive theory, on the other hand, can be tested, recalibrated, and further extended. In other words, by selecting particular phases of Chaplin's career or recurrent themes expressed throughout his films in varying degrees and applying different interpretive strategies to the subject, we treat Chaplin as both a case study and a test case. Reflecting on Chaplin's career and films through various critical lenses—phenomenology, Marxism, feminism, gender studies, deconstruction, psychoanalytic criticism, new historicism, performance studies, cultural criticism, rhetoric, as well as formal analyses of the graphic image and the intrinsic tensions between cinema's visual and sound imagery—the collaborating critics have developed sustained, theoretically informed interpretations of Chaplin's films and their cultural contexts. The results achieve two complementary objectives: (1) to highlight the understated, and often overlooked, complexity of Chaplin's filmmaking, and (2) to provide insight into both the extensive range and the limits of the critical leverage of a broad array of interpretive theories.

Complementing this range of intellectual inquiry is the wide reach of films discussed. Although *The Circus* (1928), *Modern Times* (1936), *The Great Dictator* (1940), and *Limelight* (1952) provide focal points for multiple analyses, *The Gold Rush* (1925), *City Lights* (1931), and *Monsieur Verdoux* (1947) have considerable presence in the critical conclusions. Shorter films, such as *A Burlesque on Carmen* (1915), "One A.M." (1916), "The Pawnshop" (1916), "The Rink" (1916), "Behind the Screen" (1916), and *A Dog's Life* (1918) also receive scrutiny. Moreover, some essays cite contemporary films for historical comparison or films by Chaplin's contemporaries—Buster Keaton and Laurel and Hardy—for contrast. Finally, one essay provides a unique focus by analyzing photos and magazine illustrations of Chaplin in the two travel narratives produced as companions to his promotional world tours.

These varied approaches and this range of materials have produced not only a comprehensive assessment of Chaplin but also a striking frequency of correspondences between different approaches as well as the anticipated differences in conclusions. From this interesting mix of critical collisions and concurrences, we have deliberately encouraged ourselves to address each other's positions when the opportunity arises. Our wider goal, then, has been not simply to assemble an interesting array of discrete readings of the subject but rather to foster a stimulating conversation that embodies the best inclinations of intellectual exchange.

HOW TO REFOCUS CHAPLIN

The collection presents that conversation by loosely following the chronology of Chaplin's films, but chronology is not the overriding organizational principle. In fact, several essays in the collection address a critical issue at a particular point in Chaplin's career and follow that issue's development over several films. Conversely, some essays focus mainly on one film—such as the middle three essays on *Modern Times*. Rather, the collection's organizing principle aligns with the artistic and critical development of the artist and his work. The introductory essay maps a trajectory of Chaplin's significance, followed by three essays that concentrate on an emerging cinematic giant who, by the release of *City Lights*, realized, intuitively and perhaps consciously, the artistic and commercial power of his bodily intelligence; the social, cultural, and visual significance of his female leads; and his own iconic image. The next three essays explore the richness of *Modern Times*, examining its complexity in terms of gender, technological progress, and the capitalist/worker binary. The final four essays cohere by interpreting various aspects of Chaplin the artist consciously reflecting on his mimetic presence in and influence on his art, a reflection particularly influenced by the advent of the talking picture. While the collection's unfolding chronology makes a statement about Chaplin's development, the essays need not be read in order. Each stands as its own argument, and the reader may enter the conversation at any point.

In slightly more detail, the collection unfolds as follows. Charles Maland's foreword on the "Enduring Appeal of Chaplin and Charlie" initiates our conversation. He provides important critical context for Chaplin's place as an auteur and elaborates four reasons that contribute to Chaplin's enduring influence on screen, in the film industry, and in popular culture generally, which stakes out a context for the subsequent critical consideration. James E. Caron's "Chaplin's 'Charlie' as Merleau-Ponty's Phenomenological Everyman, or, How Bodily Intelligence Manifests the Personae, Styles, and Fable of Slapstick," offers an explanation for the power of Chaplin's slapstick talent. Using the concept of bodily intelligence, derived from Maurice Merleau-Ponty's phenomenological analysis of the human body as a ground zero of intention and meaning, Caron conceptualizes the unruly nature of slapstick's comic laughter. Slapstick's comic staging of bodily intelligence makes visible that deep-seated unruliness, not only because the slapstick clown's comic appeal has its foundation in being a symbol of disorder, but also because slapstick as a mode of comic presentation plays with and thus disrupts elemental patterns of human behavior. Caron's analysis creates a taxonomy of three personae that Chaplin manifests in his presentation of the slapstick clown "Charlie": clumsy fool, eironic trickster, and comic acrobat. Teasing out this set of personae from the knockabout action of slapstick films offers a tool for analyzing specific slapstick gags as well as particular scenes. The slapstick actor comically exposes the performance dimension of every-day actions by artistically misperforming them. Slapstick is therefore struc-tured with it own peculiar paradox, for the spectacle of the clown's artistic misperformance results from careful preparation that requires superior bodily intelligence yet hides that necessity.

Moving away from the kinesis of slapstick, Lisa Stein Haven presents an unorthodox method of inquiry in "Chaplin and the Static Image: A Barthe-sian Analysis of the Visual in *My Trip Abroad* and 'A Comedian Sees the World.'" Eschewing the movement that made Chaplin such an iconic figure, Haven examines the photographs and drawings that accompanied the texts of Chaplin's two travel narratives. These texts were a kind of supplement ema-nating from two "homecoming tours" (September to October 1921 and Janu-ary 1931 to June 1932) and were published largely to promote Chaplin's recently released films—*The Kid* (1921) and *City Lights*, respectively. They were meant to fuse Chaplin's two roles, public celebrity and screen persona, into one entity in terms of personality and comportment. Haven explains how that fusion happens, using Roland Barthes's tripartite levels of meaning for the photographic image (linguistic, denotative, and connotative), with her main focus on the denotative and connotative. Chaplin's use of photographs aligns well with the travel narratives' verbal texts to achieve a marketing strategy that would conflate his public persona with his better known and more beloved screen persona. Haven's analysis demonstrates the significant role that still images—photographs and caricature illustrations—play in the narratives' overall promotional agenda, clarifying the relationship between Chaplin's cinematic and static images.

Returning to the silver screen with "A Heart of Gold: Charlie and the Dance Hall Girls," Cynthia J. Miller pairs Chaplin's Tramp figure with allur-ing females to argue that their contrasting glamour gives the Tramp an unan-ticipated beauty and grace. In effect, his retiring everyday demeanor, which always signifies the gentleman even as it implies working-class values, gar-ners some of the magic of their accentuated femininity. For Miller, dance hall girls are significant cultural archetypes that combine gender and spectacle in ways particularly well suited to Chaplin's cinematic characters and bitter-sweet comedy. Miller contextualizes her analyses with historical information about real women working in dance halls, saloons, variety performances, and brothels—work that puts them into morally ambiguous situations emphasiz-ing sexuality. Dance halls are sites where gender constructions are contested, liminal spaces where contradiction happens. As figures in a transgressive spectacle, dance hall girls challenge the stereotype of female passivity, dis-playing an agency that has often gone unrecognized in studies of Chaplin's work; they are "realized visions of a master of theatricality, carefully molded, modulated, and choreographed to highlight the poignancy and comic grace of Chaplin's signature characters" (55).

Miller's feminist analysis finds its complement in Lawrence Howe's "American Masculinity and the Gendered Humor of Chaplin's Little Tramp." This essay, one of three that concentrate on *Modern Times*, frames Chaplin's most notable film through its representation of the Tramp's troubled masculinity. Howe begins by noting that the Tramp's failure to exhibit manliness is a trademark of his misfit status. However, he argues that within the context of the Great Depression, the Tramp's serial inadequacy as a worker is not simply Chaplinesque idiosyncrasy but a comment on the effects of the Depression on American manhood, traditionally defined through the role of the breadwinner. Synthesizing historical scholarship in masculinity studies and Judith Butler's theory of gender performance, Howe interprets the Tramp's failures in the factory and success in the prison as gauges of his uncertainty in performing a socially appropriate masculine role. Yet the Tramp's potential to adopt conventional manhood turns once he meets the gamin, comically foregrounding the meaning of their struggle to perform heteronormative roles. In the climactic cabaret scene, the Tramp finally lands in an arena where his fluid movements between gendered performances are appreciated. Howe shows that the Tramp's pantomime of a seduction story, in which he enacts both stereotypical masculine and feminine roles, enables him to overcome his troubled masculinity.

Following another historical line of inquiry, A. Bowdoin Van Riper's "In the Shadow of Machines: *Modern Times* and the Iconography of Technology" examines Chaplin's iconic film within a broad social matrix of conflicting images of machines. On one hand, technology represented unforeseen power to transform the world through efficient production, as attested by a range of cultural expressions that celebrated technological advancement. "The visual language of the factory scenes," Van Riper writes, "draws on ideas about the relationship between humans and their machines that pervaded the culture of the interwar United States, manifest in the memoirs of Henry Ford, the photography of Lewis Hine, the industrial exhibits of world's fairs, and the latest newsreel footage from Hoover Dam" and "dramatizes, with uncanny precision, both the hopes and the fears that Depression-era Americans projected onto the machines around them" (83). On the other hand, industrial technology was viewed as a dehumanizing threat poised to subjugate human action in service to its power. In close readings of the film's factory scenes, Van Riper dedicates his analysis to the ways in which these countervailing perspectives on the technological changes of the day coexist within the mise-en-scène and the narrative rhetoric of the plot. Thus, in demonstrating how *Modern Times* exhibits both attitudes about technology, he argues that the film's contemporaneous audience would have understood the film's conflation of marvel and critique. His essay, then, seeks to repair the critical tendency to elevate only one of these intertwined rhetorical strands. By recovering the context documented in a wide range of sources and showing Chaplin's complex treatment of the issues, Van Riper concludes that what strikes twenty-first-century viewers as a contradiction was for a twentieth-century audience an acceptance of a dissonant paradigm.

The third in the triptych of essays on *Modern Times*, Randall Gann's "Deconstruction and the Tramp: Marxism, Capitalism, and the Trace," outlines Fordism and Taylorism to provide a historical context for what he shows is a Marxist critique of industrial capitalism foregrounded in the film's factory scenes. However, as Gann's analysis demonstrates further, the capital/labor binary central to Marxism cannot withstand the disruptions of the Tramp's subversive humor. The resulting interpretation details how Chaplin's film deconstructs the class critique he ostensibly set out to offer. Drawing on Derrida's disruptive notion of *différance*, bolstered by Michael Ryan's considerations of the Other and Jameson's application of Lacan's definition of schizophrenia, Gann interprets the Tramp's misfit status as a third category that unsettles the Marxist opposition between capital and labor. Just as Chaplin may have been ambivalent about the role of a political critique within his work as a comic entertainer, the terms and categories that Gann identifies operating within the film's representation of industrial capitalism lack the stability of a Marxist truth. What remains is the destabilizing and revealing force of laughter generated by the Tramp's resistance to both bourgeois convention and the Marxist alternative.

In various ways, the next four essays address Chaplin's increasing awareness of the consequences of the new medium, the "talkie," on his art, revealing his overlooked critical and aesthetic response to it. Rachel Joseph, in the first of these essays, "Chaplin's Presence," delivers a claim apropos to all four: "[Chaplin] offers the cinematic representation of the theatrical as space for the performer to play with the possibilities and limitations of a new medium" (131). Her essay applies Žižek's interpretation of Lacan's "traumatic Real" in order to investigate the relationship between Chaplin's theatrical presence reproduced on screen and the nature of performance. Examining *The Circus* and *Limelight*, she illustrates how presence, the traumatic Real, twists itself into the cinematic frame, asserting itself through performance. Joseph scrutinizes the chase scene and the magic act scene in *The Circus* to exemplify the struggle between theatrical presence and cinematic reproduction, which she claims is "staged upon the character of the Tramp" (119). While her initial examination highlights the inherent binaries that exist between the media of theater and cinema, revealing presence in Chaplin's performance, Joseph recognizes the complexity, perhaps even the impossibility, of cinema producing the traumatic Real. And, in her analysis of Chaplin's late film *Limelight*, she unpacks the meaning of that impossibility, arguing that Chaplin's performance as Calvero interestingly not only "prepares us for his presence but also his eventual disappearance" (140).

Marco Grosoli's "The Paradox of the 'Dictator': Mimesis, the Logic of Paradox, and the Reinstatement of Catharsis in *The Great Dictator*, *Monsieur Verdoux*, and *Limelight*" recalls Joseph's commentary on the theatrical in the cinematic. Specifically, Grosoli views these late films as a coherent trilogy, each working to "recuperate catharsis in the classical sense" and "reinstate theatricality inside cinema" (140). He begins by applying Bazin's notion of myth to establish that quality of Chaplin the icon as inseparable from his creation, the Tramp. Then, he employs Lacoue-Labarthe's interpretation of Aristotelian second-order mimesis, the "hyberbologic," which extends beyond, yet relies on resemblance to show the paradox of Chaplin the myth (persona) and Chaplin the person, defined by Lacoue-Labarthe as a movement "by which the equivalence of contraries [here: the actual face and the fake mask] is established" (144). Grosoli shows myth, mimesis, and paradox at work in both *The Great Dictator* and *Monsieur Verdoux* but claims that *Limelight* may be considered "postmythical" because it is a film ostensibly deprived of the myth of the Tramp but nevertheless, and paradoxically, reliant on it. Finally, throughout the interpretations of this late trilogy, Grosoli explores the concept of catharsis, suggesting that "by pushing the inherent link between mimesis and paradox to the extreme, these three films assert the ethical value of a representational (theatrical, cathartic) distance" (140).

The third essay in the collection's closing quadrad, "Charles Chaplin Sings a Silent Requiem: Chaplin's Films from 1928–1952 as Cinematic Statement on the Transition from Silent Cinema to the Talkies," explores the possibilities of the new medium of talking cinema that Chaplin recognized (even in his silent films) and later employed. Aner Preminger examines Chaplin's innovations in the concepts of sound that, while overlooked, nonetheless contribute greatly to the cinematic language on sound. Preminger creates three new categories to clarify the dichotomy between silent film and the talking film: audio-silent films, talking-silent films, and filmed theater. Then, applying terms from Michel Chion's *The Voice in Cinema* and *Audio-Vision: Sound on Screen*, Preminger illustrates Chaplin's emerging sophistication in using sound as both a concept and a new technological tool of his cinematic art. Tracing this emerging sophistication over four films—*The Circus*, *City Lights*, *Modern Times*, and *The Great Dictator*—Preminger reveals that Chaplin, rather than simply using the new aspect of the medium, "subtly dealt with the meaning of sound," specifically wielding the "absence of sound" to achieve that meaning (161). Through his analysis, he concludes that if *The Circus* can function as the film that "sums up silent cinema," then *Limelight* "sums up the totality of Chaplin's cinematic oeuvre" (181).

In the collection's final essay, "*The Great Dictator* as Rhetorical Encomium: Chaplin's Sound Statement on Silence," Benjamin Click argues that

Chaplin offers his most fully realized statement on limitations and possibilities of the talkie. Specifically, Click shows that Chaplin's first synchronized talkie can, and ultimately must, be read as a form of epideictic rhetoric, a statement that praises the virtues of silence and censures the dangers of sound, specifically language. Click marks off the rhetorical structure of the film's narrative and analyzes how Chaplin juxtaposes scenes of silence and sound to make that statement. He concludes the essay with a close reading of the "Look Up, Hannah" speech that applies recent criticism on the rhetoric of silence and rhetorical listening. Ultimately, much like Howe, Gann, Joseph, and Grosoli propose in their essays, Click recognizes how Chaplin's genius prevents simple binary dichotomies, in this case between silence and sound. Instead, he reveals not only Chaplin's final appeal for the value of silence but also his statement on the potential uses of speech—speech that can potentially achieve social cohesion among humans and be a contingent effort of tactical bridge building as opposed to totalization.

What emerges from the range of critical approaches offered by the collection's authors is a set of core topics within Chaplin's work. Some of these topics will be obvious: for example, the fascination and fun that the figure of the Tramp elicits, the slapstick laughter that necessarily accompanies his comic failures, and the working-class values that the figure implies. But, more subtly, the collection suggests surprising ways in which these topics can be elaborated. Thus, the onscreen and offscreen personae of Chaplin are creatures of mythic production as well as publicity campaigns, while class and gender constructions suggest not just transgressive comic gestures but deconstructive slippage. Slapstick is not just about raucous laughter but can be linked to that transgression and slippage, implying a deep structure of liminality that organizes not just Chaplin's onscreen characters, but also his cinematic presentations of important cultural themes associated with technology as well as class and gender. Just as basic to Chaplin's artistry are issues concerned with theatricality and performance, for the analyses presented here reveal that Chaplin was not simply concerned with making audiences laugh; he also used his films to foreground and explore cinema as a formal expression.

Not only has Chaplin's appeal been persistent, as Maland points out, but so too was his exploration persistent, encompassing the birth of the medium and its transformation from silent films to talkies. His dedication to expanding the opportunities of film to entertain and enlighten has contributed significantly to cinema's emergence as the signature art form of the twentieth century. Thus, the arrival of this collection of theoretically grounded, critical assessments on the eve of the centennial of Chaplin's film career is, we trust, more than fortuitous timing. If the volume fulfills its potential, it will spur further theoretical examinations of Chaplin's films and those of other cinema innovators.

Acknowledgments

This project began as a panel for the American Humor Studies Association Conference in San Diego, December 2010. So we'd like to first thank the organizers of that conference for affording us the initial opportunity, and the attendees—Ann Ryan in particular—who encouraged us to seek other contributions that could amount to something like the volume we've assembled here.

We'd also like to thank whoever came up with the idea for the Internet. The vast geography between the three coeditors spans six time zones, most of the collaborators are scattered across the United States, another began his part of the project in Italy before relocating to England, and one other is based in Israel. The ease with which we were able to share submissions, drafts, and revisions halfway across the world is a luxury not to be taken for granted. We appreciate how difficult it would have been to tackle a project like this in an earlier era.

We offer our sincere thanks to Stephen Ryan and the staff at Scarecrow for their geniality and professionalism from our first proposal to the final production. But our deepest gratitude goes to the contributors themselves, none of whom had we met prior to sending out our call for abstracts (in fact, we still haven't met in person, but we feel a common bond with them nonetheless). Randall Gann, Marco Grosoli, Lisa Stein Haven, Rachel Joseph, Cynthia Miller, Aner Preminger, and Bow Van Riper were not only excited about the project from the start but also tireless in responding to our requests for multiple revisions; Chuck Maland very generously accepted our invitation to participate considerably later in the process and in the midst of a busy sabbatical. The strength of the project is due to their collegial collaboration and their commitment to developing their shares in it, which together amounts to a whole greater than the sum of its parts.

And although we've expressed our mutual gratitude to each other private-ly, it seems only fitting to acknowledge here the good-spirited cooperation we've enjoyed in coediting this project.

LH, JC, & BC

Introduction

The Enduring Appeal of Chaplin and Charlie

Charles Maland

In 1968—four years after Charlie Chaplin published his autobiography and four years before he returned to the United States to be feted at the Lincoln Center in New York and awarded his only Oscar for his "incalculable effect in making motion pictures the art form of the century"—Andrew Sarris paid tribute to Chaplin in his bible of auteurism, *The American Cinema: Directors and Directions, 1929–1968*. In the book Sarris ranked directors in eleven categories from the most prestigious downward, and Chaplin appeared in the top category—the "pantheon." There Sarris grouped Chaplin with such directorial demigods as Griffith, Keaton, Murnau, Lubitsch, Ford, Hawks, Hitchcock, and Welles. Alphabetical order assured that Chaplin would be the first director treated in the book, yet Sarris also made clear his admiration for the director (and the actor). "Viewed as a whole," he wrote, "Chaplin's career is a cinematic biography on the highest level of artistic expression" (41).

In his preface Sarris explained the need for a new history of film by noting that Lewis Jacobs's classic *The Rise of the American Film* was nearly thirty years old and didn't discuss any films after 1939. Chaplin, unsurprisingly, figured just as prominently in that book as he did in Sarris's. Jacobs treated American movies as industry, art, and social document, yet despite his aim to write a broad history of all those areas from the birth of movies to the start of World War II, Chaplin received special treatment. Jacobs wrote complete chapters on only three filmmakers—Edwin Porter, D. W. Griffith, and Chaplin. In chapter 13, "Charlie Chaplin: Individualist," he traced Chaplin and his work from his beginnings at Keystone through *Modern Times* and ended by alluding to his as-yet-unreleased project "The Dictator." Summing up Chaplin's achievements, Jacobs wrote that "Chaplin stands out as perhaps the one unforgettable actor of the screen, the symbol of human struggle against regimentation and, now more than ever, for the rights of the individual" (247). He closed his chapter by quoting Gilbert Seldes, who had himself been celebrating Chaplin's work since the end of World War I: Chaplin, wrote Seldes, was "destined by his genius to be the one universal man of modern times" (247).

If we go forward in time from Sarris rather than back, we see that even after theorists pointed out the limitations of Sarris's auteurism and announced—prematurely, as it turned out—the death of authors, fascination with Chaplin has continued. David Robinson's accomplished *Chaplin: His Life and Art* (1985), the first biography to benefit from an examination of Chaplin's extensive studio records, helped encourage explorations into Chaplin's films: to name just a few, critical studies and biographies of Chaplin by Milton (1996), Lynn (1997), Vance (2003), Weissman (2008), Kamin (2008), and Louvish (2009), have appeared since then—and these are only some of the books that look broadly at Chaplin's whole life, body of work, and/or cultural context. A significant number of more narrowly focused studies have also appeared. Furthermore, the British Film Institute has recently added volumes on *Modern Times* (2006) and *City Lights* (2007) in their Film Classics series, and another on *The Gold Rush* is on the way. Criterion Films—perhaps the top-ranked U.S. producer of DVDs and Blu-ray disks of enduring film titles—is working its way through Chaplin's body of work, having already produced sets of *The Gold Rush*, *Modern Times*, *The Great Dictator*, and *Monsieur Verdoux*. The Cineteca di Bologna over the past decade has digitized Chaplin's studio records—the same ones Robinson drew on in his biography—which has opened new avenues of inquiry about Chaplin's aesthetic and business practices. Another landmark is the 2010 release of *Chaplin at Keystone* by Flicker Films, a DVD set of thirty-four of the thirty-five films Chaplin made at Keystone, plus footage from *The Thief Catcher*, the recently rediscovered thirty-sixth film. These films, painstakingly restored through a joint project of the British Film Institute, Lobster Films in Paris, and the Cineteca di Bologna's preservation laboratory, L'Immagine Ritrovata, now make it possible, for the first time since the Keystone films were initially released, for viewers to get a good sense of Chaplin's achievement in his first year in the movie business. All indications are that interest in Chaplin remains high.

Why this enduring fascination with Chaplin, his films, and his Tramp character Charlie, a fascination also evident in the explorations of this book? I thought about this a lot in the 1980s while researching a book about the rise and fall of Chaplin's star image in the United States, and I've continued to reflect on it since then. Here let me suggest some of the reasons why Chaplin is such an intriguing figure to study and in doing so provide some context for the rich variety of essays that follow within these pages.

First, Chaplin lived a fascinating and turbulent life, and he was not afraid to give his version of it, not only in *My Autobiography* (1964), but also, more narrowly, in *My Trip Abroad* (1922), and "A Comedian Sees the World" (1933–1934). The portrait that emerges from these accounts and the many biographies of Chaplin is of a man who endured a difficult, even Dickensian, childhood; turned early to performing on stage, soon achieving some fame as a music-hall mime; hesitantly decided to work in the movies, where he quickly became a star, a director, and eventually a major force in the film industry; successfully made the transition from silent films to the sound era; and eventually, for various reasons, lost the favor of his audience, saw his stardom crash, and ended up an exile from the country where his fame was initially achieved. This roller coaster of a life and the relationship between that life and the movies that appeared amidst it—some of which is captured in Richard Attenborough's 1992 biopic *Chaplin*—draw many to the man and the filmmaker.

Second, Chaplin was one of the first genuine celebrities in a world that has since become a culture of celebrity. Hollywood had begun to feature movie performers by name only a year or two before Chaplin arrived at Keystone in late 1913. Chaplin was a huge beneficiary of that move, becoming one of the first and eventually one of the most long-standing stars in American film history. His rapidly ascending salaries provide some indication of how his popularity exploded. Starting at Keystone at a salary of $150 a week, Chaplin jumped to Essanay for $1,250 a week: the fourteen films he made at Essanay in 1915 coincided with an epidemic of what Charles McGuirk called "Chaplinitis" in the United States (87). His salary then ballooned to $10,000 a week—plus a signing bonus of $150,000—when he signed with Mutual, for whom he made twelve films from 1916 to 1917. To top it off, in early 1918 he signed with First National Exhibitors Circuit to make eight short films for $1 million. Significantly, such was the popularity of the films that even with these rising salaries, his employers also made money. By the time Chaplin joined First National, almost every moviegoer could identify his Tramp character, and an increasing number of people knew something about Chaplin the person as well. And Chaplin's celebrity status only grew after his trips around the world in 1921 and 1931 to 1932: people around the globe, including famous artists and powerful politicians, jockeyed to get a chance to meet and rub shoulders with the world-famous filmmaker. It's true that his celebrity status took significant hits in some quarters in the 1940s and 1950s, after the filmmaker began to work more overt social material into movies like *Modern Times* and *The Great Dictator* (and to comment more willingly on current social and political topics, as he did during the

Depression and World War II), but even those shifts in his status as star and celebrity are fruitful topics of discussion.

A third reason Chaplin invites our attention is that he was shrewd enough to work himself into a position of unusual creative independence in the prohibitively expensive industry/art of filmmaking. Much of the money he made as a director/actor in the 1910s went into a wise investment: in 1917 he bought four acres of land in Hollywood, bordered by Sunset Boulevard on the north, La Brea Avenue on the west, and De Longpre Avenue on the south, and built his own studio on the site. There he made all his American films after the studio's completion in 1918. Chaplin solidified that independence even more when in 1919 he became, with D. W. Griffith, Mary Pickford, and Douglas Fairbanks, a founding member of United Artists, a company established to distribute the films that these four filmmakers produced independently. Thus Chaplin gained control of the rights of all his films from the First National period on, and all his films from *A Woman of Paris* through *Limelight* were released through United Artists. Although large-scale filmmaking is inevitably a collaborative enterprise, Chaplin, perhaps more than any other filmmaker in American film history, was able to enjoy a decades-long period of creative independence, not only as a performer, director, and writer, but also as a studio owner and—after sound came in—a collaborative composer. This independence and creative versatility make his shift to feature films, his foray into what he called a "drama of fate" in *A Woman of Paris*, his gradual and aesthetically self-aware shift to sound films, his more direct engagement with social and political concerns in *Modern Times*, *The Great Dictator*, and *Monsieur Verdoux*, and the submerged autobiography of *Limelight* and *A King in New York* even more inviting to explore and understand.

A fourth reason Chaplin has appealed to so many for such a long period is because of his most brilliant creation, the Tramp character. It's striking that Chaplin came up with the prototype of that character so shortly after he arrived at Keystone, and it's fortunate that Mack Sennett, despite his creative differences with the comedian, had enough foresight to allow Chaplin to control that character by letting the performer direct and write his own films. In his 1964 autobiography Chaplin famously described the Tramp as "many-sided, a tramp, a gentleman, a poet, a dreamer, a lonely fellow, always hopeful of romance and adventure" (144). That underdog character has resonated with audiences and critics around the globe; there's an archetypal power in the Tramp's marginalized status yet resilient spirit, and it's intriguing to watch how that character evolves from Keystone through *Modern Times*, eventually morphing into the Jewish barber, the Bluebeard Henri Verdoux, the philosophical Calvero, and the harassed King Shahdov. By conceiving the stories, performing the role, directing himself, and even—after sound came in—composing music to shape the emotional tone of the world in which the Tramp and his successors lived, Chaplin created a powerful, evolving, mythically resonant world. Sarris captures some of that achievement when he writes that "for Chaplin, his other self on the screen has always been the supreme object of contemplation" (40).

Chaplin's appeal undoubtedly endures for other reasons as well, some very personal to individual viewers. But these four reasons, I hope, help to set the context for the fresh exploration of Chaplin and his work found in this volume, articles that are informed by the vitality and diversity of contemporary film theory while they grapple with the life and art of Charles Spencer Chaplin.

Chapter One

Chaplin's "Charlie" as Merleau-Ponty's Phenomenological Everyman

*Or How Bodily Intelligence Manifests the Personae,
Styles, and Fable of Slapstick*

James E. Caron

Comic laughter signals disorderly entertainment, and a slapstick style is the very engine of such raucous amusement. In his series of two-reelers made early in his career for Mutual Films, Charles Chaplin perhaps best displays his talent for elaborating slapstick style and thus for providing the spectator a nearly nonstop ride of giggles and guffaws. The focal points of investigation for this essay offer an explanation for the power of Chaplin's slapstick talent. The first focus has a pedagogical basis: to suggest a taxonomy of three personae Chaplin manifests in his presentation of the slapstick clown "Charlie": clumsy fool, eironic trickster, and comic acrobat. By teasing out this set of personae from the knockabout action of slapstick films, I provide a tool for analyzing specific slapstick gags as well as particular scenes and thus indicate the theoretical complexity of comic laughter that Chaplin elicits from his audiences. Second, by arguing for slapstick's relation to the idea of bodily intelligence, I provide a way to conceptualize the unruly nature of comic laughter. Slapstick's comic staging of bodily intelligence makes visible that deep-seated unruliness, not only because the slapstick clown's comic appeal has its foundation in being a symbol of disorder, but also because slapstick as a mode of comic presentation plays with and thus disrupts elemental patterns of human behavior, a disruption marked by comic laughter. Finally, analysis of slapstick and bodily intelligence furthers understanding of the mystery of comic laughter.[1]

The proposed linkage of slapstick and bodily intelligence adumbrates a wide-angle perspective. Charlie comically embodies Maurice Merleau-Ponty's phenomenology of perception as its everyman, moving through space in everyday situations and performing everyday tasks. Charlie, one might say, philosophizes materially as he moves and performs, his movements and performances uncovering the Comic. This process of discovery constitutes the laughter-inducing project of a slapstick clown. I propose to use, in an initial analysis, representative examples from two of Chaplin's Mutual films, "One A.M." (1916) and "The Pawnshop" (1916), to sort out the rapidly shifting personae that Chaplin presents to the audience as Charlie maneuvers comically through ordinary situations. Theoretically, any of the physical gags or scenes in these two specific films could be classified using these personae. In addition, such taxonomy has the potential to analyze, at the level of specific gags, Chaplin's early slapstick work in particular, including all the Mutual films, as well as the onscreen antics of other slapstick film stars. Although I consider the Mutual Films to be exemplary for presenting the heuristic potential of bodily intelligence, I also briefly consider Buster Keaton and the comic duo Laurel and Hardy, as well as comment on selected slapstick moments in three of Chaplin's feature-length films—*The Gold Rush* (1925), *The Circus* (1928), and *Modern Times* (1936)—to indicate the explanatory reach of the idea of bodily intelligence for understanding the appeal of slapstick.

Understanding the significance of the relationship between slapstick and bodily intelligence begins with the postulate that intelligent movement saturates an individual's world. Innumerable and purposeful motions comprise a person's day, fill it with actions signifying intention. Many of these actions are accomplished without specific or conscious conceptual apparatus, and thus occur in what Maurice Merleau-Ponty might call a pre-reflective domain of consciousness.[2] Slapstick derives its essential comic quality by disrupting the world of intelligent movement, by apparently calling into question the existence of this pre-reflective domain. Slapstick disruption of the pre-reflective domain exemplifies Umberto Eco's idea of "the Comic and the Rule": the intelligence of the lived body represents a foundational rule for human behavior, and so the slapstick clown's cinematic disruptions have an enormous comic potential in their dramatizations of the incongruity of an individual who apparently cannot behave in conformity to that primary rule.[3]

Although theatrical pratfalls on a vaudeville stage or the silly antics of circus clowns have a similar comic potential, the movie camera early in the twentieth century was strikingly efficient in representing such disruption, for the movie camera as a new technology immediately made people more intensely aware of the human body. In addition, this awareness centered on "the kinesthetic aspects of the human form," which provided excitement for viewers.[4] The cinema necessarily highlighted the possibilities of the body as a moving form, and when spectators had exhausted their astonishment at seeing a human body in filmed motion, they were ready to be entertained. Inevitably, it would seem, much of that entertainment in early films centered on the physical quality of the human body and thus encouraged a slapstick style of presentation.

In addition, the emotional distance of the new technology, that is, the absence of any actual performing bodies, argues for an increased likelihood of comic laughter, helping to ensure that the disruptions of normalcy are not distressing or threatening to an audience. The filmed pratfall necessarily distances the spectator from the real pain possible in an actual stumble and fall. The inherent distancing advantage that film has over live theater seems ideally suited to fulfill Aristotle's dictum that a comic representation must always be without pain or distress, the implication being that the comic representation otherwise risks raising fear and pity rather than comic laughter in the audience.[5] Aristotle's distinction as well as the relative lack of distance between spectator and live performer are neatly exemplified in chapter 22 of *Adventures of Huckleberry Finn*, when Huck believes that a circus performer pretending to be a drunken audience member cannot control the horse he is riding and is in danger of falling and hurting himself. Huck cannot laugh because he fears for the clown and pities his situation. Huck has naively and all too easily collapsed the distinction between the character being performed and the performer, in part because the physical man is in front of him and his body constantly presents the danger of an actual fall.

As Huck watches, the circus clown's body moves through space, performing. In Merleau-Ponty's phenomenological account of consciousness, space has two qualities, one geometric and the second "practical." Practical space is understood as a site that shows someone relating to things, a site that harbors potential "topics" for meaningful deeds.[6] In this most practical sense, one inhabits space and renders it meaningful by one's actions. Pre-reflective or "bodily intelligence" characterizes the lived body as it displays purpose rather than the mindlessness of machinery, demarcates the body moving through and orienting within space. Bodily intelligence thus exhibits "motor intentionality," a human being performing ordinary tasks (such as picking up a pencil) and solving simple problems (such as untying a knot).[7] In addition, even much more complicated tasks, such as driving a car or executing a maneuver in a sport, can fold into this pre-reflective domain: routine can become rote memory or "muscle memory." Bodily intelligence exists a priori and therefore enables the physical gags that define slapstick. The slapstick film's audience intuitively understands normal bodily intelligence beforehand in commonsense fashion, and Chaplin disrupts that understanding with his gags as he manifests the three comic personae of Charlie.

One's personal space in a home or office, for example, exhibits basic attitudes and, along with one's body moving through space, suggests being in the world at a fundamental level. The arrangement of objects reflects one's habits and projects. Thus the basic joke in "One A.M." centers on the way that Charlie acts estranged from his own house and possessions. He is not merely clumsy and so comic because drunk; he also appears comically absentminded in a Bergsonian sense, lost in his own place and at odds with the physical objects he encounters in it, even though those objects are his possessions and their arrangement is ostensibly his.[8] The concept "bodily intelligence" captures the interplay between an individual consciousness and the objects in a perceptual field. Experience within a perceptual field thus has an embodied character.[9] Being has meaning through the temporality of the body within a pre-reflective domain.[10] Because slapstick at its core presents a disarrangement of this most basic meaning for humans, it can appeal to people of all cultures.[11]

For Merleau-Ponty, there is only a relational self. Each person's body represents his or her own ground zero of intention and meaning, through which he or she achieves an orientation to the surrounding environment. A silent conversation with things exists, what Richard Shusterman calls the body as silent cogito.[12] This fundamental reciprocity with the world and others is exemplified by touching one's own body, an action in which one experiences the sensation of touching and being touched simultaneously. One's image in a mirror works similarly: one sees and has the sensation of being seen simultaneously. Another Mutual film, "The Floorwalker" (1916), has a scene in which Charlie and a look-alike store manager act as though they are looking in a mirror. Their mutual mimicking of the other can be read as a comic presentation that momentarily makes visible the irreducible fact of a relational self.[13]

Inadequate bodily intelligence manifests clumsiness. Extraordinary bodily intelligence manifests grace, agility, and strength. The trick of the slapstick clown that so delights an audience is a display of both sides, often in quick succession—in effect, an oscillation of opposed ability that creates appropriate comic personae, clumsy fool and comic acrobat. Most *lazzi* or comic routines with physical objects manifest these two opposed personae. However, the eironic trickster (who demonstrates a clever yet foolish playfulness) completes my proposed roster. The eironic trickster delights the audience because it marks the pivot from performing bodily intelligence inadequately to performing bodily intelligence extraordinarily. With this persona, the slapstick clown expresses an unexpected cleverness of gesture within the situation. The suddenness of that gesture is such that the two opposing sides of underperforming and overperforming bodily intelligence seem fused. However, that apparent conceptual fusion is better understood as liminal, thus defining a boundary. The eironic trickster, then, embodies the boundary between the clumsy fool and the comic acrobat. Theoretically, all *lazzi* could be understood as dynamically creating these three slapstick personae.[14]

The default persona for the slapstick clown is the clumsy fool, a role whose inadequate bodily intelligence demands pratfalls and mistakes. This role also most clearly manifests Henri Bergson's idea of comic absentmindedness. To the extent that a character seems to be without the mindfulness of bodily intelligence, he or she becomes comic in a manner that appears rigid and mechanistic. Actions deteriorate into mere motions. Objects around the character become impediments that thwart plans and balk progress. Intention disappears. Thus the spectator discerns the comic butt, a figure who creates the laughable situation (e.g., clumsy or absentminded) or makes it worse (e.g., stupid or drunk). This persona triggers comic laughter in an audience because people directly understand themselves as superior to the clown. When the slapstick clown manifests extraordinary bodily intelligence, he or she displays the grace and agility of the comic acrobat. The body's motions are thoroughly controlled and superbly directed toward a clear goal. The comic acrobat persona represents flashes of mastery over the material world as the body moves through space and interacts with objects. Audience laughter generated by this role emphasizes delight and wonder rather than superiority.

When the figure appears both clumsy and clever, when he pivots in unforeseen ways from clumsy to clever behavior, the slapstick clown reveals the eironic role of the clown as trickster. Actions fulfill plans and intentions fitfully. The eironic trickster clown represents the most complicated of the three persona: a figure doubly liminal, a clown within a roster of clowns, not only signifying the boundary between serious and nonserious domains, but also falling in between the clown as fool and the clown as acrobat, presenting neither constant entanglement with objects nor efficient mastery of them.

In his slapstick moments, Chaplin as Charlie (and by extension other filmed slapstick clowns, perhaps especially Buster Keaton) enacts the fable of the individual pitted against a world that seems malevolent when it is not just indifferent or hindering. His situation resembles that of a character in a naturalistic, Darwinian landscape but without the usual dire consequences.[15] As trickster or acrobat, the slapstick clown displays degrees of comically playful escapes from a world of objects that appears determined to reduce him or her completely to its own merely material order.

For the slapstick clown, a process of interaction represents being-in-the-world. The body of the slapstick clown manifests a fundamental temporality through its relationship to objects and location as well as to others. For example, the slide step Charlie exhibits when he shadowboxes outside the pawnshop becomes a diversionary dance step when a policeman shows up, but the dancing looks foolish when he moves inside the shop and continues it in front of the boss. The same physical gesture therefore changes meaning depending on a location and upon who and what is present in the perceptual field (i.e., the camera frame) with the clown. The clown's sliding movement is not a true step nor is it quite dancing. Rather, it exists between the distinction Paul Valery made: prose as walking and poetry as dancing.[16] The slide movement thus signifies a fundamental liminality and as such epitomizes the slapstick clown.[17]

Bodily intelligence as a heuristic for analyzing slapstick suggests a fundamental reason for Chaplin's enormous popularity both in the United States and abroad.[18] No language barrier impedes understanding at this most basic level of motor intentionality. Everyone everywhere apprehends the joke of individual-as-comic-fool, someone who seems to be less than a human being because he or she manifests not just a lack of fundamental skills to manipulate a given object or to solve a specific task, but someone who also demonstrates an impaired bodily intelligence and thus is in danger of being unable to remain literally upright, that is, to maintain the unique stance of *Homo sapiens sapiens*.

Examining a few representative examples in some detail will make these theoretical statements concrete. First, there is the clumsy lout or fool, what should be understood as the default persona for the slapstick clown and what one usually means when saying "comic butt," the figure Aristotle no doubt had in mind when he declared that a character is comic because of a lack. The comic butt or comic fool lacks bodily intelligence. In "One A.M.," Chaplin manifests this persona as a drunk. The overarching joke centers on his altered state having alienated him from his own house. Charlie's interaction with his stuffed animals provides some of the funniest moments in the first half of the film, but other features of the house also function as key obstacles to his intentions, for example, the rugs, the table when it spins, and the shower. The absurdly large clock pendulum hinders him by repeatedly knocking him down. The pull-out bed behaves with a special malevolence. In these moments, Chaplin also develops a theme of the recalcitrance of material objects; that is, Charlie appears comic, in part, because his reactions suggest not the clumsiness he exhibits but his feeling that inanimate objects are hostile.

An excellent example of the comic fool persona occurs early in the film when Charlie goes back outside immediately after finding his house key, even though he is already in the house. Moreover, he uses the window to exit, ensuring that he will again step into the fish bowl, as he did when he first used the window to enter the house. For Charlie, even walking upstairs is problematic in this film, with one of the cleverest *lazzi* involving the rugs on the stairs, a sequence that ends with him rolling himself up in the rug when he falls down the stairs for the last time. Perhaps the best example of the clumsy lout who makes the situation worse occurs when Charlie destroys his top hat by repeated and violent efforts to free it when it is pinned to the floor by the leg of the bed.

In "The Pawnshop," the comic butt or clumsy lout appears over and over: (mis)handling a ladder, stepping into a bucket of water, drying plates and his hands with the clothes wringer, making a bigger mess when attempting to sweep up a long string, crashing into a bass fiddle and destroying it. In an extended scene involving a customer trying to pawn a clock, Charlie destroys the clock as he examines it. An echoing scene follows when Charlie almost kills a fish by attempting to put acid into the fish bowl that the customer wants to pawn.

Theoretically, other slapstick films could also be analyzed with the three comic personae schema not only as a way to discern difference in the flow of slapstick gags, but also to discriminate slapstick styles. Buster Keaton brilliantly manifests all three personae, yet with different emphases. In the feature-length film *The Seven Chances* (1925), for example, Keaton as comic fool runs straight into a barbed wire fence and does not notice at first that the police squad surrounding him has disappeared when they see the mob of angry prospective brides coming after him. In the two-reeler "The Neighbors" (1920), Keaton shows us the comic butt when he has a pratfall on the stairs in his house, and during the wedding scene there is an extended *lazzo* with his outsized pants repeatedly falling down because his suspenders do not work properly. However, that *lazzo* also suggests how his character is often not so much clumsy or absentminded as unlucky or overwhelmed by circumstance. The same effect happens when the antagonist father of his next-door sweetheart hangs him from the clothesline by his shoes, and Keaton's body appears objectified as another laundered item of clothing. When his sweetheart's angry father transfers Keaton to his own backyard, still hanging upside down, his father accidently beats him instead of the rug he has hanging up because Keaton arrives at the precise moment and in the particular place on the clothesline to receive the blow.

Although silent film has an advantage over sound film as a comic form insofar as it suggests the possibility of a universal appeal, the triad of personae offers insight for slapstick sound film as well. For example, we might note how Laurel and Hardy's art as a slapstick duo completely leaves out extraordinary bodily intelligence in favor of dueling dumbness and petty one-up-manship. Laurel and Hardy with their *lazzi* emphatically display the comic butt, elaborated a priori because doubled with two foolish characters. In their award-winning short film, "The Music Box" (1932), for example, the *lazzi* with hats (repeatedly mixing them up) epitomizes their status as comic butts.

The main comic business of "The Music Box" can be described as an extended *lazzo* of the stairs and a heavy object: attempts to move a piano up a long set of stairs on a hill to deliver it to a customer's house fail repeatedly. When the postman shows them the road they should have used to bring the piano to the house, their endeavors are capped with the stupidity of taking the piano back down the stairs, though they finally had successfully reached the top. Other stupidities manifesting the comic fool persona include placing the piano on Ollie's back and mounting a block and tackle on a flimsy awning. Ollie and Stan continually demonstrate clumsiness by routinely destroying objects unintentionally.

Both of Chaplin's Mutual films examined here provide few but notable examples of the comic acrobat who manifests extraordinary bodily intelligence, the opposite of the comic butt or foolish clumsy lout. In "One A.M.," Charlie uses a rug to slide across the floor on two occasions, once to the door and later toward the stairs, appearing deliberate and almost graceful. After he climbs on the table and it begins to spin, just maintaining his balance on the spinning table for a moment suggests the comic acrobat. The best example in this film, however, is when Charlie climbs on the hat rack to reach the second floor, a maneuver he performs twice. Notable in "The Pawnshop" is Charlie's clever use of his feet. During a fight with his adversarial coworker, Charlie displays physical dexterity in the moments when he boxes with his feet, and he appears graceful when he employs his slide step and dance. That dancing returns for a moment at the very end of the film, when Charlie has vanquished the bad guy: it is almost a bow. However, the clearest instance of comic acrobat in "The Pawnshop" occurs when Charlie is outside the shop on a ladder. As he reaches to clean the three globes comprising the pawnshop's sign, he rocks the ladder and falls off, yet easily lands on his feet, as though deliberately dismounting.

Keaton as comic acrobat in "The Neighbors" repeatedly flashes into view: when he climbs the brick wall of the house to see his sweetheart, jumps over the fence dividing the two backyards to elude her father, and climbs telephone poles to escape policemen. A particularly dramatic example occurs when Keaton takes off his tie and uses it to slide down a telephone pole's supporting wire to the ground and away from trouble. Nevertheless, this display of physical mastery does him no good. The camera frame when he lands on the ground is at first empty of people except for him, implying a successful escape. However, the tracking shot as he walks away quickly reveals a waiting police van. The most spectacular example of the extraordinary bodily intelligence of the comic acrobat in this two-reeler, however, occurs when Keaton teams up with two other men to perform as acrobats would, stacked one on top of the other's shoulders. The three traverse back and forth between the two houses, retrieving luggage and then the sweetheart, and finally providing escape from her father. In *The Seven Chances*, the comic acrobat appears repeatedly during the long chase scene near the end, but most dramatically in the crane sequence, when Keaton holds on as a crane swings around a railroad yard and then dangles him over the sidewalk. Once he realizes that the crane has positioned him on the other side of the fence from his pursuers, Keaton releases his grip and easily drops unharmed to the ground, escaping them. Keaton's slapstick style more often emphasizes

Figure 1.1.   Charlie as comic acrobat in "One A.M." From the archives of Roy Export Company Establishment.

extraordinary bodily intelligence within a domain of prominently displayed objects, especially in his two-reelers.

Turning to Chaplin's comic trickster persona, the foolish-yet-clever or suddenly playful figure, we have only one clear moment in "One A.M.," when Charlie deliberately flips his top hat onto the stuffed ostrich's head, a gesture that suddenly seems to belie all of the clumsiness witnessed to that point. Above all, this film demonstrates the comic butt who not only has rendered himself impaired due to drinking, but who repeatedly makes situations worse with his clumsy choice of actions as he tries to execute simple tasks, such as lighting a cigarette or walking up the stairs. In "The Pawnshop," much more of the character Charlie fits the trickster clown category, a dominance signaled at the outset when Charlie, as he walks toward the entrance to the pawnshop, pulls himself over the curb. The gesture registers as comically clever even as it suggests that Charlie recognizes his basic clumsiness and worries that his feet will trip over the curb. The many fights with his coworker also mostly manifest this persona: though the first fight shows extraordinary competence by boxing with his feet, this gesture might also be glimpsed as tricky; the second encounter more obviously exhibits a foolish cleverness when he takes advantage of his coworker being stuck in the ladder; and the third fight shows Charlie initially thumping the coworker yet then switching to a feigned victimhood when he sees Edna coming, thus garnering her sympathy.

When Keaton shows us the eironic trickster in "The Neighbors," the trickiness of the persona uniformly fails. Whereas Charlie has success in his oddly playful moments, fooling Edna or besting his pawnshop rival, Keaton's tricky maneuvers provide only one moment's respite from his predicament before a new circumstance traps him. When he leaps out the window of his sweetheart's house to elude her father, using the clothesline that connects her house with his own, his momentum does not put him safely back home, but instead returns him to her house and into the clutches of her father. Later, Keaton may be able to distract and confuse a policeman with his face half-painted black and then elude him when he climbs a telephone pole, but a second officer grabs him as he descends. Moreover, though this new circumstance of the second officer provides the opportunity for Keaton to try his version of the clown's slide step—a kind of rocking motion created when he first almost hops toward the policeman and then hops back—an equivocal motion that turns into explicit dance moves, the effort does not result in escape, as it did for Charlie. Misdirection dominates "The Neighbors," both for the characters and the audience, as what appears within their perceptual fields and within the camera frame consistently proves otherwise than what the first glance indicates. Keaton achieves more of Charlie's success in *The Seven Chances* when he is stuck on a hillside between an avalanche of boulders and the mob of angry prospective brides, avoiding yet not avoiding the boulders, his dexterity vividly evident, but the sense of his power at the same time diminished by the wide-angle shot that renders his body small and vulnerable. These differences suggest that Keaton's films more obviously enact the slapstick fable of the individual pitted against a naturalistic world that always seems hindering if not malevolent.

That contrast with Keaton's slapstick style can also be discerned in the way that Charlie's play with certain objects cleverly misuses and so transforms them. In these instances, Charlie's quirky playfulness signals an unexpected and superior mindfulness we should recognize as imaginative. In "The Pawnshop," Edna's biscuits become weightlifting equipment to indicate how poorly they are made; the dough and a ladle become props for Charlie as a singing gondolier to indicate his intent to woo Edna. The wringer for drying clothes suddenly functions as a rolling pin for the pie dough. When Charlie examines and destroys a customer's clock, the manner of examination also imaginatively transforms it so that the clock becomes a fine watch (the telephone mouthpiece used as a jeweler's glass) or a human heart (tapping on the clock and listening as a doctor would tap on a patient's chest and listen to the heartbeat). The best example of this odd and sometimes destructive playfulness, which happens suddenly and just as suddenly disappears, occurs when Charlie attempts to sweep up a long string: his efforts cause the string to stretch across the floor rather than push it together in order to put it into a trash can. Once he realizes that he has extended rather than contained the disorder, Charlie suddenly lifts the broom and uses it as a balancing beam, pretending that the string is a tightrope that he is crossing.

This moment of Charlie's playing with disorder hints at a special quality of the slapstick clown, its potential status as a "lord of disorder."[19] An exemplary moment signifying this status occurs in "The Pawnshop" when Charlie uses the feather duster to clean up and instead creates a bigger mess. He not only misuses the feather duster by spreading dust around instead of containing it, but when he sticks the feather duster into a fan and does not notice that he is thereby destroying it, scattering bits of feather all over the backroom of the pawnshop, he reverses the function of the cleaning tool. With this gesture, Charlie becomes a lord of disorder, symbolizing an inversion and subversion of normalcy; that which is meant to clean instead spreads dirt, as anthropologist Mary Douglas would define it: the disorder of matter out of place.[20] In "The Music Box," Laurel and Hardy as clowns symbolic of disorder also demonstrate this ultimate moment of foolishness. Having destroyed much of the living room of their piano customer, they insert a music roll and stage a clean-up of their destruction that cleans up nothing. They dance to the music during multiple crossings of the room, but in doing so, each one continually deposits what he has picked up on his side of the room onto the floor in the other's part of the room, self-defeating behavior that echoes Charlie destroying the feather duster in "The Pawnshop."

This essay has thus far focused on Chaplin's two-reelers for Mutual Films in order to demonstrate how bodily intelligence might be used to analyze slapstick. Samples of slapstick moments from *The Gold Rush*, *The Circus*, and *Modern Times* suggest ways that Chaplin continued to use and develop the three slapstick personae in his more ambitious feature-length films.

Chaplin frames *The Gold Rush* with the default persona for the slapstick clown: the clumsy fool. The opening shots of Charlie as a lone prospector hiking through the snow immediately evoke this persona as a visual gag: his tramp outfit with cane and bowler hat and no overcoat seems ridiculously out of place. After the camera follows him hiking on a mountain trail, a medium shot shows Charlie pausing for a moment on a snow-covered hill to lean on his cane, with the predictable result of the cane disappearing into the snow and Charlie falling. At the very close of the film, when Charlie sails homeward as a millionaire, he falls down a gangway and then tumbles into a giant coil of rope that hides him completely. Significantly, just before this pratfall, he has changed out of his fancy clothes and back into his tramp outfit to pose for a rags-to-riches newspaper photo. Revealing more foolishness than those pratfall moments, however, is a close-up in the opening outdoor scenes of Charlie apparently consulting a map. When the camera zooms in, the paper is revealed as no map at all but features instead the cardinal points of a compass, hand-drawn. Charlie turns the paper in his hand, as though it were an actual compass and then places the paper back in his coat.

In *Modern Times*, Chaplin again readily presents Charlie as the clumsy fool. For example, when Charlie imagines a dream house for himself and the gamin (Paulette Goddard), the scene dissolves into a portrayal of the couple living in it. In the first moment Charlie appears on camera, he starts to walk across the living room but trips over a footstool. When Charlie and the gamin take possession of a shack for their actual house, he repeatedly looks clumsy, struck on the head multiple times by a swinging board, smashing a table when he sits on it, and falling out the back door into the water that borders the shack. Similar to the paper compass, this last instance provides an opportunity to underscore Charlie as fool. Falling into what turns out to be about a foot of water does not stop Charlie from subsequently diving into the water and trying to have a morning swim.

Chaplin's intentions in *Modern Times* for the slapstick clown as clumsy fool, however, center on Charlie's jobs. This focus starts with the famous initial factory scenes and continues when Charlie finds a job in a boatyard, when he is given another job assisting a mechanic who is bringing the machinery of an idle factory back to serviceable status, and when Charlie follows the gamin to the Red Moon Café and is hired as a singing waiter. In every instance, Charlie proves to be incompetent and disruptive, even destructive. He only lasts about five minutes on his first job after he is released from jail, working at a boatyard. When asked by his foreman to find a wedge resembling the one in his hand, Charlie uses a sledgehammer to retrieve a similar wedge, one that is holding up a half-built ship. Once Charlie knocks the wedge loose, the ship, released from its scaffolding, slides into the water and promptly sinks. After his nervous breakdown, Charlie is especially prone to being the clumsy fool when he works as an assistant to a mechanic. His assistance results in the mechanic being caught in the machinery, echoing the famous moment early in the movie when Charlie's body goes through the giant gears. Charlie compounds his foolish help when the lunch whistle blows. Rather than take a minute to operate the machine and release the mechanic, Charlie chooses not only to leave him in place during the lunch break but also to feed him, even though he is supine in his trapped position and his mouth is therefore oriented upward. The comic results again echo the film's early factory scenes, this time when Charlie is force-fed by a machine. Charlie's assistance to the mechanic retards the required work to restart the machines. His actions repeatedly destroy objects. Moreover, when he causes the tools meant to repair and maintain the machines to be destroyed by them or when the tools damage the machines, Charlie manifests the clown as a lord of disorder. His persistent hindrance of the mechanic inverts Charlie's job: the assistant becomes a comic saboteur.

The notable exception in *Modern Times* to Charlie being clumsy and foolish at work happens when he is a night watchman and he straps on roller skates. He immediately demonstrates his skill and grace as a skater. Then, as if to belie all his earlier clumsiness, he dramatically blindfolds himself to show off the acrobatic quality of his skill to the gamin. At the same time, however, Charlie fails to see the danger posed by the nearby construction of stairs, with the floor presenting a large hole without a barrier, and he repeatedly skates near the edge. Ultimately, his foolish aspect prevails in this job, too, and he is fired. Chaplin thus organizes the night watchman sequence as a whole by shifting slapstick personae dramatically, both in quick succession and in much wider intervals.

The length of feature films provides Chaplin with such opportunities to organize extended sequences by shuffling slapstick personae. All three personae can be seen in the opening factory scenes in *Modern Times*, though Chaplin structures the entire factory sequence to manifest the eironic trickster: Charlie rebels against his body functioning as a metaphoric gear in the production line and thus ends up behaving as a deliberate saboteur. The sequence begins with Charlie trying to keep pace with the assembly belt, a pace that the factory boss raises more than once. Machinelike absentmindedness provides some of the basis for the clumsy fool persona, but the opening scene creates a variation, for lack of mindfulness has been transformed into something productive (though dehumanizing) for industry. Thus, Chaplin exploits the lack of bodily intelligence at the base of the clumsy fool twice, first using it to signal nonhuman behavior and so comment satirically on modern industry and then garnering further laughs as Charlie fails to be mechanically productive and disrupts the assembly line. As the sequence unfolds, comic failure becomes trickster disruption, the pivot coming after Charlie is retrieved from the giant gears of the assembly line, as though momentarily seeming to be part of the machinery enabled a transcendence from it. Suddenly, all the movements of Charlie create comic disruption to deny the routinization of bodily intelligence—replete with playful disruptions and skillful, tricky gestures to evade capture, capped by his acrobatic moment swinging from a crane above the factory floor. As comic choreography for an eironic trickster, Charlie's disruptive gestures demonstrate not the deadening routinization of mechanical repetition, but rather the enlivening patterns of aesthetic movement.

In *The Gold Rush*, Chaplin again structures important scenes by alternating slapstick personae in successive iterations. Slapstick organizes much of the action in the three dance hall scenes, for example. In the first of these scenes, Charlie switches roles repeatedly to create a variety of audience reactions. When he first starts dancing with the beautiful dance hall girl,

Georgia (Georgia Hale), he is clearly competent though dazed by her attention. However, this sympathetic image turns into the comic fool persona when his belt falls off and his pants threaten to follow. Suddenly using his cane to hold up his pants brilliantly flashes the eironic trickster, and the audience would presumably continue to admire his quick improvisation when he finds a rope to substitute as a belt. Of course, when a dog is revealed on the other end of the rope, Charlie the eironic trickster turns back into the clumsy lout. When the dog chases a cat and pulls Charlie to the floor, causing the entire crowd of dancers to laugh at him, his return to the status of comic butt is complete. Notably, this public humiliation only comes immediately after Charlie demonstrates the apex of his abilities as a dancer. Though the dog initially is in tow as he dances, he briefly moves around the dance floor displaying graceful flourishes that suggest the comic acrobat persona.

Charlie as comic acrobat occurs much more clearly in one memorable moment in *The Gold Rush*. When Georgia agrees to come to dinner on New Year's Eve, and then leaves, Charlie is so happy that he begins to dance and jump about the cabin, knocking over objects. He then attacks the pillows on his bed, destroying them and releasing feathers that coat everything in sight, including him, as though his exuberance is so great that it cannot be contained in his body and so spills out in childishly destructive gestures. In the midst of his antics, however, he jumps from the bed and grabs a rafter and swings on it like a gymnast on a high bar. Charlie's behavior registers as both comic acrobat and lord of disorder at this point in the scene, but when Georgia returns to the cabin to retrieve her gloves, what she sees is only the madcap figure of disorder, the cabin and Charlie covered in feathers as though he had made it snow inside.

Charlie as eironic trickster is obvious in *The Gold Rush* when he lays down in the snow outside a cabin in a theatrical bid for a meal. Charlie's body appears frozen stiff when the kind miner picks him up and brings him inside, but when he starts to give Charlie a taste of hot coffee, Charlie switches from frozen to agile and suddenly puts sugar into the coffee. Perhaps the best example of Charlie as the trickster clown, however, happens shortly after a starving and delusional Big Jim has made yet another attempt to kill him. Charlie has fended off the axe-wielding Jim with the shotgun, and when Jim gets into bed and appears to sleep, so does Charlie. The camera fades to black and when the next scene begins, we see Jim in his bed and Charlie in his, covered completely by a blanket except for his feet, one in a shoe and one swathed in cloth—he and Jim have eaten the other shoe. The feet poke out from the blanket on the end of the bed nearest to Jim. Apparently, Charlie has let his guard down and is again in danger: a close-up shot shows that Jim is only pretending to be asleep. As Jim eyes his intended victim, Charlie's feet wriggle in his sleep. In the next moment, however, Charlie's head pops out from the blanket, apparently between his feet, which are now revealed as his hands, one inside his shoe and the other in the cloth that had been covering his shoeless foot. The image is startling and wonderfully comic in its incongruity. Charlie has clearly not let his guard down, though he had deliberately given that impression. The famous dinner rolls scene, in which Charlie rhythmically manipulates forks stuck into bread rolls to resemble dancing legs and feet, should also be understood as an aspect of eironic trickster behavior, showing an imaginative transformation of objects through an unexpected and extended playfulness that recalls scenes in "The Pawnshop."

Chaplin has an important twist to his presentation of the slapstick clown, a meta-gesture about performance. As Alex Clayton has noted, figures in a fiction film are ontologically dualistic: they are both characters behaving and actors performing.[21] The essence of acting is to present that duality as unified so that the spectator perceives only Charlie behaving, not Chaplin acting, just as Huck Finn reacts to the horseman in the circus. However, Chaplin in "The Pawnshop" gives the whole game away when he has Charlie reveal that a hammer is mere rubber, just after striking an irate customer with it, by bending both ends with his fingers. In this moment, Chaplin dissolves the character's presentational unity: the figure in the film is exposed as both character and performer. The gesture shows the spectator that the character reacting painfully to the blow is of course an actor pretending to be in pain.[22]

The Circus provides an exceptional opportunity to understand how the meta-gesture of the rubber hammer in "The Pawnshop" reveals performance. Indeed, much of the action of the film explores the meta-gesture's revelation of the paradox that structures performance.[23] Chaplin performs Charlie to make the character appear as though Chaplin is not performing, which is what all good actors do: maintain presentational unity of character and performer. The biggest joke in the film is the way that the theater of the circus exposes that illusion. When Charlie evading the policeman appears in front of the circus audience, his actions to the spectators are not real but theatrical: he is part of the show. From Charlie's perspective, however, he is actually being chased and will go to jail if he is caught. An intertitle reveals that the circus audience calls Charlie "the funny man," which is precisely why the circus owner wants to hire him. The running joke for the film audience is that Charlie fails to be consciously funny: as the unconscious clown, Charlie must not try to be funny in order to be funny. Charlie being funny by not trying exhibits the same paradox found in the command, "be spontaneous!" No one can plan spontaneity, yet that is the task of the slapstick clown: to appear comically spontaneous despite rehearsals, to be laughably clumsy through a disciplined practice, to display bodily intelligence by not displaying it. By convincingly pretending to be unconsciously funny, Chaplin also points the film audience to how conscious he must have been during rehearsals in order to perform Charlie as the clumsy fool.

Similarly, the brilliance of the tightrope sequence is not that Chaplin demonstrates directly the comic acrobat persona, but that his superb physical skills allow him to *appear* to the film audience to be in danger as he performs Charlie the unconscious clown. However, for the circus audience, that performance of apparent danger becomes a sense of actual danger. Once the monkeys enliven the scene, members of the circus audience have the same concern as Huck when he watches the performer he takes to be an actual drunk man ride the horse; they are aware of the apparent danger within the scene for the clumsy fool Charlie. Actions that retain their comic slapstick status for the film audience suddenly thwart laughter at Charlie for the circus audience. In addition, an especially concerned audience exists within the story world of the film: the stagehand Charlie pays to maintain the supporting wire. When the wire slips off Charlie, the stagehand clearly behaves like Huck, full of pity and fear. The circus audience's fears for Charlie are seen too, in a long shot and then a close-up of one row, once the trapeze strikes Charlie. The structure of the doubled audience for Chaplin's performance in *The Circus* insists upon the presentational fusing of performer and character that causes the circus audience to worry about Charlie, even as it invites the film audience to indulge in the fusion yet ultimately ignore it and laugh at Charlie's self-inflicted predicament, its laughter signaling an appreciation of how Charlie the clown is also Chaplin the acrobat. The scene stages the potential advantage filmed slapstick has over its live performance: an emotional distance provided by the fact that no actors' bodies are present for the film audience. This difference helps to maintain the comic possibilities of any scene or action that presents physical pain or danger. Like the literal slapstick when wielded on stage, slapstick on film as a mode of comic presentation functions to both hide and flaunt a performative illusion meant to make people laugh.

Chaplin in *The Circus* provides another explicit slapstick twist to such meta-joking about performance when he rehearses for the William Tell act with one of the clowns after watching his rehearsal of the scene with a partner. Charlie unconsciously adds a funny bit to the act beyond what he saw and is trying to copy. When he walks across the ring to take his place with the apple on his head, Charlie falls over the short barrier that forms the ring, which the original clown did not do. With this pratfall, Charlie is doing what the circus owner wants—being funny—but without trying and only for the film audience. Ironically, the circus owner wants Charlie to mimic the first clown completely even though the clowns' routines have been failing with paying audiences. Thus Chaplin aims to be funny by pretending not to be funny through a character who is unintentionally funny in a scene in which he is supposed to be trying, that is, rehearsing to be funny. The same meta-gesture happens when Charlie replaces the worm-eaten apple with a banana: like falling over the barrier, using the banana is funny to the film audience because laying flat on his head, it presents an impossible target, but not to the spectators within the story world of the film watching the rehearsal because Charlie changes the gag. Indeed, during the William Tell act and the subsequent barbershop act, only Charlie laughs. These moments again foreground the two layers of spectators constructed by *The Circus*, one within the film and one watching the film.

Staging rehearsals on camera is already a doubled operation: pretending to practice in the story world while such scenes are also the actual act—the filmed performance. Comically revealing the magician's tricks to show what is behind the act functions similarly, exposing what ought to stay hidden. Such extravagant and elaborate meta-gestures, like demonstrating the hammer is rubber, expose for laughs the fundamental artifice of staged performance. The circus ring and its spotlight both signify performance, and as long as Charlie does not recognize the special nature of that space, does not know himself as a performer but is nevertheless mistaken by the circus audience as such, he is funny. When he considers himself as a performer during rehearsals, he fails for the immediate story world audience. To enact the clumsy fool persona, the slapstick actor hides his bodily intelligence, which creates an image of failure. In *The Circus*, Chaplin cleverly doubles that process by having the slapstick clown fail at being the slapstick clown. Bodily intelligence must be hidden twice and uncovered twice. The conscious efforts of Charlie to be funny fail onscreen, parodying the offscreen conscious efforts in rehearsal as they simultaneously present them and their success at making the circus audience laugh. The film audience's laughter would signal the success of the complete process and thus its knowledge that the hammer is just rubber, that all gestures are staged. This playing with the presumed unity of character and actor uncovers the art of performance in slapstick fashion.

The exposure of performance replicates the dynamic of exposure that slapstick works on bodily intelligence. Audience laughter signals bodily intelligence performed by its absence. Just as slapstick uncovers bodily intelligence by performing its absence, Chaplin exposing himself as the actor performing the character Charlie uncovers not just the theatrics of the filmed slapstick clown, but also the fact that performance underlies all actions. Any action implies the skill to execute it, what Richard Shusterman would call a "somaesthetics." At the highest level of a performative somaesthetics are actions within disciplines devoted to bodily strength and skillful maneuvering, such as athletics or martial arts. Dancing and acting are disciplines that also demand a body in motion, a body performing more artistically than athletically, though there is obvious overlap.[24] We can also speak of the everyday performance of people demonstrating bodily intelligence. The slapstick actor comically exposes the performance dimension of everyday actions by artistically misperforming them. Slapstick is therefore structured with its own peculiar paradox, for the spectacle of the clown's artistic misperformance results from careful preparation that requires superior bodily intelligence yet hides that necessity. Noting the disciplined practice required to be an athlete, a dancer, or an actor indicates a hierarchy of conscious effort in the performance of human actions, a hierarchy that must include the acts of an individual going about his or her everyday routine. Slapstick reveals the fact that even at this lowest level of performance, discipline and skill are required to perform well. The appeal of slapstick as a mode of filmed representation is its comic operation at and on this most ordinary level of human action.

As a comic performer of Maurice Merleau-Ponty's argument for the existence of a bodily intelligence, the filmed slapstick clown narrates a body inhabiting and moving through space, rather than presenting a body in static display. The slapstick clown cannot be immobile, is not to be found on a beach boardwalk, striking a statuesque pose to show off a well-muscled, tattooed figure. Rather, the filmed slapstick clown tells the tale of a kinetic relationship to objects within his or her perceptual field, a relationship mimicked by the perceptual field of motion offered through the movie camera's lens. The clown's body comically demonstrates the phenomenological reciprocity or exchange between self and world because the human body inhabiting the world implies motion in this exchange, its pre-reflective habits both positing and generating significance. When the clown fails in some way to enact that exchange, he or she has violated, disturbed, or negated those basic meanings that precede reflection and conscious experience. The importance of identifying three slapstick personae is that the range of competence in their actions provides a comic complexity to the reciprocity of exchange between self and world. Taken together, the three slapstick personae suggest Susanne Langer's definition of the buffoon, a comic figure she links to folk theater: "the indomitable living creature fending for itself, tumbling and stumbling [as the clown physically illustrates] from one situation to another, getting into scrape after scrape and getting out again, with or without a thrashing."[25]

The slapstick clown necessarily emphasizes the human body, which in effect narrates itself continually through the duration of the film rather than being momentarily highlighted in the mode of Mikhail Bakhtin's concept of a "material bodily lower stratum,"[26] as it is in a farce, for example, in the sham urine-drinking scene of Moliere's one-act play, *Le Medicin Volant*, with references to Gargantua's monstrous consumption of food in François Rabelais's *Gargantua and Pantagruel*, or through the emphasis on farting in Mark Twain's "1601: Conversation, as It Was by the Social Fireside, in the Time of the Tudors." The clown's body, therefore, does not so much narrate the fully developed plot of a story as it tells about a necessary series of interactions with objects and people, showing the human body's continuous stagings of its place in the physical world at large. This difference between a storyline narration and a slapstick narration means that slapstick as a mode of comic presentation is as likely to abandon as it is to further a plot, allowing random action and mere motion to overtake and supplant a sense of events being plotted. This fundamental disinterest in maintaining a plot provides a directorial motive for scenes that essentially halt storytelling for any number of extended *lazzi*, such as a food fight, complete with pie throwing, or a chase. Chase scenes are particularly interesting in this light because they can be motivated by plot—the hero wants to escape from the villain or imminent danger—yet they can easily engulf a story and become the plot, with its own twists and turns. Keaton transforms his feature film *The Seven Chances* in this manner for a substantial portion of its second half, more than ten minutes, or one full reel in all.

Slapstick's dynamic of exposure typically uncovers bodily intelligence by performing its absence: the pratfall is its paradigmatic gesture and the clumsy fool its signature figure. When Charlie tangles with the pull-out bed in "One A.M.," for example, the audience laughs as the bed repeatedly seems to outwit him. The audience laughs at Charlie because he makes the situation worse, a judgment that taps a preexisting store of common sense that Charlie clearly lacks. In another gag found in the opening sideshow sequence of *The Circus*, Charlie embodies directly the Bergsonian absentmindedness that manifests the mechanical encrusted on the living. As part of his strategy to escape both the policeman and the pickpocket chasing him, Charlie stands next to a life-sized automaton just outside the funhouse and mimics its machine movements. At first, this mimicking is simply a single shift from facing front to facing to one side. However, when the pickpocket spots him, Charlie takes the thief's truncheon away from him as he gestures toward the policeman waiting at the bottom of the stairs, which convinces the thief also to pretend to be an automaton. The immediate visual gag is that of Charlie hitting the pickpocket with the truncheon and then turning to face the camera and laughing. Chaplin's ability to appear to be an automaton is uncanny, so that the gag simultaneously manifests the less-than-human mechanical behavior of inadequate bodily intelligence and the superior bodily intelligence of the comic acrobat. Once again Chaplin creates an exemplary moment of performing inadequate bodily intelligence perfectly and thus paradoxically signifying, in part, its opposite, the disciplined bodily intelligence of a well-rehearsed actor. Moreover, when Charlie hits the pickpocket, another layer to the meta-joke appears: for the sake of fooling the policeman, Charlie as mock-automaton must pretend to hit the thief to suggest that they are both true automatons and to continue hiding in plain sight, but Charlie, within the story world of the film, strikes him and the thief falls—but of course he is just an actor pretending to be struck unconscious. The same dynamic structures the famous scene of the tipping cabin in *The Gold Rush*, which shows human bodies apparently overwhelmed by natural forces, placing Big Jim's as well as Charlie's actions into the category of the clumsy fool in a naturalistic story world. Charlie at first even mistakes the instability of the cabin as his own physical state, hung over from his drinking binge the night before. However, the scene forcefully presents the physical dexterity of both actors by their performing its absence so relentlessly.

This doubled operation—make something visible by performing its absence—bears an affinity with Georges Bataille's discussion of comic laughter in his essay ruminating about a philosophy of unknowing (*non-savoir*). Comic laughter as a certain kind of behavior defines this philosophy; that which induces comic laughter is unknowable, asserts Bataille. Moreover, this unknown nature is not accidental but essential to comic laughter. Comic laughter, then, is an important manifestation of encountering the unknowable. Bataille wants to emphasize the intoxicating quality of comic laughter, and ultimately this aspect links comic laughter to his explorations of sacred or ecstatic states.[27] My essay argues for an understanding of laughter that moves in the opposite direction, linking it to the most mundane of human actions. However, the structure that defines the relationship between slapstick and bodily intelligence resembles Bataille's claim that comic laughter signifies the unknowable. As such a sign, comic laughter expresses the ultimate transgression against philosophy, the discipline devoted to wisdom and knowledge, by apparently existing outside the domain of philosophy, yet comic laughter necessarily produces effects within that domain: the realm of knowledge must contain an unknowing.[28] Similarly, slapstick presents itself as outside bodily intelligence, yet its operation as a comic mode of action produces that which it apparently denies; that is, it brings the thoughtful spectator to a cognizance of the practiced and complicated bodily intelligence of the slapstick clown.

The relationship of slapstick and bodily intelligence thus exhibits the structuring dynamic Bataille identifies for a philosophy of unknowing, and the result in both cases is comic laughter. In such a philosophy of unknowing, the slapstick clown would seem to be the necessary philosophizing agent, not in the usual sense of an intellectualizing consciousness, but rather as an embodied intelligence whose phenomenological being comically tells about that which is otherwise hidden, if not unknown. For Bataille, comic laughter tells about a philosophical un-knowing that functions as a comic matrix.[29] Perhaps comic laughter and the comic operation of the unknowing resembles the necessary mystery of a black hole that sits at the center of a galaxy and so structures it: one can observe the stream of radiation emanating near or from the black hole, but the hole itself, the singularity, cannot be observed. Thus comic laughter emanates from an enabling yet mysterious place, somewhere "below" even the primary level of consciousness implied by bodily intelligence, from the singularity of nonintelligence. Slapstick, then, provides the initial visible form, organizing with its *lazzi* that streaming energy radiation called comic laughter, an energy that can be anarchic and thus destructive of routine social habits and routine modes of thought. Charles Spencer Chaplin and his cinematic colleagues present a clownish liminality through their slapstick personae, personae that display a capacity to be radical symbols of disorder, or even of unknowing, perhaps bringing us closest to the mystery of what makes people laugh.

NOTES

1. I use the generic "Charlie" to refer to Chaplin as a slapstick clown, rather than "the Tramp," because Chaplin, in some of both his two-reelers and feature films, does not portray his usual tramp figure. In naming the second persona "eironic trickster," I wish to evoke the classic Greek comic figure of the *eiron*, who seems less than he is but often bests his opposite, the braggart *alazon*, and compound that figure with the mythic proportion of the trickster archetype. These figures embody the primal quality of comic laughter in ways that are reiterated by the filmed slapstick clown. I have borrowed the term "bodily intelligence" from Noel Carroll's study of Buster Keaton, *Comedy Incarnate: Buster Keaton, Physical Humor, and Bodily Coping* (Malden, MA: Blackwell Publishers, 2007). Carroll mentions several sources for his use of this term (4–6), but he relies especially upon Maurice Merleau-Ponty's argument that consciousness is immanent in the human body.

2. Merleau-Ponty does not use this term so much as imply it. His project shows how to "picture consciousness in the process of perceiving." *The Phenomenology of Perception*, trans. Colin Smith (London: Routledge & Kegan Paul, 1962), 53. His emphasis on the experience of perception leads to an insistence that a species of knowing exists prior to any conscious reflection, philosophical or otherwise. The body is "a first opening upon things without which there would be no objective knowledge" (96). Richard Shusterman, *Body Consciousness: A Philosophy of Mindfulness and Somaesthetics* (Cambridge: Cambridge University Press, 2008), elaborates four levels of consciousness, two of which fit into this pre-reflective domain of the body (54–56).

3. Umberto Eco, "The Comic and the Rule," in *Travels in Hyperreality*, trans. William Weaver (San Diego: Harcourt & Brace, 1986), 269–78.

4. Jonathan Auerbach, *Body Shots: Early Cinema's Incarnations* (Berkeley: University of California Press, 2007), 6, 7.

5. Aristotle, "Poetics," in *The Complete Works of Aristotle*, ed. Jonathan Barnes (Princeton: Princeton University Press, 1984), 2:2319.

6. David Morris, "Body," in *Merleau-Ponty: Key Concepts*, ed. Rosalyn Diprose and Jack Reynolds (Stocksfield, UK: Acumen Publishing, 2008), 115.

7. Merleau-Ponty, *Phenomenology of Perception*, 110; cf. Morris, "Body," 115–16.

8. Henri Bergson, *Le Rire: Essai Sur La Signification du Comique*, 7th ed. (Paris: Félix Alcan et Guillaumin Réunies, 1911), 88–89; "Laughter," in *Comedy*, ed. Wylie Sypher (Baltimore: Johns Hopkins University Press, 1980), 117.

9. Merleau-Ponty, *Phenomenology of Perception*, 137; cf. Morris, "Body," 128.

10. Morris, "Body," 114.

11. The comic laughter generated by such disarrangements is predicated upon an axiomatic principle that people find pleasure in nonthreatening presentations of comic chaos. See James E. Caron, "From Ethology to Aesthetics: Evolution as a Theoretical Paradigm for Research on Laughter, Humor, and other Comic Phenomena," *Humor: International Journal of Humor Research* 15, no. 3 (2002): 274.

12. Shusterman, *Body Consciousness*, 49.

13. This scene anticipates the famous mirror *lazzo* in the Marx Brothers' *Duck Soup* (1933), which in turn inspired Lucille Ball's version with Harpo on her TV show *I Love Lucy* (1955). Kyp Harness claims a French comedian, Max Linder, as a precursor to Chaplin for this gag, and

notes such *lazzi*'s probable origin in music hall routines. *The Art of Charlie Chaplin: A Film by Film Analysis* (Jefferson, NC: McFarland, 2008). I will use the term *lazzo* to refer to specific gags as a deliberate nod toward *commedia dell'arte* and its organization of slapstick into specific actions or *lazzi*, generally thought to be a corruption of "*l'azione.*" See Mel Gordon, *Lazzi: The Comic Routines of the Commedia dell'arte* (New York: Performing Arts Journal Publications, 1983). The mirror scene early in *The Circus* apparently also suggests the reciprocity of self and world or the relational self, the sensation of seeing and being seen simultaneously. However, the multiple images of more than one person intimates not a representation of the relational body, but rather bodies displaced by images in a gesture that anticipates a postmodern aesthetic. The phenomenological body as the center and initial point of identity transforms into a camera shot of infinite images in which characters and audience are amazed, diminishing any sense of orientation and threatening its extinction. See Rachel Joseph, "Chaplin's Presence," in this volume, which makes a similar point.

14. Adam Clayton develops a similar point about Chaplin's slapstick films, Charlie presenting "a fluid movement" between the extremes of a pratfall and a virtuoso action. *The Body in Hollywood Slapstick* (Jefferson, NC: McFarland, 2007), 37. Noel Carroll makes the same claim for Keaton (6). Clayton characterizes Chaplin's performance as a parody of the Cartesian duality of mind and body (28) and invokes Merleau-Ponty's critique of that duality to claim that Chaplin's performance presents unity, not duality, the mind perfectly visible in the body's movements. My use of "bodily intelligence" emphasizes the mind's pre-reflective domain. Also, neither Clayton nor Carroll presents a third persona. In addition, Clayton understands the incompetence/virtuosity drama as a general comic incongruity, whereas I argue that the incompetence of the clumsy fool already presents a comic incongruity, that is, a violation of bodily intelligence. I also emphasize the audience's or spectator's variety of laughing responses to the personae, which neither Carroll nor Clayton consider.

15. I have in mind here the presentation of literary naturalism in which human intention is thwarted or destroyed, often by a combination of social and natural forces as well as mere chance. The link between comic laughter and naturalism is developed in James E. Caron, "Grotesque Naturalism: The Significance of the Comic in *McTeague*," *Texas Studies in Literature and Language* 31, no. 2 (1989): 288–317. Tom Gunning reaches a similar conclusion in his argument for the basis of all gags: gags function as "crazy machines" that invert purposes and projects; they create a "pitfall between agent and purpose." "Mechanisms of Laughter: The Devices of Slapstick," in *Slapstick Comedy*, ed. Tom Paulus and Rob King (New York: Routledge, 2010), 140.

16. Paul Valery, "Poetry and Abstract Thought," trans. Charles Guenther, *Kenyon Review* 16, no. 2 (spring 1954): 223–24.

17. See James E. Caron, "Silent Slapstick Film as Ritualized Clowning: The Example of Charlie Chaplin," *Studies in American Humor* 3, no. 14 (2006): 5–22.

18. Charles J. Maland provides an in-depth look at Chaplin's popularity in the United States throughout his career. His coverage of the period while at Mutual in particular notes the huge crowds Chaplin drew at war bond rallies. *Chaplin and American Culture: The Evolution of a Star Image* (Princeton, NJ: Princeton University Press, 1989), 25–44. An obvious indication marking Chaplin's early popularity was the adulation he received from crowds at train stations during his 1916 journey to New York from Los Angeles in pursuit of a contract with one of the studios courting him. See Kenneth S. Lynn, *Charlie Chaplin and His Times* (New York: Simon and Schuster, 1997), 171–72; David Robinson, *Chaplin: His Life and Art* (New York: McGraw-Hill, 1985), 156. John McCabe notes Chaplin's appearance at the New York Hippodrome after he signs with Mutual: the crowd fails to recognize Chaplin out of his Tramp costume until he suddenly pantomimes the Tramp's walk, at which point "the audience exploded." *Charlie Chaplin* (New York: Doubleday, 1978), 82. Chaplin's autobiography recounts the unceasing American public attention at the time. *My Autobiography* (New York, Simon and Schuster, 1964), 175–78, with similar reaction in France after World War I (275). Though Chaplin was criticized in the British press during the war for not enlisting, Lynn points out how much the average British soldier loved Chaplin's films (176) and notes that the French filmmaker Jean Renoir fell under the spell of Chaplin's comedies while recovering from wounds

received at the Western front (147). Chaplin recounts how a German soldier greeted him enthusiastically in Berlin after the war (279).

19. Cf. Wolfgang M. Zucker, "The Clown as the Lord of Disorder," in *Holy Laughter: Essays on Religion in the Comic Perspective*, ed. M. Conrad Hays (New York: Seabury Press, 1969), 75–88.

20. Mary Douglas, *Purity and Danger: An Analysis of the Concepts of Pollution and Taboo* (London: Routledge, 1991), 2, 35.

21. Clayton, *Body in Hollywood Slapstick*, 43.

22. Oliver Hardy routinely provides similar moments. Ollie inevitably takes the hardest knocks, while Stan causes much of the trouble and always makes the situation worse. This dynamic allows Ollie his signature comic moment, looking at the camera/audience, as though to say, "look what I have to put up with," a facial gesture that functions in part as the revelatory meta-gesture about performance, even as it also implies the audience's complicity with Ollie's point of view.

23. Rachel Joseph's analysis of *The Circus* explores in more detail the idea that the film is about the "rules" of performance. For different views on Chaplin's personae and the issue of performance, see also the essays in this volume by Lisa Haven and Cynthia Miller.

24. Schusterman, *Body Consciousness*, 23–30.

25. "The Great Dramatic Forms: The Comic Rhythm," in *Feeling and Form* (London: Routledge & Kegan Paul, 1953), 234. Langer goes on to call the buffoon "the personified *elan vital*." This link to Bergson correctly underlines the buffoon or clown's indomitability, an aspect that Chaplin as the Tramp portrays admirably, perhaps best at the end of *The Circus*, but misleading in that Bergson posits the basic comic butt as lacking *elan vital*.

26. Mikhail Bakhtin, *Rabelais and His World*, trans. Helene Iswolsky (Bloomington: Indiana University Press, 1984), 18–23, 373–74.

27. Georges Bataille, "Un-Knowing: Laughter and Tears," trans. Annette Michelson, *October* 36 (spring 1986): 98, 99–100; cf. Lisa Trahair, "The Comedy of Philosophy: Bataille, Hegel, and Derrida," *Angelaki: Journal of the Theoretical Humanities* 6, no. 3 (2001): 156, 159. Bataille's essay talks about "laughter" rather than "comic laughter," as I have been doing. I make this distinction, even when borrowing from Bataille, because there are pathological forms of laughter that I wish to exclude, though Bataille's larger perspective on forms of behavior apparently outside rationality could be seen as denying the distinction. See Donald D. Black, "Pathological Laughter: A Review of the Literature," *The Journal of Nervous and Mental Disease* 170, no. 2 (1982): 67–71, for an overview of the phenomenon of pathological laughter, and Josef Parvizi et al., "Pathological Laughter and Crying: A Link to the Cerebellum," *Brain* 124, no. 9 (2001): 1708–19, for more recent findings.

28. Trahair, "Comedy of Philosophy," 156.

29. Bataille, "Un-Knowing: Laughter and Tears," 100.

Chapter Two

Chaplin and the Static Image

A Barthesian Analysis of the Visual in My Trip Abroad
and "A Comedian Sees the World"

Lisa Stein Haven

In his autobiography, Charlie Chaplin makes this statement about his early business inclinations: "There was a strong element of the merchant in me. I was continuously preoccupied with business schemes. I would look at empty shops, speculating as to what profitable businesses I could make of them, ranging from fish and chips to grocery shops" (60). Chaplin proved adept at marketing both his image and his films, despite his lack of prior experience. It's not surprising, then, that Chaplin used what he termed his two "home-coming tours" (September to October 1921 and January 1931 to June 1932) and the travel narratives that emanated from them largely to promote his newest films—*The Kid* (1921) and *City Lights* (1931), respectively. As a screen artist, Chaplin and his publicity team would have found it essential to complement such narratives with visual elements in order to accomplish a conflation of the Little Tramp (the screen Chaplin) with Chaplin the man (the public Chaplin).[1] This chapter, through a Barthesian analysis of visual elements, concretizes the significant role these images—photographs and illustrations—play in the narratives' overall promotional agenda, one dependent on this conflation. Through this determination, then, the relationship between Chaplin's cinematic and static images is also clarified.

Both travel narratives were written (or in the case of the first one, "influenced"[2]) by Chaplin himself, *My Trip Abroad* (Harper, 1922)[3] and "A Comedian Sees the World,"[4] published in *Woman's Home Companion* over the course of five months, from September 1933 to January 1934. *My Trip Abroad*, for instance, reveals the fact that Chaplin attended premieres of his

work on this trip and, significantly, carried his films into Germany for the
first time. The business correspondence of the Chaplin Studios during this
time documents that the second tour's itinerary was planned with the intention of staging premieres of *City Lights*, which the public Chaplin would
attend and enhance with his own particular charisma. Letters to Chaplin and
his representative at the United Artists' New York office, Arthur Kelly, from
Chaplin's European United Artists representative, Boris Evelinoff, written
and sent the same day (December 12, 1935)[5] promise that "it is not difficult
to reconstruct the great popularity and enthusiasm around the genius of our
great patron 'Charlie'"[6]—the same publicity as Chaplin had for the
1931–1932 tour on what Evelinoff calls "un voyage de propagande en faveur
de Charlie."[7] Chaplin managed to rest and relax on the beaches of the French
Riviera and the slopes of St. Moritz, but these occasions were beside the
point of the trip. Both the 1921 and 1931–1932 tours were clearly arranged
for promotional reasons.

   According to the book contracts, the text documenting each tour proved a
very lucrative venture on its own; *MTA* alone went through several printings
in the United States and was being translated and published in twelve foreign
countries. The contract for *MTA* guaranteed more than $15,000 for Chaplin
and earned him much more than that;[8] the contract for "ACSTW" paid
$50,000.[9] In comparison, David Robinson reports that Chaplin received an
advance of $1.5 million plus 50 percent of the net from First National for *The
Kid*.[10] *City Lights* made $400,000 at just the Cohan Theatre in New York
during its first twelve weeks[11] and soon claimed more domestic rentals than
The Circus (1928) and 90 percent of rentals claimed by *The Gold Rush*
(1925)—all during the height of the Great Depression.[12] From this comparison, it is clear that the texts were created and disseminated largely for publicity purposes.

   Chaplin's publicity machine was well aware of the fact that in order for it
to be a success, it had to convince Chaplin's audience of the conflation just
discussed—that the public and screen Chaplins were fused into one entity in
terms of personality, demeanor, comportment, and so on. But as far as signification is concerned, how does that work? How would an independent-
thinking filmgoer be persuaded to believe in this conflation? One of the most
important means is through the static image, a product that the publicity
machine endeavored to control at all costs. Roland Barthes works out the
image's process of signification convincingly in his book *Image-Music-Text*.
Therein, he delineates three levels of meaning for the photographic image:
(1) linguistic, (2) denotative, and (3) connotative. The linguistic level Barthes
asserts is present for every image—"as title, caption, accompanying press
article, film dialogue, comic strip balloon"[13] and attempts to "fix" the floating chain of signifieds of the photographic message by identifying "purely
and simply the elements of the scene and the scene itself."[14] Because the

relationship between the caption and photograph is not often simple, I will selectively examine the caption (the linguistic message) as it colors the reading of Chaplin's photographs and illustrations in his two travel narratives. However, because many of the captions for "ACSTW" are quotes pulled from the body of the narrative, my main focus in this essay will be the denotative and connotative levels of meaning. The denotative message allows the photograph its semblance of truth-value.[15] Barthes calls this level both the denotative and the literal; it is one in which the relationship of the signifieds to the signifiers is one of "recording"; "the scene is *there*, captured mechanically, not humanly (the mechanical is here a guarantee of objectivity)."[16] The denotative level of meaning allows the photographs included in Chaplin's narratives to achieve two of three tasks: (1) to confirm the rhetoric of authenticity achieved in the written text of the narrative and (2) to confirm Chaplin's status as a celebrity. With the power of this denotative meaning, the photographs become referents and thereby validate the narratives as historical factual accounts. The final level of meaning for Barthes is the connotative or symbolic. This level guarantees not one reading, but infinite readings that vary according to the individual reader. Susan Sontag provides a clear definition of this connotative message, explaining that "any photograph has multiple meanings; indeed, to see something in the form of a photograph is to encounter a potential object of fascination. . . . Photographs, which cannot themselves explain anything, are inexhaustible invitations to deduction, speculation, and fantasy."[17] It is this connotative meaning that is the hardest to manipulate for both the model and the photographer. In essence, then, Chaplin's use of photographs aligns itself well with his marketing agenda for the verbal texts that make up the travel narratives (the photographs' third task): to conflate his public persona with his better-known and more beloved screen one.

One of the oldest tools for film celebrity promotion is the formal photographic portrait, usually disseminated in the form of five-by-seven fan photos sent gratis on request as well as published by the media. This tradition made its way to the publicity departments of Hollywood studios from the stage, where cabinet photos and cartes de visite[18] had promoted the popularity of prominent performers since the mid-nineteenth century. Chaplin sat for such photographic portraits as a headliner for Karno's London Comedians in 1909. Even in these early days of his career, he was sitting for portraits both in and out of costume, thereby beginning a tradition of linking the faces and costumes of those characters with his own public persona. While such sittings would seem like the perfect opportunity for Chaplin to exert his directorial expertise (to "forge a photographic self-image"), the testimony of one photographer suggests otherwise. Chaplin sat for Edward Steichen twice, once in 1925 and again in 1931—both times for *Vanity Fair* magazine and both times in New York when Chaplin was in the city to promote a film.

Although such sittings were requirements of life as a film celebrity, Steichen insists that Chaplin exhibited unfamiliarity and lack of ease in his particular studio, relating that for the 1925 sitting Chaplin was delivered to his studio by his secretary (probably Carlyle Robinson) and then put himself completely in Steichen's hands for the shoot itself:

> When we got in the studio and started to arrange the lights, he froze. I dismissed my assistants and tried to work alone with him, but nothing happened. Finally Chaplin said, "You know, I can't just sit still. I have to be doing something. Then I'm all right." . . . Then I started to talk to him about his films, and as I waxed enthusiastic about *The Gold Rush*, the film he had just released, he loosened up and became enthusiastic in turn. I called the men in and in a few minutes I had a half-dozen portraits of Chaplin relaxed and himself, the image of a dancing faun.[19]

Steichen offers here an account of a Chaplin who has no particular agenda in terms of what sort of image he hopes to project in the portraits. Yet, as "himself" (his public persona), or who Steichen believes him to be, Chaplin is "the image of a dancing faun"—in other words, the Little Tramp. In fact, the two portraits from these sessions Steichen published in *Vanity Fair* achieve a conflation of Chaplin's public persona with the Little Tramp within the photo itself more than any of his other formal portraits. A 1925 portrait depicts Chaplin in street clothes, but its composition works to achieve a conflation of his two personae through its connotative message. The cane and hat are not those of the Little Tramp, but Chaplin's posture in the photo is. The shadow cast by his diminutive figure (made smaller by the large amount of dark background that frames him) looms large and menacing over Chaplin, almost overtaking him. In this shadow the viewer sees the typical posture of the Little Tramp (hand on hip), the outline of the hat (a homburg), and the curly hair that becomes exaggerated in size and shape by the shadow. The white background becomes a movie screen and Chaplin's own body reflects the image of his film creation upon it.

Despite Steichen's account, it is hard to believe that Chaplin, the master self-promoter, would have had no hand in the final product, especially considering his use of visual elements in the two travel narratives. Perhaps Steichen's version reflects only an artist's territoriality over his own work. It is more likely that Chaplin played a large role in shaping the image that emerges from his portraits in order to "maintain a kind of 'authorship' of self-image."[20] In accordance with Walter Benjamin's conclusions in "The Work of Art in the Age of Mechanical Reproduction," such portraits seem to express that "one of the immediate dangers of the infinitely reproducible image is the loss of control over that image when it is released to the public."[21]

In fact, Chaplin's publicity machine used similar formal photographic portraits in the original edition of *MTA* released in the United States in February 1922. In addition, the book contains both press photographs and film stills. There are twenty photos in all, twelve of which are press photographs of Chaplin out of costume, three are portraits (two in costume and one out of costume), and five are film stills that depict Chaplin in costume. *MTA* contains one formal portrait of Chaplin out of costume and two in costume as the Little Tramp. The denotative message of Chaplin's portrait out of costume is that Chaplin exists. Linda Haverty Rugg reiterates the denotative message of the photograph in general: "photographs as evidence re-anchor the subject in the physical world, insisting on the verifiable presence of an embodied and solid individual."[22] In this role as referent, the photographic portrait accomplishes its first task—confirmation of the authenticity of the written text. However, this portrait seems to be a counter-text to the written narrative, because the public Chaplin depicted in the photo doesn't look like the film persona. This portrait, positioned opposite page 8, is one taken before Chaplin's film career.[23] The linguistic message of the photograph, "As I Look When I Am Serious," focuses on Chaplin's dour expression. In this photo his hair is parted in the middle and slicked down on either side, thereby effectively hiding his trademark curls. He is hatless. His "serious" expression also provides a stark contrast to the lighthearted demeanor of the Little Tramp. In fact, this grave expression is further exaggerated by the dark Edwardian necktie he wears, which makes him appear almost neckless.[24] The connotative message of the photo, then, implies that this young man takes himself very seriously and that he is *not* the Little Tramp. Compared to one of the portraits depicting Chaplin in costume, found opposite page 126, the contrast is striking. Here Chaplin wears the trademark Little Tramp costume—derby hat, toothbrush moustache, conspicuously curly hair, ragged clothes (the viewer sees only a small portion of the shirt, vest, and jacket). His expression is almost mischievous; his smile is tentative. A conflation of the public and screen Chaplins has not been accomplished between these two photos, given this stark contrast.

While press photos of Chaplin out of costume are more numerous than those in costume in *MTA*, the familiar face of the Little Tramp—more familiar than Chaplin's own—appears frequently enough to be useful to the conflation agenda. The concurrence of portraits of Chaplin both in and out of costume in the same volume, despite the formal portrait's threat as possible counter-text, in fact, assists the efforts of the written text to rhetorically conflate Chaplin's public persona with his screen persona. The stark contrast between the public Chaplin and the screen Chaplin is one the reader is expecting. He or she has seen the public Chaplin in the papers, in magazines, and in newsreels. The formal portrait of the serious young Chaplin assists the conflation achieved in the written narrative, because it refers to the image of

the public Chaplin, one who, as the written narrative insists, behaves, responds, thinks, acts, and moves like the screen Chaplin despite his physical
contrast. The conflation is assisted not by a one-to-one correlation of the
appearance of the actor with the Little Tramp, but by correspondences in
behavior, movement, and action between the two, for a juxtaposition of
verbal or visual images of Chaplin in and out of costume only reinforces the
strategy of reversible metamorphoses[25] employed in the films. The affluent
public Chaplin—the one out of costume—works simply as another role or
shape into which the screen Chaplin has temporarily metamorphosed.

The inclusion of images of the screen Chaplin in *MTA*, film stills from his
recent movies, such as *A Dog's Life* (1918) and *The Kid* (1921), furthers this
project quite effectively by keeping the image of the Little Tramp constantly
within easy access. The cover design (figure 2.1), however, is the element
that brings these disparate images together on one page. This publicity portrait of Chaplin as the Little Tramp together with his dog from *A Dog's Life*
is featured in the center position. Just below the image is a facsimile of
Chaplin's famous signature that is embellished with Chaplin's own caricature of his film persona—a sort of sketched montage of the iconic elements:
the shoes, the derby, the cane, and the "important" elements of his expression—the eyebrows and moustache. This signature acts as an authentification
stamp on the work (it appears again just inside the front cover on the page
facing the flyleaf). These central elements are then framed on each side by a
section of fabricated filmstrip in which Chaplin can be seen out of costume at
various venues on his tour. While it would have been possible to view the
public Chaplin on film—in newsreels, for instance—the fabricated "film"
depicted on *MTA*'s cover moves the public Chaplin to the screen Chaplin's
home—the celluloid—thereby demonstrating yet again the facility with
which each persona could move into the place of the other.

Different from the publicity photograph and film still in terms of signification is the press photograph, partly because the photographer in most cases
is unknown or not commissioned by the artist and, therefore, outside of the
control of the subject being photographed. Still, *MTA* utilizes this type of
image most frequently. Perhaps this is due to the press photograph's attribute
of candidness, one that adds to the perceived authenticity of the image. The
press photograph, in other words, more than the portrait, is evidence of the
existence of a living body in a certain time and place. The press photographs
chosen for *MTA* potentially provide evidence of two aspects of Chaplin's
narrative through their denotative objectivity. First, they act as referents for
the actions and events detailed in the text of the narrative. Second, they help
to provide evidence of Chaplin's celebrity status both before, during, and,
presumably, after the tour. The press photo's role in providing evidence of
Chaplin as a celebrity is especially important because it verifies this phenomenon as it is appears rhetorically in the written text.

Figure 2.1. *My Trip Abroad* cover art. Courtesy of Roy Export S.A.S. and Jessica Buxton.

Figure 2.2, for example, shows the mayor of Southampton, England, greeting Chaplin. A nattily attired public Chaplin stands hatless in the center of the photo, surrounded by members of his diverse audience, clasping the mayor's hand in welcome. He looks at a seemingly boisterous individual standing just next to the mayor who, open-mouthed and with hands outstretched, may represent the typical fan experiencing and sharing his excitement in the presence of others. Just barely visible near the bottom edge of the photo, Chaplin's left hand (his dominant one) clasps his cane tightly—the only sign of the Little Tramp in sight, but one that subtly evinces the ever-present link between the two. Two other press photographs depict Chaplin in similar situations on his tour. Repetition of such images, of course, enhances the power of any one image to lend credence to its denotative message.

Other press photos in *MTA* work to provide similar evidence of Chaplin's celebrity status. One photo depicts Mutual Studios head John Freuler, Sydney Chaplin, and Charlie signing his $670,000 contract in 1916 in New York City. Interestingly, this event had nothing to do with the tour and occurred more than five years prior to it; thus its presence in the narrative can only be justified by its ability to prove Chaplin's importance in the film industry, however gratuitous this may seem. Press photos depicting Chaplin in the company of other well-known figures of the time such as German actress Pola Negri, H. G. Wells, and boxer Georges Carpentier also effectively es-

Figure 2.2.   "I Am Welcomed by the Mayor of Southampton, England," from *My Trip Abroad*. Courtesy of Roy Export S.A.S. and Jessica Buxton.

tablish his position as a celebrity of a merit at least equivalent to theirs. The fact that Chaplin eclipsed these individuals in terms of popularity and importance by 1932, just over ten years later, suggests strongly that the conflation agenda was successful, at least at this point in his career.[26]

The visual components of "ACSTW" have some commonality with those of *MTA* in that they include press photographs. However, the color illustration supplants the photograph in importance in this narrative. This privileging of illustrations over photographs may be due only to the design concept and tradition of the *Woman's Home Companion*. A quick survey of other articles in the five issues in which Chaplin's series appears shows that almost all of them used color or black-and-white illustrations exclusively. Due to this stark difference in visual components, my analysis must be modified to accommodate it. Barthes accounts for just such an accommodation in his analysis, writing that the drawing must be considered very differently from the photograph, for the operation of the drawing (the coding) immediately necessitates a certain division between the significant and the insignificant: the drawing does not reproduce *everything* (often it reproduces very little), without its ceasing, however, to be a strong message. In other words, the denotation of the drawing is less pure than that of the photograph, for there is no drawing without style.[27]

The denotative message of the illustration is also less pure because of artist ownership. The Peter Helck illustration for Chaplin's final installment (January 1934) recently sold at auction as a work of art—one totally separate from the narrative it illustrated, except for its subject matter. This fact demonstrates that the Chaplin company, though it embellished the first page of each installment with its familiar copyright stamp (Copyright, 1933, by Charles Chaplin Film Corporation), did not own the rights to the illustrations published as part of that installment and therefore did not control the content of those illustrations. In some sense, then, the illustrations for "ACSTW" become each artist's personal interpretation of the events and experiences of Chaplin's tour as related in the narrative but also his or her interpretation of the Chaplin-as-tourist (the public Chaplin's) persona. These dual perspectives are especially important when considering how well most of the illustrations work to further Chaplin's promotional agenda for the work (despite his approval or disapproval of them).[28]

The brilliantly colored cover by Welsh in the September 1933 *Woman's Home Companion* for the premiere installment of the series begins a message that is communicated consistently by most of the various illustrators for the series—that it was as much the screen Chaplin on tour as the public Chaplin. Although photographs might allow the viewer to see Chaplin's cane and derby, traditionally signifiers of wealth and status, as important echoes of the Little Tramp in the actor, the illustrator can make the conflation more overt and obvious. In figure 2.3, Chaplin is depicted as the Little Tramp tourist,

Figure 2.3. "A Comedian Sees the World" cover art of *Woman's Home Companion*, September 1933. Courtesy of Roy Export S.A.S.

wearing the familiar costume, except that it has morphed here into the costume of a sort of Great White Hunter. His usually shabby suit now seems pristine and is white except for his black necktie, with even his derby now a white pith helmet, and his baggy pants a pair of fashionable harem trousers.

His chest is adorned with a *Legion d'Honneur* medal, one the public Chaplin actually received on the tour. He's depicted in action; the scarf on his helmet cascades behind him, as does his camera case. The camera case is only one piece of evidence that Chaplin is in tourist mode. Unlike the penniless Little Tramp that he appears to be in the films, here he is accompanied by an assistant, a valet of some ethnic origin (he appears in colorful traditional dress, perhaps Turkish—Chaplin never visited Turkey), who totes Chaplin's sticker-covered suitcase and golf clubs. Chaplin raises his hat in a characteristic style and looks straight ahead, as if deferring to some unseen acquaintance. The Turk looks down on him from his greater height with an expression of deference and respect. This depiction of an affluent Little Tramp, almost a symbol of aristocracy and imperialism (on the connotative level), attempts to reconcile the stark disparity between the public Chaplin's wealth and social status with the screen Chaplin's poverty. He looks and carries himself like the Little Tramp, but he obviously has the advantages of money and influence. This hybrid figure represents, if nothing else, a unique attempt to overtly conflate the two personae, one that can only help this goal of the narrative.

Inside the first installment are three large tricolor illustrations (blue/black/white or brown/black/white), the first labeled with a microscopic caption that reads "Drawn from photographs by Shapi." These illustrations try to capitalize on the denotative message of the press photograph—that the physical Chaplin was in this place, at this time, meeting with this person—by representing press photograph scenes realistically. Still, as Barthes warns, the artist *selects* what he or she will represent. The first photograph reproduced is of a line of policemen holding back a London crowd. Chaplin does not appear either in this illustration or in the original photograph. While Shapi has been mostly true to that original representation, he chooses, in this instance, to add to it by sketching in, just under the policemen's feet at the far right of the scene, the Little Tramp's iconic props—the cane, the shoes, and the derby. Therefore, while the policemen in the original photograph hold back the crowd in order to protect the body of the public Chaplin, the policemen of the illustration seem to protect *only the Little Tramp's props* as if these were the most tangible signs (iconic) suggested by the name "Chaplin" printed on the other side of the same page. If the caption, "Drawn from photographs," is read at all, it must allow the drawings some status as referents for the reader, thereby lending a level of authenticity to the text. The drawing just described, then, asserts Chaplin's status as a celebrity attraction, an attribute also supported by the two other drawings in this installment, one of Chaplin and Ramsay MacDonald, the British Prime Minister at the time, and the other of Chaplin and Bernard Shaw at the premiere of *City Lights* in London.

The second installment, which appeared in October 1933, utilizes press photographs, not by reproducing them in illustrations but by manipulating them into a sort of postcard booklet. Along the left margin of the first page, the photographs have been cropped into approximately one-by-two-and-a-half-inch trapezoids onto what looks like either a gold ribbon or an accordion-shaped postcard folder. If a postcard folder, the effect is that Chaplin has collected these images as documents of his own encounters with celebrities, reinforcing the public Chaplin as tourist. Whatever the connotative message, the denotative one—again, that Chaplin was there at this time—provides a semblance of truth-value to the narrative. All the photos on this page depict Chaplin in the company of an easily recognizable male (no captions necessary), with the largest and most prominent one depicting Chaplin with the Prince of Wales, thereby solidifying his celebrity status. On the two succeeding pages, however, the photographs are cropped into the shape of circles, surrounded in large blue type by the names of the cities in which each was taken. Each of these round photos provides evidence of Chaplin's celebrity status at each venue.

In the third installment, which appeared in November 1933, the illustration supplants the photograph entirely—the first such visual strategy of the series—allowing a closer connection to be made between the screen and public Chaplins. The full page of illustrations (see figure 2.4) featured on the second page of the article is especially important because it affirms the rhetorical work of the narrative in the fox hunt episode in forging correlations between the behavior and actions of the actor with typical behavior of the Little Tramp. The focal point of the page is a large, realistic (almost photographic) drawing of Chaplin in his hodgepodge huntsman's outfit drawn by Rodrogin. Chaplin, in his narration of this episode in the series, sets up the coincidental conflation of his public and screen selves:

> The duke was dressed in huntsman style, a red coat and a hard, plush jockey cap. I felt a little *de trop*, not having the correct costume. I had hurriedly bought riding breeches and boots, but no coat or helmet. However, the duke provided me with a rig-out. I wore Sem's little red coat which made my breathing difficult, and one of the duke's helmets, also his waistcoat.
>
> I might mention the duke is a man about six feet three and thickset in proportion, and so his waistcoat hung to the level of my knees. In reaching for a match from the pocket, I looked as though I were pulling up my socks. And the duke's gloves were so large I found I could close my fist inside without disturbing the fingers. The tightness of Sem's coat seemed to give the waistcoat a ballet-skirt effect. It stuck out in folds.[29]

The illustrator Wallace Morgan, who would become famous later for his war illustrations, creates a sort of cartoon of this hunting episode that moves from the top center of the page, down the left margin, and then to the right along

Figure 2.4. "A Comedian Sees the World," from *Woman's Home Companion*, November 1933. Courtesy of Roy Export S.A.S.

the bottom border to its conclusion. The story is told in seven distinct frames, making it the most cinematic of the illustrations included in the series. The focus of the first five frames is Chaplin's interactions with the horse and with other riders. In the final two frames, however, the public Chaplin visually becomes the Little Tramp when he is depicted hatless with a shock of dark curly hair (the public Chaplin was silver-haired by this point, and recognizably so). The final frame expands on this assumption when it depicts Chaplin with his back to the viewer, hands on hips, curly black hair asserting itself, and feet splayed outward—all typical attitudes of Chaplin's film persona. The illustrations by Rodrogin and Win (separately) on the next page abandon Chaplin's public persona altogether and depict Chaplin's characters (Rodrogin depicts Chaplin's Karno persona "the Inebriate" and Win a collection of nine Little Tramps from his films). The emphasis in all of this illustration, which almost overwhelms the text, is that the narrating subject of "ACSTW" is the Little Tramp of the films, that they are the same person. The assertiveness of this imagery must assist the efforts of the written narrative, then, to achieve the conflation of these two personae and, for some more visual "readers," may even substitute for it.

As in the first two, the December 1933 installment features illustrations that utilize actual publicity photos, this time cropped according to illustrator Robert Gellert's specifications. The title page begins with a banner similar to the one for October in that it depicts the iconic props (hat, cane, and shoes), but here they become Christmas ornaments (even hanging off of a pine bough) and the laurel wreath a Christmas garland. Gellert creates an interesting effect with his illustrations, all done in blue-green ink. He creates a sort of montage by interweaving postcard-type scenes of recognizable European cities with iconic features of those cities, such as a bullfighter for San Sebastian and a dancing bear for Biarritz. The more solid blue band (the "road" taking the public Chaplin from place to place), which links the images, is drawn upon in white with images of transportation and travel, such as a valise, a Pullman car, and a limousine. Gellert then employs the publicity photos by superimposing disembodied Little Tramp heads onto each venue. These illustrations, consistent with the others in the series, promote the conflation of Chaplin's public and private personae. They also work to promote the image of the Little Tramp as tourist. Interestingly, what is missing from Gellert's message is Chaplin's status as a celebrity attraction. By using only the Little Tramp's head (and face), Gellert adds further evidence to my assertion that Chaplin's audience is not swayed so much by a similarity in looks between the public Chaplin and the Little Tramp, but by a similarity in behavior, gesture, and comportment, because the focus is on the Little Tramp's varied facial expressions. The connotative message in this element of the illustration is that the reader need only recognize this photograph of the Little Tramp's characteristic grimace or smirk placed here next to Biarritz and there next to London to believe both that he was in these places and that Chaplin's narrative of the trip is also his (the Little Tramp's).

The final installment (January 1934) continues the strategy of combining illustration with altered press photographs. The illustrator for this issue is Peter Helck, most famous for his drawings of modes of transportation (especially cars). The title page illustration depicts a very tiny Chaplin out of costume moving quickly out of the frame of the illustration in a rickshaw pulled by a Ceylonese man in a straw hat. Chaplin's brother Sydney is seated at his side (an attempt at realism). The rest of the illustration is filled with figures of the Ceylonese—the working Ceylonese—who abandon their work to give chase. These are the frenzied crowds that the narrative only depicts in Europe, but this illustration argues that Chaplin's appeal to the common man (his celebrity) is worldwide. The only evidence of the Little Tramp here is Helck's embellishment of the first letter of the title ("A") with a derby hat and an Asian artifact depicted in perspective behind it, a subtle artistic touch, which, however small, still keeps the conflation agenda before the eyes of the reader. The second page includes only a press photo of Chaplin at a Japanese tea ceremony, cropped into a circle and captioned with a pull quote, "In the sanctity of peace you refresh your troubled mind in liquid jade." The effect here is to ascertain Chaplin's presence in Asia and his willingness to participate in and experience the local traditions, no matter where he is; that is, it depicts Chaplin as tourist.

The third page, shown in figure 2.5, is complex and rich in signification. The rectangular frame at the top left of the page shows two Balinese folk dancers performing. The public Chaplin is visible in the audience, positioned at the top right corner of the illustration. He stands out among the dark-skinned natives because he glows white—his suit is white, his hair is white, and his face is white (a depiction of his public persona that reflects back to the "Great White Hunter" illustration on the cover of the premiere issue). This contrast is made especially noticeable because Helck draws Sydney beside him in more muted tones. Chaplin is depicted in the posture of someone totally engrossed in the performance; his shoulders are hunched forward as if he desires to be as close as possible to the action—the enthusiastic tourist experiencing what he believes is an authentic ethnic performance.

The large frame of this illustration is embedded into the illustration behind it. Whereas the frame just described is a dark and colorful scene, this background illustration is light—almost a sketch. It shows the public Chaplin arriving back in America. He is a small, dapper figure stopping near the end of the gangway to wave to the press and the swarming public. Above the porters on the ship's deck are Chaplin's shipboard companions, admirers as well, who even after all this time still climb on the railings or crane their necks in order to catch one final glimpse. This illustration, then, ends the series with an image of Chaplin's celebrity, a position he has occupied consistently throughout the sixteen months of the tour and will continue to occupy in the months and years to come.

Figure 2.5. "A Comedian Sees the World," from *Woman's Home Companion*, January 1934. Courtesy of Roy Export S.A.S.

While illustrations cannot offer a written text the level of authenticity afforded by photographs, the fact that many of the illustrators used press photographs (although altered) in conjunction with their illustrations may allow these illustrations more documentary value (Barthes's truth-value) than others, which are solely artistic inventions. Besides these photographic elements, the illustrations seem to project the message that the subject on tour was both the public Chaplin and his film persona in one, thereby assisting this agenda of the written text. And overall, the illustrations enhance and even exaggerate Chaplin's status on the tour as a celebrity attraction.

Chaplin was a visual artist, an artist of film, and as such it would be hard to imagine any creative product of his that tried to stand alone without a visual component. As promotional texts, the travel narratives use whatever means at their disposal to achieve their marketing usefulness for Chaplin and his film creation. Just as the Little Tramp appears in nearly every scene of his films, so, too, must he be visually accessible in his written texts. Chaplin and his publicity machine understood the rhetorical usefulness of the visual image and capably employed it both to market the films and to keep the iconic image of the Little Tramp alive in the minds and hearts of his audience, thereby solidifying his legacy.

Visual images of Chaplin as the Little Tramp on film or even in photos have inspired volumes of written commentary, thereby demonstrating a close affinity between these two types of texts. Even Lucia Joyce, James Joyce's daughter, begins her short tribute to Chaplin[30] for *Le Disque Vert* in 1924[31] with looking at a photograph: "The photo of Charlie is on my table. His intelligent and sad eyes look at me while I search for a way to express to you my admiration for this great and small comic actor."[32] The denotative message of the photograph makes Charlie (the Little Tramp) seem alive to her, even allowing him to meet her gaze with his own. Because of the vitality of the Little Tramp created by these images, the public Chaplin must perform the Little Tramp in order to be accepted. As Rugg asserts, as the physical body's aura increases with the reproduction and dissemination of its images, its audience begins to identify the "presence of humorous entertainment with the presence of the body, and if they were disappointed in that hope, they might begin to suspect that the *body* before them was a fake, a counterfeit. The image, on the other hand, could not be. [Therefore], it becomes the body's task to approximate its images."[33] As was the case for Samuel Clemens's Mark Twain, the physical body of Chaplin must perform or impersonate the Little Tramp in the travel narrative and in the photograph in order to succeed, for the pseudonym (the fictional creation) has become more alive in the minds and hearts of the public—more real—than the man who created him.

NOTES

1. A celebrity may comprise many personae. In this chapter, I distinguish the screen Chaplin (the Little Tramp persona) from the public Chaplin (the persona Chaplin presented to his public—also performative) and the private Chaplin (one that existed away from the public eye). For a more developed discussion of the verbal aspects of the narratives and their role in this conflation, see my dissertation: Lisa Stein, "The Travel Narrative as Spin: Mitigating Charlie Chaplin's Public Persona in *My Trip Abroad* and 'A Comedian Sees the World'" (PhD diss., Ohio University, 2005).

2. *My Trip Abroad* was written by then-journalist Monta Bell, later a Chaplin Studios employee, then a director in his own right.

3. Charles Chaplin, *My Trip Abroad* (New York: Harper, 1922). Hereafter referred to as *MTA*.

4. Charles Chaplin, "A Comedian Sees the World," *Woman's Home Companion* (September 1933): 7–10, 80, 86–89; (October 1933): 15–17, 102, 104, 106, 108; (November 1933): 15–17, 100, 102, 104, 113, 115, 116, 119; (December 1933): 21–23, 36, 38, 42, 44; (January 1934): 21–23, 86. Hereafter referred to as "ACSTW."

5. Boris Evelinoff, Letter to Arthur Kelly, 12 December 1935, Charlie Chaplin Archive, Cineteca di Bologna, Bologna, Italy.

6. Translation by Lisa Stein Haven.

7. Evelinoff, Letter to Charles Chaplin, 12 December 1935, Charlie Chaplin Archive, Cineteca di Bologna, Bologna, Italy.

8. *My Trip Abroad* Contract, Harper and Brothers Publishers to Charles Chaplin, 20 January 1922, Charlie Chaplin Archive, Cineteca di Bologna, Bologna, Italy.

9. David Robinson, *Chaplin: His Life and Art* (London: Penguin, 2001), 479.

10. Robinson, *Chaplin,* 277.

11. Robinson, *Chaplin,* 441.

12. Charles J. Maland, *Chaplin and American Culture: The Evolution of a Star Image* (Princeton, NJ: Princeton University Press, 1989), 121.

13. Roland Barthes, *Image-Music-Text,* ed. and trans. Stephen Heath (New York: Hill and Wang, 1977), 38.

14. Barthes, *Image-Music-Text,* 39.

15. Barthes, *Image-Music-Text,* 44.

16. Barthes, *Image-Music-Text,* 44.

17. Susan Sontag, *On Photography* (New York: Farrar, Straus and Giroux, 1977), 23.

18. CDVs were the first affordable type of photographs and as such brought photography and the owning/collecting of photographs to the masses. First patented by Disdéri in 1854 in France, CDVs were, as John Tagg relates, "paper prints from glass negatives, mounted on card and produced by use of a special camera with several lenses and a moving plate holder. With such a camera, eight or more images could be taken on one plate and the prints from it cut up to size" (48).

19. Edward Steichen, *A Life in Photography* (Garden City, NY: Doubleday, 1963), no page.

20. Linda Haverty Rugg, *Picturing Ourselves: Photography & Autobiography* (Chicago: University of Chicago Press, 1997), 3.

21. Rugg, *Picturing Ourselves,* 43.

22. Rugg, *Picturing Ourselves,* 2.

23. The photo was probably taken in 1910 or shortly thereafter, when Chaplin worked as a music hall comedian for the Karno Company in London.

24. In his 1940 review of the just-released *The Great Dictator,* entitled "Chaplin Draws a Keen Weapon," Robert Van Gelder notes the contrast between Chaplin's thick neck and the rest of his physique, a comment supported by Chaplin's own words: "His physique is unusual. His hands and feet are small, very finely made. His body is lithe, and its movements are perfectly coordinated. But his neck is out of proportion—thick, when compared to the rest of him. 'I have a bull neck,' [Chaplin] commented. 'Always have had. Yes, it's been useful with all the knocking around I've taken. But it is out of character for the Weak little tramp.'" (*New*

York Times, 8 September 1940, n.p.) Chaplin's admitted knowledge of this contrast suggests that he fully understood the conflation agenda his images needed to achieve.

25. Francis W. Dauer offers a general schema of the Little Tramp's visual rhetorical strategies in his essay, "The Nature of Fictional Characters and the Referential Fallacy," *The Journal of Aesthetics and Art Criticism* 53, no. 1 (1995): 31–38. As he explains, "At the broadest level, the humor of Chaplin's films is principally achieved through dazzling sequences of incongruities" (33). The problem, he argues, with this sort of comedy is maintaining the continuous humor. Chaplin does it, he suggests, by relying "on a series of reversible metamorphoses" (34).

26. Maland makes reference to a *New York Times* article from January 1932 entitled "Ten Men Who Stand as Symbols" in which Chaplin is included, along with the Prince of Wales, Mussolini, Stalin, the Pope, Henry Ford, Gandhi, Charles Lindbergh, Albert Einstein, and George Bernard Shaw (*Chaplin and American Culture*, 132).

27. Barthes, *Image-Music-Text*, 43.

28. Chaplin's approval or disapproval of these illustrations is unknown.

29. Charlie Chaplin, "A Comedian Sees the World," 15–16.

30. I include Lucia Joyce's tribute because it begins with the photograph, moves to remembrance of the Little Tramp on film, and ends with Joyce's brief encounter with Chaplin on the Champs Elysees during his 1921 tour (she was just fourteen). Most importantly, she begins her quest to meet Chaplin, hoping to meet the Little Tramp, and finds him, not in Chaplin's appearance, but in his gestures and attitudes.

31. Lucia Joyce, "Charlie et Les Gosses," *Le Disque Vert* 3, nos. 4–5 (1924): 76–78.

32. Translation by Lisa Stein Haven.

33. Rugg, *Picturing Ourselves*, 43.

Chapter Three

A Heart of Gold

Charlie and the Dance Hall Girls

Cynthia J. Miller

> There she stood, her loveliness lighting the room, filling his soul with the
> music of romance for which he was so ill-suited.
> —*The Gold Rush*

It's not surprising to see Charlie Chaplin fall in love with a beautiful girl on
the silver screen—even a tramp needs a little tenderness. Overlooked,
shunted aside, and ridiculed, Chaplin's forlorn signature characters—the
Tramp, the Little Fellow, the aging Clown—all reside at the margins of their
fictional worlds, inhabiting the insignificant corners of the narratives' social
landscapes. They are drawn to beautiful, seemingly unattainable women and
ultimately win them over—at least, in part—with a sensitive, comic humanity that blurs the boundaries of appearance, status, and class. The objects of
their affections, however, whether vulnerable waifs, down-and-out working
girls, or flamboyant coquettes, provide his hapless characters with much
more than fleeting affection. Far from what has been described as "ornamental heroines,"[1] each of Chaplin's onscreen partners contributes to his films'
narratives and to the construction and reception of his personas in ways that
define and highlight Chaplin's iconic traits. One pairing that repeats several
times throughout Chaplin's career—from early silent films, such as *A Dog's
Life* (1918) and *The Gold Rush* (1925), to his last directing effort, *A Countess
from Hong Kong* (1967)—is "Charlie" and the dance hall girl. Seldom considered in examinations of Chaplin's work, dance hall girls are significant
cultural archetypes that combine gender and spectacle in ways that are particularly well suited to his cinematic characters and bittersweet comedy. In
some cases, as in *A Burlesque on Carmen* (1915), they are flamboyant wom-

45

en of questionable morals; in others, as in *Limelight* (1952), their circumstances are deceiving. In all cases, however, their iconic characters provide
not only visual and symbolic contrast for Chaplin's downtrodden figures, but
also function in support of his underlying social and political commentary.
Though typically cast in narratives of "difference"—glamorous and self-
assured in contrast to his world-worn demeanor—these transgressive charm-
ers are aligned with Chaplin's characters as kindred spirits on the margins of
polite society and also similarly challenge the taken-for-granted values of
class, gender, and demeanor that form the basis for his comic critiques. This
essay, then, will explore the significance of these relationships between Chaplin and the dance hall girls, examining the various ways in which these
socially, culturally, and visually significant female figures contribute to the
construction of both Chaplin's character and his films. The glamour and
femininity embodied by the dance hall girls inspire both boldness and vulnerability in his downtrodden figures, causing him to seek out an intimacy that
transcends the dictates of class and caste.

CONJURING GENDERED SPECTACLE

Dance hall girls, in their many forms and guises, come from a long and rich
lineage of women who have existed outside the moral conventions of their
communities—working jobs that brought them into intimate contact with
men and that emphasized sexuality and a loosening of conventional social or
moral restraints—beginning with the saloon girls of the Western frontier.
Often referred to as "painted ladies" because of their use of makeup, saloon
girls could be seen decked out in bright colors, sequins, and ruffles, exposing
bare arms, stocking-clad legs, and cleavage.[2] Vibrant symbols of "lively
pursuits," the bold statement made by their appearance was given form
through their behavior as women who would drink, dance, and talk with
strangers—practices that set them apart from the "respectable" women of
their communities and established them as icons of female sexuality. Bold,
confident, and sensual, saloon and dance hall girls were found in abundance
in the Western territories and mining towns, intermingled in the public consciousness with other "fallen" women, such as variety performers and prostitutes. However, most were women who had simply fallen on hard times—
poor, displaced, or widowed—or were youthful adventure seekers. They
were lured to the job—one of the few means of earning a living open to
women in the nineteenth century—through the advertisement of high wages,
easy work, and fine clothing.[3] Their stories were not very different from the
urban dance hall girls who would follow them into the twentieth century, in
cities such as New York and Chicago, as women pushed the boundaries of

appropriate behavior and staked their claims to both the risks and benefits of commercial entertainment.

Departing from early theatrical and courtly stages for dance associated with nobility and privilege, such as ballet where tightly constricted notions of femininity were enforced and promoted, dance halls of the nineteenth and early twentieth centuries served as complex sites where female identities were contested.[4] They stood among the earliest forms of commercialized entertainment where, as Kathy Peiss notes, "female participation was profitable and encouraged." [5] This migration of young women into the public sphere was fostered by a collision of economics and social change, creating what sociologist Paul Goalby Cressey cites as "the drive toward casual association" found in areas of growing population.[6] For unmarried working-class women, dance halls embodied notions of leisure, modernity, individuality, and, of course, social interaction with men. In symbolic terms, they are what Victor Turner sees as "liminoid" space: carefully bracketed cultural locations where improbable and often contradictory experiences occur; spaces animated by the opportunity to challenge the norms of everyday life, without the uncertainty of actual change.[7] Similar to dime museums, variety halls, carnival sideshows, and theaters, dance halls were social spaces where taboos of expression and association were defied, but upon further analysis, such defiance occurred only in ways that highlighted and reinforced the most fundamental of gender norms: the pursuit of romantic partnership and the showcasing of heightened femininity.

In this specific form of defiance, the dance hall played one of its most important roles: as a context within which femininity was constructed, elaborated, and displayed. The women who worked in these establishments were transgressive women, to be sure, but that is not their most important quality. The dance hall girl is an icon of female spectacle—part of a long lineage that not only encompasses saloon girls, bordello queens, and other "working girl" archetypes, but also extends to female stage performers from burlesque, music halls, variety shows, and the follies. They are "public women"—not in the limited sense of the harlot, but in the broader sense, as women whose gender is on display, in public—and their performance of femininity speaks to an enhanced or ideal type: a spectacle of curls and curves, whether accompanied by wide eyes or knowing smiles.

This notion of gendered spectacle is a complex constellation of sexuality, high and low culture, theatricality, and social commentary—a combination of institutionalized social roles and insubordination that is typically associated with the women of burlesque, vaudeville, and the follies.[8] Feminist critic Laura Mulvey argues that such icons of gendered spectacle do not contribute to the construction of the narrative, but rather hinder it, bringing little more to the stage or screen than a focal point for male desire:

Woman displayed as sexual object is the leitmotif of erotic spectacle: from
pin-up to strip-tease, from Ziegfeld to Busby Berkley, she holds the look, plays
to and signifies male desire. The presence of woman is an indispensable element of spectacle in normal narrative film, yet her visual presence tends to
work against the development of the story line, to freeze the flow of action in
moments of erotic contemplation.[9]

However, this approach overlooks many of the social complexities of gendered spectacle by dehistoricizing it, removing it from the wider implications
of its social milieu and collapsing issues of agency, social hierarchy, and
conceptualizations of masculinity into a narrow reading of visual presence.
The female performers in each of the genres relying on gendered spectacle,
however, brought an image of femininity to the American stage that chal-
lenged prevailing notions of respectability, refinement, and the boundary
between public and private in the lives of early-twentieth-century women. At
one pole, female-managed burlesque troupes, such as the renowned Lydia
Thompson and her British Blondes, took urban centers by storm and gave
"low" culture—the popular culture of the masses—a voice on stage. Their
performances featured parodies of gender roles and sophisticated entertainment, along with brazen humor emanating from voluptuous, feminine working-class women.[10] The other, high budget, "high culture" productions, such
as the Ziegfeld Follies, laid claim to "Glorifying the American Girl," as each
performance showcased dozens of unattainably beautiful chorines baring
their breasts in the name of "art."[11] As Kathryn Oberdeck has noted, even
vaudeville—which struggled to find a middle ground by providing entertainment that bridged the differences between high culture and low, Anglo and
immigrant—claimed to uphold genteel cultural sensibilities, yet mocked
upper-class refinement as so much "hackneyed Victorian prissiness."[12] It
thus provided a spotlight for transgressive female performers such as Julia
Arthur and Ruth Budd, who were as iconic as they were controversial. In
return, these female performers, "placed at the outer limit of civil life,"
became objects of fascination, longing, and desire.[13]

From the girl in the frontier dance hall, to Lydia Thompson's British
Blondes at New York's Winter Garden, to Little Egypt at the Columbian
Exposition, these women all contributed to the sense of wonder, mystery, and
romance of feminine archetypes in the late nineteenth and early twentieth
centuries. Their presence and evolution in American performance culture
functioned to provide glamour, alongside a palpable tension derived from
irony and parody, on stage and screen, while also serving to define the roles
and reception of their male counterparts. And while female spectacle may be
found in both high culture entertainment, such as the Ziegfeld Follies, and its
low culture counterparts, it is the latter that speak directly to portrayals of the
dance hall girl in Chaplin's films, with their direct address of working-class

issues and working-class values. Although the Tramp was a character "that compelled attention and laughter simply by being,"[14] these archetypes of femininity would highlight the very qualities that made him and his kindred characters both memorable and endearing. Their glamour—whether smoldering and subtle or bawdy and blatant—gave the Tramp an unanticipated beauty and grace all his own, as his retiring demeanor and artful pantomime contrasted with their accentuated femininity.

Walter Kerr observes that "[t]he secret of Chaplin, as a character, is that he can be anyone."[15] However, in the public consciousness, Chaplin the actor was inextricably linked to Charlie, the character of the downtrodden Tramp—the Little Fellow, the dejected Clown—a gentle, often bittersweet figure of comic spectacle in his own right. Adaptable as Chaplin was in his craft, these signature characters were constructions that were dependent, in both their narrative and visual presentation and reception, on their historical, social, and ideological contexts in ways that corresponded to the gendered spectacle of the dance hall girl. In his examination of the ways in which the character of Chaplin's Tramp, working-class values, and productive labor are bound together, Charles Musser discusses at length the importance of such contexts, and the discussion holds equally true for gender archetypes. The character of the Tramp has deep roots in the performative traditions of vaudeville and variety—as well as in low culture literature, such as comics, newspapers, and pulp novels—making him a familiar figure to the working class. This working-class popularity allowed the character of the Tramp an easy transition to motion pictures, as well, until, at the turn of the century, as Musser notes, "almost every production company had its tramp comedies."[16] None, however, were as durable or had the same impact on popular culture as Chaplin's.

More a character of inspiration than intention, Chaplin's Tramp was born in a dressing room, cobbled together from bits and remnants borrowed from others: Roscoe "Fatty" Arbuckle's capacious trousers, Charles Avery's coat, Arbuckle's father-in-law's derby, a tuft of crepe hair affixed beneath his nose with spirit gum, and a bamboo cane. The laughter he evoked was some of the first of his as-yet lackluster cinematic career. As Mack Sennett, founder of Keystone Studios, recalls: "Charlie fumbled his way out of the dressing room, walking with a splay-footed shuffle we had never seen before." He looked "like a shabby-genteel sparrow."[17]

Seldom the serious romantic lead but always the gentleman, Chaplin's Tramp brought the comedic irony of burlesque and vaudeville to his amorous encounters as he strategized, strained, and pratfalled in attempts to display his masculinity and bask in the light of his beloved. Chaplin's inventiveness and wit brought an element of constant surprise to the stage that harkened back to the touring companies of *commedia dell'arte* in sixteenth- and seventeenth-century Italy. For *commedia*'s actors, each scene acted as a canvas upon which their task was to paint the brilliant colors of their craft, making laughter ring or tears flow, to playfully spar "like a merry game of ball or spirited sword-play, with ease and without a pause."[18] Much like Arlecchino, the harlequin figure of *commedia*, Chaplin's presence created comic magic: "I pluck a limp, wrinkled rainbow from my trunk and endow it with my shape, and beholding it, the world can only rejoice."[19] But unlike the brightly colored harlequin, Chaplin's quiet, understated magic is at its best when viewed in contrast with the glamour of spectacle.

CHARLIE'S "ANGELS"

Chaplin's early cinematic encounters with feminine spectacle are found in films like his 1915 two-reel production *A Burlesque on Carmen*, his thirteenth film for Essanay.[20] In true burlesque tradition, the film parodies earlier cinematic renditions of Bizet's comic opera *Carmen* (1875), spinning a tale of the beautiful Gypsy woman who seduces an awkward and inexperienced Spanish officer in order to facilitate a smuggling run.[21] Here, we find Chaplin's enduring costar Edna Purviance playing the glamorous, sultry temptress of the title (see figure 3.1). In this highly sexualized role, Purviance seduces Chaplin's officious and inept border guard, Darn Hosiery, with come-hither looks, teasing caresses, passionate kisses, and a table dance not at all unlike the "cooch dance" of turn-of-the-century burlesque. The exotic sophistication of the gypsy Carmen, with her bold, almost flapper-like demeanor, is in sharp contrast to the severely limited masculinity of the diminutive border guard. This effect is especially clear in scenes where hypermasculine Gypsy men—Carmen's counterparts and roguish masculine equivalents—surround him, creating a contrast that heightens Chaplin's parody of the opera's character Don Jose. Purviance's Carmen is all confidence, while Chaplin's Darn Hosiery—of visibly smaller stature—fumbles with his sword, fails in his repeated attempts to lift her onto a table for her dance, and then loses himself in enthusiastic but clumsy mimicry of her graceful movements while she looks on. He is overeager while she is self-possessed, earnest while she is guarded and reflexive. As Dan Kamin observes, Purviance "anchored Chaplin's performances both physically and emotionally. She brought a great dignity to her roles, as well as a concentration on Chaplin that helped the audience focus on his more subtle movements."[22] In the absence of this contrast between the robust, sexualized Gypsy and the ineffectual guard, much of the burlesque's mockery of "high art," masculinity, and social class would have been lost.

Although Purviance appeared with Chaplin in nearly all of his pictures for Essanay, the Carmen role was a sharp departure from any of those in which she had previously been cast. However, Chaplin's initial attraction to her as a

Figure 3.1.   The seductive Carmen (Edna Purviance).

costar—and a love interest—had its roots in the very qualities that supported her portrayal of this archetype of gender spectacle. Her sensual, ethereal beauty and bold confidence made her a natural complement to his hapless characters. The two worked together in much the same way that Chaplin's forlorn characters offset the vibrant, ongoing rhythm of the day-to-day lives around them—silence drawing attention to sound, darkness accentuating color.

Chaplin's leading lady from 1915 to 1923, Purviance made her next foray into this archetype of feminine spectacle three years later, in *A Dog's Life*. In this, one of Chaplin's most well-known films, the Tramp ventures into the Green Lantern saloon—a disreputable dive where Purviance's character, "Edna," is employed as a singer. In this film, she is stripped of the radiant confidence and charm that propelled her portrayal of Carmen, and her performance harkens back to her earlier Essanay roles as a fragile woman in need of rescue. Edna may be a dance hall girl, but only reluctantly so, and it is precisely that reluctance that works against type here. She is unschooled in the art of seduction and too fearful to comply with her employer's instructions to graciously accept the sexual advances of the tavern's patrons, thus framing her as victim rather than agent in the film's narrative. Her passivity, often identified with traditional mainstream female roles, particularly in early-twentieth-century entertainment, positions her as simply supporting the existing character construction of Chaplin's Tramp, rather than challenging it or throwing it into relief as do the more vibrant, transgressive dance hall figures.[23]

Edna, then, is every bit as shy and retiring as the Tramp himself, short-circuiting the potent comic and dramatic contrast between the two iconic types. Unlike the temptress Carmen, she denies her own sexuality and rejects men who would draw the archetypal qualities to the forefront of her character. She intrudes upon, rather than owns, the space of the dance hall stage and fades into a corner, her sensuality cloaked in drab attire and seldom even hinted at through direct eye contact. The singer's awkward attempt to flirt—as ill fitting as any of Chaplin's—presents a parody of the "public woman," rather than an illustration. When she finally draws him into a dance, dog in tow, the Tramp secures the canine's rope leash about his waist to free his hands for the encounter. His four-legged companion, however, has other ideas, and soon exits the scene, dragging the surprised suitor behind him, leaving the dance hall and romance behind. A failure at her attempts at seduction—and as an archetype of feminine power—Edna's impact on Chaplin's Tramp is thus minimized, upstaged, in good vaudeville fashion, by a dog. Her inability to engage with the power of her archetype positions her as a subordinate to his comic antics, rather than as a counterpoint; her muted glamour fails to provide the spotlight in which the Tramp and his antics truly shine.

In *The Gold Rush*, however, Chaplin's narrative returns to a more powerful, direct use of feminine spectacle in the character of "Georgia," played by Georgia Hale (see figure 3.2). The film was one of Chaplin's favorites: "This is the picture that I want to be remembered by," he stated in one of the film's pressbook advertisements, a full-length feature comedy masterpiece.[24] Inspired by the Donner party disaster (1846–1847) and, as some scholars have suggested, Erich von Stroheim's *Greed* (1924), the film follows Chaplin's Tramp to the Yukon, where he intends to strike it rich during the Klondike gold rush.[25] The vast Arctic wilderness accentuates the Tramp's isolation and ineffectuality; his small figure is overwhelmed by the landscape and its perils, setting the stage for the narration of Chaplin's main theme: the "utter insignificance" of the Tramp in the face of the "vast indifference of the universe around him."[26] Yet even in the struggle to survive, the Tramp creates transformative comedy, as a boiled boot becomes a sumptuous Thanksgiving dinner, and forked potatoes dance like chorus girls across the table. The Tramp is, himself, transformed, however, when amid the action and intrigue of larceny and lost claims, he is smitten with the vivacious dance hall girl, Georgia.

Hale's casting brought an additional spark to the dance hall girl archetype, as Hale delivered her role with "a sultry, defiant hint of vulgarity" that did not come naturally to Chaplin's other leading ladies, such as Edna Purviance.[27] Typifying the "new woman" of the 1920s, Georgia is characterized by the intertitles as "quick and impulsive; proud and independent"—a wom-

Figure 3.2.   Sultry and vivacious, Georgia Hale adds fire to Chaplin's dance hall girl archetype in *The Gold Rush* (1925).

an who works in the evening in "the beacon light of pleasure, that retreat of lost dreams"—the dance hall.

In the beginning of the scene, Chaplin's character moves, unnoticed, through the dance hall, alienated from the laughter and merrymaking that surround him. He scans the room for glimmers of welcome but finds none. Not, at least, until his attention shifts to Georgia. Dressed in multicolored spangles that reflect the dance hall lights, she stands out like a beacon in the midst of winter wool and leather around the dance hall's bar. His spirits lift as she moves toward him with a smile, but his hopes are dashed when he realizes that the warmth of her greeting is meant for someone else—Jack, whom the intertitles signal is a "ladies man." In spite of this disappointment, he is love-struck. Even as she looks right through him, he returns her gaze with adoration.

Georgia's character harkens back to those found in *commedia dell'arte*—flirtatious, keen-witted and worldly—a robust Columbina to Chaplin's clownish Arlecchino.[28] When she asks the Little Fellow to dance in order to spite her burly would-be suitor, the two make an awkward pairing: Georgia, in her festive party dress, and the Little Fellow, in his mismatched shoes and drab, ill-fitting secondhand clothes. His pants, held up by a rope, become a comic prop as he struggles to keep them up, ultimately reprising scenes from *A Dog's Life*, when the canine at the other end of his improvised belt develops a mind (and direction) of his own. Georgia's easy laughter accentuates the Little Fellow's earnestness and her worldliness emphasizes his insecurities in the same way that her polished presence later redefines the primitiveness of his borrowed cabin. Only at the film's end, when the Little Fellow has struck it rich and is, in effect, her social "better," does the light of Georgia's glamour dim, her iconic feminine spectacle no longer necessary in the construction of his character.

The use of such feminine spectacle to foreground Chaplin's character is not limited to dance hall girls or other "tarnished" character types. In the 1952 motion picture *Limelight*, the last American-produced film of Chaplin's career, we find a different sort of Chaplin complemented by a different sort of feminine spectacle—one that is no less powerful but differs in its interrelationships of gender, performance, and social hierarchy. Here, we find Chaplin as Calvero, a complex music hall clown in the twilight of his career, alienated from the art that gave him life: isolated, old, and no longer able to "see the joke." Like the Little Fellow in *The Gold Rush*, Calvero recognizes his invisibility, but as a more mature Chaplin character, he holds an abiding awareness that "survival" is not enough: "As a man gets on in years, he wants to live deeply," he confesses. "A feeling of sad dignity comes upon him, and that's fatal for a comic." Calvero's gradually emerging story is interwoven with another—that of the film's heroine, Terry (Claire Bloom)—a character who complements this world-worn Chaplin figure. "What a sad business, being funny," she muses as Calvero reflects on his life. Terry is, in many ways, a culmination of several of Chaplin's characters' earlier attempts at love, sharing many of their traits and circumstances: She is reminiscent of Merna (Merna Kennedy) of *The Circus*, a troubled and vulnerable performer compromised by material reality, and also of the blind flower girl (Virginia Cherrill) in *City Lights* (1931)—both of whom are rescued by Chaplin's characters. As Kyp Harness notes, Terry is faintly tinged with the aura of the "fallen woman," like the dance hall girls played by Purviance and Hale—and also Marilyn Nash in *Monsieur Verdoux* (1947)—but here, we find that circumstances can be deceiving.[29]

As the film opens, a drunken Calvero stumbles home. The odor of gas in his apartment building rouses him to action, and he prevents Terry's attempted suicide. The aging Clown moves the mysterious woman to his apartment, where he nurses her back to health. Both Calvero and his landlady assume that Terry is a prostitute. The landlady warns: "You watch out for that hussie—she's no good. And what's more, she's been sick ever since she came here." Later, only after Calvero intimates that the illness she suffers from is syphilis, does she reveal that she is, in fact, a ballet dancer, whose past—troubled by poverty and a sister who walked the streets to finance her sibling's dance lessons—has left her emotionally and physically paralyzed.

Unlike films such as *The Gold Rush*, however, *Limelight* employs a high culture female archetype as the counterpart for Chaplin's character. While perhaps falling victim to popular suppositions about the loose morals of women involved in performance, Terry is a practitioner of one of the high arts associated with sophistication, breeding, and education, rather than a woman whose association with the stage falls on the wrong side of the high culture/mass culture divide and suggests low moral standing. However, her dance scenes, both in Calvero's dreams and in reality, offer prime examples of female spectacle intended to highlight and complement the figure of the faded comic star rather than to upstage him. In scenes that overtly reference *commedia*, from which their characters are loosely drawn, the glitter and gracefulness she brings to the stage draw attention to his understated demeanor, much as musical notes draw attention to the silence of a rest that falls between them. In her precise and fluid movements, clothed in crisp white, she is all virtue, all art, all refined femininity. In the final scenes of the film, even Calvero draws attention to the existential gulf between his clownish parody of a gentleman and the ballerina's unattainable (to him) perfection, observing: "even you make me feel isolated."

Weissman has suggested that the relationships between Chaplin's cinematic personas and characters such as Terry have more to do with re-creating the actor/director's inner world than with creating performative contexts and contrasts.[30] In each of these pairings, Weissman sees Chaplin's attempts to rescue and "rehabilitate" ostensibly fallen women as reflecting, retracing, and correcting the circumstances of his own mother's decline. Certainly, no analysis of Chaplin's work would deny that he, like any other actor or film-maker, brought elements of his own character and experience to his projects. Many commentators—such as Maland and Harness—have discussed at length the larger autobiographical interweaving of Chaplin's iconic personas with his own life and career, and as Kamin notes, in *Limelight*, "the cross-overs between art and life are vertiginous" and resonant with meaning.[31] However, while dance hall girls, prostitutes, and other afflicted heroines are recurrent themes in Chaplin's oeuvre, reducing their significance to merely that of externalized artifacts of psychological discomfort is to diminish both the careful construction of the characters and his comic genius as an actor and filmmaker. The dance hall girl stands as a particularly potent female archetype in an era of shifting gender identity, at once both challenging and reinforcing prevailing notions of class and propriety. From his early days at Mack Sennett's Keystone Film Company onward, Chaplin displayed his mastery of imagery—not just physical virtuosity of movement and gesture, but of framing, context, and contrast—and no discussion of the dance hall girls, prostitutes, or women of the stage in Chaplin's films is complete with-out such a consideration.

Just as Chaplin's signature characters—the Clown, the Tramp, the Little Fellow—were enhanced by sharing the screen with female characters con-nected to the powerful archetype of the dance hall girl, they also brought a gentleness and comic grace to the relationship that gave the ladies' glamour an air of magic—a sparkle that dimmed a bit without him when Chaplin matched them with other onscreen counterparts. This absence of contrast is apparent first in *A Woman of Paris* (1923), which paired Edna Purviance with both Carl Miller and Adolphe Menjou, and then, more than forty years later, in Chaplin's final film, *A Countess from Hong Kong* (1967), when he brought one last dance hall girl to the screen—Natascha, a 50-cents-a-dance countess, played by Sophia Loren—who sneaks aboard a ship bound for the United States to avoid being forced into prostitution. An actress widely ac-knowledged as embodying fantasies of an ideal female type—charismatic, bold, voluptuous, and alluring—Loren brought all of the qualities of gen-dered spectacle to her role of the impoverished stowaway Russian countess. She is transgressive, however, in image only. Much like Terry in *Limelight*, in fact, the countess is desperately attempting to *avoid* transgression, humor-ously sidestepping moral compromise and bringing a virtue to the role of the dance hall girl that others of Chaplin's wayward-seeming female characters do not. Both are, at the core, representatives of high culture, standing apart from Chaplin's more working-class female figures. Through a series of Key-stone-inspired antics, Loren brings comedy as well as archetypal grace to her role, as she evades both detection and the amorous advances of her husband-of-convenience (Patrick Cargill) during her bid for passage into America.

But the leading man—her benefactor and coconspirator, Ambassador Ogden Mears—is played by the equally dynamic Marlon Brando, rather than Chaplin, causing both Loren's portrayal of the feminine archetype, as well as its narrative impact, to appear muted; the feminine spectacle it attempts to employ lacks luster in the absence of its downtrodden comic counterpart. As Kamin observes, "the film is more a tribute to Chaplin's appreciation of female beauty than his ability to create a world illuminated by that beauty."[32]

SPOTLIGHTING THE TRAMP

Charlie and the dance hall girls—the understated and the exotic—did not come together lightly or incidentally in his films. Their pairings were not merely the products of a storyteller's imagination, or art configured to imitate life, but the realized visions of a master of theatricality, carefully molded, modulated, and choreographed to highlight the poignancy and comic grace of Chaplin's signature characters; to ensure that the quiet charm of the Tramp, so easily passed by in the narrative worlds of his films, would not be overlooked. The women of Chaplin's films were not cast as ornamental objects recruited to entertain the sexualized gaze—or as symbolic figures conjured in the service of publically working out his inner world—but rather, as part of the process of creating and deepening an enduring cinematic icon.

Carmen, Georgia, and Terry, along with several other of Chaplin's key female characters, were all archetypes of feminine spectacle—women defined by their glamour and the power of their iconic femininity. These characters, in both demeanor and action, explore that power of bold femininity and its impact on traditional narrative and character formation. At their fullest expression, Chaplin's dance hall girls call into question the notion that the concept of "feminine spectacle" denotes passivity and objectification by the male gaze. They are, rather, embodiments of spectacle's visual, social, and imaginative power, capable of evoking wonder and fascination. Through their femininity, they transcend the everyday, in which Chaplin's personae are so firmly rooted, and are mesmerizing . . . fascinating . . . compelling—qualities that scholars such as Camille Paglia have linked to contemporary reconsiderations of the "goddess."[33] They are, in a sense, magical—not as manifestations of the supernatural, but as embodiments of longing. Magic, as Marcel Mauss has observed, is inextricably linked to the wish—the desire for fantasy to be fulfilled—the attempt to make manifest longings, dreams, and visions, and move beyond the realm of known possibilities into the desired unknown.[34] Chaplin's dance hall girls—from the ephemeral Terry, as she glides across the stage, to the exotic gypsy Carmen, queen of the tabletop cooch dance—evoke and make manifest such dreams and visions, not only through their glamorous appearances or their bold return of the male gaze, but through the spectacle of the dance itself.

We see this clearly in Carmen's signature dance scene in the tavern. Carmen, who is, as the intertitles narrate, "loved by all men under the age of 96," is the epitome of powerful femininity. She is unflinchingly flirtatious, never failing to meet the gaze of her would-be suitors full-on, yet unattainable. As she dances atop one of the tavern's tables, her movement unfettered by either appropriate attire or social convention, her arms wave and hips gyrate to the delight of the men around her. Even as she draws Darn Hosiery close for a kiss, it is *he* who is objectified, rather than her. Carmen easily maintains control of the male crowd that gathers, however, beckoning them close, then turning away, bestowing her attention like a rare gift. Chaplin's ineffectual soldier competes to capture her interest, attempting to match her captivating power with a dance of his own and fails, appearing all the more comic in the process.

A similar dynamic inheres in the tavern scene of *The Gold Rush*, as Georgia, who appears luminous through the eye of the camera—sleek and sophisticated, amid a sea of flannel and three-day beards—uses the dance to assert her power over the establishment's wilderness Romeos, drawing Chaplin's unassuming Little Fellow into intimate physical contact, while he struggles to maintain his facade of composure and engaging "equality" with this woman whose star clearly outshines his own. Georgia is all poise and confidence, gracefully moving across the dance floor, while the Little Fellow cannot even maintain control of his pants with her in his arms. The result, once again, is one of Chaplin's most widely recognized comic scenes.

Whether high culture or low, Chaplin's dance hall girls were thus vital to the construction of his comedy and of his comic persona, as well. Bringing to life roles that carried expectations of passivity and objectification, these female leads subverted those expectations and held the key to the trajectory of Chaplin's character development wherever they appeared, crafted not simply to reflect his talents but to shape and channel them, as well. Their confidence, boldness, glamour, and grace gave them an agency that has often gone unrecognized in studies of Chaplin's work. They were female figures whose main roles were not simply to create comedy, drama, or narrative tension, although they did that as well, but more significantly, they served to create a powerful contrast—to act as the spotlights that made a Little Fellow appear larger than life.

NOTES

1. Dan Kamin, *The Comedy of Charlie Chaplin: Artistry in Motion* (Lanham, MD: Scarecrow Press, 2008), 90.

2. See Michael Rutter, *Upstairs Girl: Prostitution in the American West* (Helena, MT: Farcountry Press, 2005).

3. See Alton Prior, *Bawdy House Girls: A Look at Brothels of the Old West* (Sacramento, CA: Stagecoach Publishing, 2006); Lael Morgan, *Good Time Girls of the Alaska-Yukon Gold Rush: Secret History of the Far North* (Kenmore, WA: Epicenter Press, 1999); Mary Murphy, *Mining Cultures: Men, Women, and Leisure in Butte, 1914–1941* (Champaign: University of Illinois Press, 1997).

4. Ballet, with its origins in Renaissance court pageantry, for example, was associated with nobility, and advanced a singular notion of ideal femininity marked by control, discipline, and training—not only in the dance, but the body and demeanor of the dancers, as well.

5. Kathy Peiss, *Cheap Amusements: Working Women and Leisure in Turn-of-the-Century New York* (Philadelphia: Temple University Press, 1986), 6.

6. Paul Goalby Cressey, *The Taxi-Dance Hall: A Sociological Study in Commercialized Recreation and City Life* (Chicago: University of Chicago Press, 2008), xvii.

7. For discussion, see Robert C. Allen, *Horrible Prettiness: Burlesque and American Culture* (Chapel Hill: University of North Carolina Press, 1991).

8. See M. Alison Kibler, *Rank Ladies: Gender and Cultural Hierarchy in American Vaudeville* (Chapel Hill: University of North Carolina Press, 1999).

9. Laura Mulvey, "Visual Pleasure and Narrative Cinema," in *Issues in Feminist Film Criticism*, ed. Patricia Erens (Bloomington: Indiana University Press, 1990), 33.

10. Allen, *Horrible Prettiness*.

11. See Ethan Mordden, *Ziegfeld: The Man Who Invented Show Business* (New York: St. Martin's Press, 2008).

12. Kathryn J. Oberdeck, "Contested Cultures of American Refinement: Theatrical Manager Sylvester Poli, His Audiences, and the Vaudeville Industry, 1890–1920," *Radical History Review* 66 (1996): 42.

13. Peter Stallybrass and Allon White, *The Politics and Poetics of Transgression* (Ithaca, NY: Cornell University Press, 1986), 191.

14. Charles Musser, "Work, Ideology, and Chaplin's Tramp," in *Resisting Images: Essays on Cinema and History*, ed. Robert Sklar and Charles Musser (Philadelphia: Temple University Press, 1990), 42.

15. Walter Kerr, *The Silent Clowns* (New York: Alfred A. Knopf, 1975), 85.

16. Musser, "Work, Ideology, and Chaplin's Tramp," 40.

17. Mack Sennett, *King of Comedy* (Garden City, NY: Doubleday, 1954), 158.

18. Theater historian Karl Mantzius, quoted in Robert Barton and Annie McGregor, *Theater in Your Life* (Belmont, CA: Wadsworth Publishing, 2008), 234.

19. David Madden, *Harlequin's Stick, Charlie's Cane* (Bowling Green, OH: Popular Press, 1975), 26.

20. The film was later recut and rereleased on four reels in 1916. Chaplin's original version is now widely available.

21. Earlier cinematic versions were directed by Cecil B. DeMille (1915) and Raoul Walsh (1915). Chaplin's version virtually recreates the DeMille film scene-by-scene, including the intertitles. See Kyp Harness, *The Art of Charlie Chaplin* (Jefferson, NC: McFarland, 2008); Theodore Huff, *The Early World of Charles Chaplin* (New York: Gordon Press, 1978).

22. Kamin, *The Comedy of Charlie Chaplin*, 91.

23. During this period in both burlesque and vaudeville, female roles had transitioned from those of assertive agency to more passive support of male performers—particularly as the brunt of male comics' humor. Female performers were increasingly silent and objectified to the point where a woman with significant dialogue was referred to as "Talking Woman."

24. Charles J. Maland, *Chaplin and American Culture: The Evolution of a Star Image* (Princeton, NJ: Princeton University Press, 1986).

25. Maland, *Chaplin and American Culture*, 77; Harness, *The Art of Charlie Chaplin*, 117–18. However, in *Tramp: The Life of Charlie Chaplin* (New York: HarperCollins, 1996), Joyce Milton suggests that the film's inspiration, at least in part, was a script circulated by Chaplin's longtime friend, theatrical entrepreneur Sid Grauman (224–25).

26. Harness, *The Art of Charlie Chaplin*, 118.

27. Harness, *The Art of Charlie Chaplin*, 122.

28. For an in-depth comparison between Chaplin's characters and Arlecchino, see David Madden, *Harlequin's Stick, Charlie's Cane*.

29. Harness, *The Art of Charlie Chaplin*, 188

30. Stephen M. Weissman, "Charlie Chaplin's Film Heroines," *Film History* 8, no. 4 (1996). www1.american.edu/academic.depts/soc/heroines.html.

31. Kamin, *The Comedy of Charlie Chaplin*, 190.

32. Kamin, *The Comedy of Charlie Chaplin*, 94.

33. See Camille Paglia, *Sexual Personae: Art and Decadence from Nefertiti to Emily Dickinson* (New York: Vintage Books, 1991).

34. Marcel Mauss, *A General Theory of Magic* (London: Routledge, 2001).

Chapter Four

American Masculinity and the Gendered Humor of Chaplin's Little Tramp

Lawrence Howe

SCREENING AMERICAN MASCULINITY

Early filmmakers understood that they would best utilize the visual medium of silent film to appeal to audiences by creating spectacles that featured bold actions. In the early twentieth century, bold action was commonly—indeed, almost exclusively—associated with the exploits of men. Thus, since its inception, American cinema has emphasized images of stereotypically masculine action: a fireman's heroic rescue, the cold-blooded daring of train robbers, acts of battlefield bravery, or the racist triumph of the Ku Klux Klan. Comedy in silent cinema also relied on physical action, but did so most often by flouting the conventions of masculine heroics. Successful comic screen figures such as Laurel and Hardy, Harold Lloyd, Buster Keaton, and Roscoe "Fatty" Arbuckle created personae often ill-suited to the norms of manly action, characters awkwardly placed in dangerous or emasculating situations. Perhaps the most iconic of the silent film comedians, Charlie Chaplin projected a screen identity in the Little Tramp whose comic effects also stemmed from his amusing failure to embody the masculine ideals of the culture. His undersized jacket and oversized pants and shoes are clear semiotics of costume conveying the degree to which his physical stature simply does not fit the conventions of the masculine role, and his timidity and recurrent failures to adapt to norms of masculine behaviors maximize the comic potential of a figure who does not measure up to the standards of manhood.[1]

In this essay, I examine the gendered basis of the humor Chaplin creates in his Tramp persona; moreover, I show how the significance of the Tramp's compromised masculinity becomes magnified in the era of the Great Depression. In *Modern Times* (1936), especially, the backdrop of the Depression transforms this endearing comedian's signature gags into a subtle though expansive cultural critique of a social construction that scholars now term "hegemonic masculinity" operating within the normative "heterosexual matrix for conceptualizing gender and desire" in modern American society.[2]

Over the last several decades, scholars in the emergent field of gender studies have provided insight into the history and meaning of masculinity in American culture. The most recent work in gender theory and criticism highlights the conflicts even within such a powerful social formation as hegemonic masculinity.[3] Michael Kimmel, for example, points out a division in the evolving notion of American manhood, reflecting a history of energy and excitement, of sadness and silence—a history of fears, frustration, and failure.

> At the grandest social level and the most intimate realms of personal life, for individuals and institutions, American men have been haunted by fears that they are not powerful, strong, rich, or successful enough. And many of our actions, on both the public and private stages, have been efforts to ward off these demons, to silence these fears.[4]

Chaplin's comedy, I contend, taps into these contradictions and the anxieties that arise from them in complex ways. And the relevance of the Tramp's conflicted masculine identity assumes even greater relevance in the period of the Great Depression. The Tramp embodies many of the attributes that men feared and, in response, ridiculed in others. But in projecting a persona at whom audiences might laugh, Chaplin also invited his audiences to identify with many of the foibles and weaknesses of the Tramp, as well as to delight in his remarkable ability to endure and to overcome the ridicule and abuse that befalls a man who fails to live up to the ideals of masculine power.

Chaplin's film narratives consistently place the Tramp at odds with more powerful individuals. These stories usually resolve with the Tramp managing to find a way around the superior power of his adversaries. Fisticuffs, which had such a prominent place in early silent shorts for their physicality, manageably confined settings, and readily legible narrative appeal, recur in Chaplin's early humor as well. In a two-reeler like "The Pawnshop" (1916), for example, when the Tramp fumbles through his duties as an assistant pawnbroker, his fellow clerk, annoyed by the Tramp's disruption, physically assails him. The Tramp, after trapping his adversary between the rungs of a ladder, retaliates by delivering a torrent of boxing blows on his coworker. When a policeman happens on the scene, as so often occurs in Chaplin films, the Tramp quickly converts his somewhat cowardly retribution on his opponent into an effeminate capering dance, skipping away from the policeman's gaze. His unsettled masculinity continues throughout this slapstick comedy when he meekly hides from his irate coworker late in the narrative. However, when the Tramp springs from his hiding place to foil a robber, the story's final resolution reverses his timidity: he is rewarded with the pawnbroker's gratitude and his daughter's affection.

In other instances, the Tramp's masculine deficiencies are offset when the more imposing figures that threaten him are rendered comparatively impotent in a context that provides him an advantage, such as in "The Rink" (1916). Here the Tramp's clumsiness as a waiter and his subordinate class status in the first act gives way in later scenes; his discovery that some of his clients are engaged in marital infidelity tips the balance in his favor. He foils their attempt to silence him by eluding them through his agility on roller skates, a prowess, if not a power, that trumps his adversaries whose greater physical and social power are negated by their precariousness on wheels. Thus the humor stems from the Tramp's unlikely success after having been denied comfortable acceptance in a society that grants other men positions of power and respect that enable them to get away with morally suspect behavior.

As has been widely noted, the popular art form of cinema arrived in an era that ensured its success.[5] Social mobility created large urban concentrations that promoted mass communication technologies and demands for inexpensive entertainment; the arrival of immigrants who did not speak English gave the universal appeal of silent film a ready boost. In a similar concurrence of social circumstance, the comic appeal of the marginalization that the Tramp represents on screen arrived in an era ripe for this kind of entertainment. The late nineteenth and early twentieth centuries were marked by sociological changes that had a profound impact on the masculine identities of working men. And the "work ethic" defined the identity of American men long before it was characterized by modern and postmodern sociologists. Max Weber, in his foundational study, *The Protestant Ethic and the Spirit of Capitalism*, locates the importance of work to American culture in the ethos of Benjamin Franklin. To Franklin, work was not simply necessary for production but was an important constituent to character formation. He held that a man who displayed his commitment to the work ethic would project an identity that others would admire and trust, a notion whose influence endured throughout the nineteenth century, to be sure, and later to varying degrees.[6] Defining masculine identity in terms of the work ethic and the role of the breadwinner implicitly underscored autonomy as a constituent feature of manliness and dependence as insufficiently masculine, if not womanly. Thus the inability of Chaplin's onscreen persona to adapt to work environments is not simply a comic trope; rather his portrayal of ineptitude ironically dovetails with the cultural emphasis on the work ethic, thereby framing the Tramp as a portrait of troubled masculinity.

In "Behind the Screen" (1916), David (Chaplin), a hardworking assistant stagehand on a movie set, single-handedly performs the work assigned to his lazy boss, Goliath (Eric Campbell). The comic angle on David's assiduousness often relies on the disruptions that result from his energetic activity, such as interfering with camera set-ups as he moves awkward and heavy scenery from one place to another, displaying Chaplin's uncanny talent of the bodily intelligence that James Caron shrewdly investigates in his essay. The comic irony is maximized when the film's producer finds David resting after his solitary exertions and accuses him of being a loafer. More often, though, Chaplin's persona portrayed ineptitude and thus turned the work ethic on its head for comic effect. In "The Fireman" (1916), he plays the title character but as a consistent failure in contrast to the heroism of Edwin Porter's landmark "The Life of an American Fireman" (1903). In *Shoulder Arms* (1918), a film about the masculine arena of warfare, Chaplin plays a doughboy in the "Awkward Squad," whose only heroism occurs in his dreams. Finally, in *Modern Times* (1936), the Tramp's serial incompetence in all manner of work is direct evidence of his masculine shortcomings.

The workplaces in *Modern Times* are notable for the specificity of tasks delegated to workers. Prior to the expansion of modern industrialism, American manhood was measured in the degree of autonomy one experienced and in the range of personal control one exercised over one's life.[7] But modernization of production labor led to increased corporate power and, correspondingly, less autonomy and personal control by the individual over one's work, as fewer and fewer workers owned their own shops or small farms. To be sure, economically independent men had long been vulnerable to the turmoil of the marketplace, and men with families to support knew the heavy responsibility of the role of breadwinner. But by the 1890s, workers came to see their dependence on employers pejoratively, comparing their conditions to wage slavery or prostitution.[8] Even worse, unemployment was perceived as a form of utter emasculation, of one's failure to provide manfully for oneself and one's family.

The increasing influence of women through reform movements, especially over suffrage, won them greater participation and authority in areas where men had held exclusive control, including the workplace.[9] The cultural sense that manliness was under attack by economic and social forces was converted to open hostility toward anything viewed as womanly, such as homosexual men, whose presence in America's growing cities had been noted with degrees of tolerance since the end of the nineteenth century. Indeed, by the 1920s, as George Chauncey's history of New York gay society shows, Prohibition, spearheaded by women's temperance activism, had helped to advance the influence of homosexual culture in the entertainment industries, including film. Strikingly similar to the interest that many white patrons showed in black culture during the Harlem Renaissance, heterosexual audiences actively supported performances of drag shows and other entertainments featuring gay performers to a level of creating what was known as a "pansy craze."[10] "Behind the Screen," the film in which Chaplin uncharacteristically plays a stagehand's hardworking assistant, acknowledges the presence of homosexuality in the entertainment industry, in what is perhaps cinema's first explicit screening of a gay theme. When Goliath discovers David kissing another stagehand (Edna Purviance), an out-of-work actress who has disguised herself as a boy in order to be hired on the set, Goliath, believing he has discovered David's secret passion for the "boy," mocks his overworked assistant. Although David's kiss comes only after he has detected the girl behind the disguise, he does not reveal her identity, honorably accepting Goliath's misplaced ridicule in order to protect her secret. The episode acknowledges the tolerated presence of homosexuality in the industry by having the antagonist Goliath perform the role of macho bully, while still emphasizing David's heteronormative attraction to the girl disguised as a boy stagehand.

By the 1930s, however, the tenuous tolerance of homosexuality pivots 180 degrees, coinciding with the growing fear about the diminishing power of manhood generally. Kimmel observes that, as the Depression took its toll on employment, working-class heterosexual men, sensing their loss of economic and social power, "had begun to define themselves in opposition to all that was soft and womanlike," and argues further that the reverence for manly virtue stressed the need for deliberate performance: "men felt themselves on display at virtually all times. . . . To be considered a real man, one had better make sure to always be walking around and acting 'real masculine.'"[11] This historical observation aligns with Judith Butler's influential insight about the role of performance in the formation of gender: "[t]here is no gender identity behind the expressions of gender; that identity is performatively constituted by the very 'expressions' that are said to be its results."[12] This provocative revelation resonates remarkably with Chaplin's persona, especially in the context of *Modern Times.*

The cultural requirement for men to act masculine is exhibited by a wide range of characters who surround the Tramp, especially in the factory scenes. The Tramp's inability to fit into the hypermasculine world of the factory and his anomalously masculine performance in the prison demonstrate how Chaplin sets up the Tramp's otherness to question hegemonic gender norms. The Tramp's awkward failure to perform masculinity sets up the narrative premise that turns when he and the gamin (Paulette Goddard) embark on their markedly innocent, though no less heteronormative, relationship. A close examination of the gendered cultural codes embedded in the film's unfolding narrative of their evolving relationship will show how Chaplin calibrated his humor to address the stiffening gender categories of the Depression era.

To be sure, the Tramp's antics in *Modern Times* are consistent with Chaplin's well-established screen persona; his divergence from masculine norms had long defined Chaplin's comedic identity. But the historical context of the Great Depression placed the Tramp's troubled masculinity in an enhanced light. The era of economic deprivation had inspired Chaplin's critique of capitalist greed in *City Lights* (1931), to which the Tramp's selfless generosity in paying for the operation that restores the blind flower girl's sight is such a contrast. But the Depression-era setting of *Modern Times*, his most politically engaged film up to that point, added powerful social relevance to the gendered basis of his signature comic antics, making the Tramp's complex relationship to masculinity more explicit. For the collapse of industrial society had far-reaching effects secondary to the economic impact: the inability of men to find work was an assault on an American concept of manliness so closely aligned with the work ethic. [13]

Nor was the effect limited to the cinematics of Chaplin's Tramp. Depression-era films like *My Man Godfrey* (1936) and *Meet John Doe* (1941) address the problem of men's alienation from the ideals of masculinity by showing the resilience of their male protagonists when women with more powerful social positions attempt to exploit them. The gendered meaning of the Depression is still legible in recent films set in that period. Films like *Seabiscuit* (2003) and, to an even greater degree, *Cinderella Man* (2005) have not only highlighted the way in which the Depression impacted men's sense of themselves as inadequate providers, as broken men, but also melodramatically represented their protagonists' triumphs as moments of reclaimed masculinity through which unemployed men, specifically, and the culture, generally, can identify with the underdog heroes and the powerful appeal of their narratives. The title *Cinderella Man* itself calls attention to the complex gendered implications of this period and the narrative's purpose in leveraging the tensions embedded in gender roles. In *Modern Times*, Chaplin's Tramp evokes a related form of pathos, thus synthesizing his comedian's desire to make audiences smile, as his signature theme song makes clear, or better yet, laugh, with a newly awakened sense of social responsibility to make films that respond to the conditions of the era.

MASCULINITY ON THE ASSEMBLY LINE

Chaplin's complex portrait of the Tramp repeatedly shows him lacking the requisite skills and qualities necessary for inclusion in the prevailing masculine categories—working man, organization man, empire builder—that social scientists and social critics were positing to define the qualities of

American masculinity in the modern age.[14] However, the cultural undercurrents of troubled masculinity roiling just beneath the surface of the narrative of *Modern Times* emerge explicitly in several key episodes to highlight, question, and ultimately reinforce gender conventions that are integral to the film's rhetoric. The factory sequence reestablishes the Tramp's long-running conflict with the masculine ideals of the culture. This episode, not only the longest and the most frequently referenced of *Modern Times*, is also one of the more complex. Despite the film's release in the midst of the Great Depression, the opening montage suggests that the action unfolds in an earlier time, during an economic boom signaled by the rather sizeable army of workers who are gainfully employed. Among them is the Tramp, one of many at work on an assembly line in the gleaming high-tech factory of the Electro-Steel Corporation. In addition to being organized by class, the factory is a highly masculinized space, dominated by men engaged in various mechanical tasks. The factory's foreman (Sam Stein), carrying out the orders of the company's president (Allan Garcia) by literally controlling the levers of power in the factory, is a brawny icon of masculine power, an image reinforced by his otherwise inexplicable shirtlessness. In contrast to him and the other diligently occupied workers, Chaplin's diminutive Tramp is out of place, struggling to keep up with the repetitive rigors of automated factory work. As the army of workingmen maintains their focus on their respective tasks, the Tramp is continually distracted, once by a buzzing bee, and more often by his own body—a sneeze, an itch, and the desire for an unscheduled cigarette break from the hectic pace of the factory belt. He is also harassed by the demands of his coworkers further down the assembly line who harangue and threaten him when his failure to keep up with the mechanized pace of work interferes with their sequenced tasks.

This first scene is a prelude to the more dramatic and more complicated confrontation later in the day. In the second assembly line scene, as the factory boss orders "more speed," the Tramp futilely struggles to perform his role in the chain of factory operations. Overtaxed by the escalating speed of production, he becomes obsessed with the single-mindedness of his bolt-tightening duty and dives headlong into the bowels of the factory mechanism in pursuit of his fleeting piecework, bringing the entire production line to a halt. When he emerges, he is transformed from frenzied mechanic to deranged saboteur. Chaplin derives significant humor from the Tramp's mischievous interference with the regulated productivity of the factory, in part by exploiting the regimentation of the coworkers who try to subdue him. Whenever they are about to apprehend the Tramp, he simply turns the factory belt back on, and they return to their mechanical tasks as if by Pavlovian conditioning.

Although the disorder that the Tramp wreaks upon the scene is an unmistakable critique of the dominance of Taylorism and Fordism on the quality of life of working people, as Randall Gann points out in his contribution to this volume, his subversive behavior inverts the value attributed to autonomy as a masculine trait, for the Tramp's antics distort the notions of personal control formerly associated with manliness. Moreover, the gendered quality of his behavior when unleashing the mayhem deserves attention that heretofore has been absent in the critical commentary of *Modern Times*. In tandem with the Tramp's disruption of the industrial order, the episode's humor stems equally from his carnivalesque transgression of rigidly defined gendered behavior. After emerging from the disorienting machinery, his posture and gestures are highly feminized, even balletic, as he lithely prances around the factory floor *en pointe* (see figure 4.1). Pirouetting beyond the grasp of his frustrated coworkers, he twists one's nose or another's nipple with his two wrenches or squirts an oilcan into his coworkers' annoyed faces, one after another. Accompanying his effeminate disruptions in the masculine workplace, the musical soundtrack shifts from the heavily accented regular rhythms and deeper brass tones of the orchestra to legato strings with trilling piccolo flourishes whenever the Tramp mockingly gestures to one of his factory adversaries.

But effeminate interference is not the Tramp's only stance; when the boss's secretary (uncredited) walks through the factory scene, the Tramp's eyes light up in salacious desire; he dangles his wrenches by the sides of his head like Pan's ears, connoting the lasciviousness of a satyr driven by testosterone-fueled lust. As she attempts to elude him, he notices the hexagonal buttons on the back of her skirt, and their resemblance to the nuts that he repetitively tightens on the assembly line reawakens his mechanical fixation. With twitching wrenches firmly grasped in his extended hands, he chases her out of the factory, stopping only when he notices the hex nuts on a nearby fire hydrant. This distraction lasts only until he notices a full-figured woman (Juana Sutton) walking toward him. Her comically designed costume includes black hexagonal buttons in obvious double array down the front of her light-colored dress. As the Tramp trains his gaze on the two most prominent buttons on her bosom, his wrenches twitching, mechanical obsession and masculine erotic fixation are conflated. When she flees apprehensively, he renews his pursuit, only to have this phase of the chase reversed when she seeks the protection of a passing policeman.

Having escaped the policeman by retreating to the factory, the Tramp resumes the antics that disrupt the masculine project of the factory but now extends them to the entire plant. Moreover, his sabotage not only iterates his earlier exaggerations of gendered derangement but also includes rapid oscillations between polarized gendered behaviors. Intruding on the bare-chested foreman who controls the power dynamo, the Tramp playfully flips a switch here, turns a dial there, and pauses to languidly pose over an extended crank lever. All the while, the flustered foreman attempts to restore the steady operations of the factory but to no avail; the Tramp's spectacular sabotage

Figure 4.1.   *Ballet Mécanique*. Courtesy of Photofest.

spews billows of roaring flame from the disabled dynamos. (See figure 4.2.) As the full workforce now seeks to contain this imp of chaos, he fends them off by squirting them with oilcans and eluding them aloft on a gantry. When finally apprehended, he is escorted off to a mental hospital. In this last phase of the sequence, his demeanor swings wildly from manic effeminacy to the kind of bold masculine action that Chaplin's friend Douglas Fairbanks made

Figure 4.2.   Confronting the foreman. Courtesy of Photofest.

famous in numerous swashbuckling title roles in films such as *D'Artagnan* (1921), *Robin Hood* (1922), *The Thief of Baghdad* (1924), and *The Black Pirate* (1926). The Tramp's abrupt shift from femme-frolic to macho derring-do signals the extremity of his trauma. But more importantly, the construction of gender is held up for scrutiny in this extended action sequence. For the Tramp's comic mayhem disassembles the behavioral conventions through which gender norms were enforced. American culture had instituted complementary spheres of industrial and social order: the regimentation of the assembly line was designed to achieve efficient industrial productivity, and clearly legible gender normativity sought to make masculinity and femininity distinct. In this cultural scheme, the disruption that the Tramp introduces to both spheres must be contained and its agent diagnosed as sick and remanded to treatment that will attempt to cure the Tramp's perverse gender confusion, thus reinforcing hegemonic masculinity. From this perspective, any man who cannot participate normatively in the arena of man's work requires adjustment to regain his masculine bearings. Although we do not see the Tramp's treatment, we might safely infer that his diagnostic work-up would have included one of the tests devised to inventory gender traits. In

1936, the year *Modern Times* was released, the creator of the Stanford-Binet IQ test developed an "M-F" scale for measuring attitudes and behaviors plotted in terms of masculinity and femininity.[15] Although the scale potentially heralded the recognition that gender identity is not simply an opposition but could be mapped on a continuum, as it is widely regarded in our current era, the scale was devised to identify areas that could be strengthened or discouraged in order to orient an individual toward a clearer performance of normative gender in the direction of one pole or the other.

Upon his release from a sanitarium, the Tramp is declared fit to reenter society, but he is no more able to conform to hegemonic masculinity now than he had been prior to his treatment. In quick succession, he loses another job due to his failure to conduct himself effectively as a shipwright's helper, and then in an innocent attempt to return a signal flag that has fallen from a passing truck, he is mistaken as the leader of a Communist uprising. Deemed a political threat to the economic order, the Tramp is now viewed as a criminal agitator and sentenced to the most exclusively masculine of institutions: the prison, a significant narrative setting because it also unsettles the gendered expectations of the culture. Initially, the Tramp is just as awkward in this environment as he was on the outside, easily bullied by his glowering cellmate (Dick Alexander). But in the dining hall scene, contraband cocaine, unwittingly ingested, chemically transforms the Tramp into a man of action—one who, first, assertively challenges the power of his erstwhile dominant cellmate and then foils a prison break single-handedly after fearlessly dodging bullets from the would-be escapees. Although the Tramp's action upholds the rules and objectives of order in the prison, his behavior, which James Caron's analysis highlights as "bodily intelligence" in the first essay in this collection, warrants comparison to his culminating acts in the factory. In each, he is jolted out of his baseline inability to embody manliness. In the factory, machine-induced trauma prompts his manic derangement into a performance of bipolar gendered behavior, whereas in the prison, a mind-altering substance dislodges him from his characteristic timidity and fuels his autonomic performance of hypermasculinity. The notion suggested in these scenes is that, for a figure like the Tramp, whose gender identity is not emphatically defined, gender itself may be subject to outside interference.

However, the film's construction of the prison scenes complicates masculine identity in the characterization of two figures. The first is the Tramp's burly cellmate, whose physically imposing, even menacing, masculine presence is contradicted by his indulgence in the feminine handicraft of needlepoint. The second complicating figure in this exclusively masculine environment is an inmate (uncredited) whose effeminate gait makes him stand out among the file of convicts marching back to their cells from the dining hall. This inmate's unmistakable sashaying body language—one hand on his hip, the other tracing a ninety-degree arc to his side as he walks—subtly suggests the commonplace assumption about prison life as a perverse replication of heterosexual domesticity in which male convicts play either masculine or feminine roles. Not unlike Chaplin's inclusion of homosexuality in "Behind the Screen," it is reintroduced here but more explicitly characterized as perverse, especially within the context of a film that emphasizes the thematics of masculine performance in an era in which manliness is perceived to be under attack by the emasculating forces of the Depression. In contrast to these complicating figures, then, the Tramp's drug-induced hypermasculinity establishes a parallel to his mania in the factory setting. In both instances, his gendered response overturns the contextual expectations.

The domesticity figured by the burly cellmate is ironically iterated in the Tramp himself. His uncharacteristic heroism in foiling the prison break earns him a privileged place in the prison's society as a model inmate. Rewarded with a private, single-occupancy cell, he transforms it into a model domestic space: furnished with a bureau topped with books, a vase of flowers, and an alarm clock, while a needlepoint sampler reading "Home Sweet Home" and a portrait of Abraham Lincoln decorate the walls. In sum, his cell replicates the kind of home decorating that was generally the province of women as organizers of the domestic sphere, as Thorstein Veblen points out in explaining the woman's responsibility for "household adornment" in the consumer economy.[16] As the Tramp lounges on his bunk reading a newspaper whose headline reports the strikes and bread riots that roil the society beyond the walls, the prison affords him not only the comforts of home and a stable routine, but also the gratification of being recognized as a competent and conforming member of a community.

Indeed, he is so comfortable here that he is taken aback at the news of his release. He asks, "Can't I stay a little longer? I'm so happy here," anticipating the struggles that await him in the tough economy on the outside. Contrary to society's view of him as a rehabilitated criminal, he is an ordinary, albeit idiosyncratic, citizen who has simply found the environment that suits one with his diffident quirkiness. Sheriff Coulson (Ed LeSainte) issues the Tramp a letter of introduction attesting that the Tramp is an "honest and trustworthy man," but his assessment is drawn from a rather narrow experience in which the Tramp exhibited masculine prowess while under the influence. Outside the prison, a man's worth is measured in more than these two virtues; he must also be capable of work that contributes to the economy. Despite his observations of the Tramp, the sheriff has no knowledge of whether the Tramp can fulfill the role of "man" in a conventional workplace. The Tramp, on the other hand, knows that he is alienated from the modern world, even if it were functioning prosperously; thus he understands that his reentry into society in the midst of the Depression holds out even less likelihood of success than his earlier efforts. In short order, the Tramp hatches a plan to satisfy his renewed desire to return to prison.

MANLINESS, BREADWINNING, AND THE DOMESTIC SPHERE

For all the comic distance that the Tramp's masculine failure achieves for the audience, his alienation from the world of work also strikes a chord of recognition for those who have become dispossessed by the Great Depression. Sherwood Anderson's examination of the cultural malaise of the Machine Age, titled *Perhaps Women*, explicitly names Chaplin as the personification of alienation through modern technology. After visiting several factories in which Anderson observes a sublime beauty, one night he encountered a road-making machine whose frighteningly human appearance terrified him; he recollects:

> I became a Charlie Chaplin that night by the mill gate. I was, to myself at least and for the time there in the half darkness, just the grotesque little figure Chaplin brings upon our screen.
> . . . the little figure with the cane, putting the hat back correctly on his head, pulling at the lapels of his worn coat, walking grotesquely, standing blinking thus before a world he does not comprehend, can not comprehend—
> Brushing his clothes, as I was doing with a soiled pocket handkerchief— "he would have been" I thought, "just the one to run as I had done from an idle road-making machine, thinking it a man, his quick rather fragile mind and feeling upset—his eyes distorting things as I so often do."[17]

That Anderson sees the Tramp as the epitome of modern man—a "grotesque" figure who flees from an idle machine—and identifies with his sense of alienation and emasculation underscores Chaplin's ability to personify the troubled masculinity that was increasingly widespread in the Depression. The crippling distortions that mechanized society imposed upon men, Anderson conjectures, might only be remedied by women, as he alludes in his title. Having escaped the dehumanizing experience of mechanized factory labor, women, he reasons, have maintained their connection to nature and thus may serve to reconnect men to nature, to their essence as men, rescuing them from their condition as the mechanized beings into which they have been transformed.[18]

Chaplin encodes the salutary influence of women in *Modern Times*, as well, for the Tramp's relationship with the gamin inspires him to forsake his plan to return to the reliable though modest comforts of prison and provides his first motivation for being in the world despite his inadequacies. While Chaplin's earlier films sometimes showed how the Tramp could be influenced by the affection of or his attraction to a woman—perhaps most clearly in *City Lights*, his film immediately prior to *Modern Times*—his relationship with the gamin is a notable development, granting him an opportunity to express masculinity defined by its heteronormative relationship to the corresponding gender category.[19] Yet the desire of the gamin and the Tramp to

settle into heteronormative domesticity is not easily fulfilled, and the difficulty they face in adapting to the conventional roles of domesticity is the
basis of the comedy in the second half of the film.

The film's narrative structure prepares for the characters' partnership as
awkward participants in a heteronormative couple: the gamin is first introduced when her story is intercut into the film narrative, first, immediately
after the Tramp's mistaken arrest as a Communist agitator, and then in her
family tragedy, alternating with scenes of his prison experience. In contrast
to the inept innocence he exhibits, the gamin is shown taking matters forcefully into her own hands, boarding a boat to steal and distribute bananas to
other hungry waifs, her trusty knife clenched between her teeth pirate-style
while she tosses the looted nourishment to the delighted children. When
discovered and pursued by the boat's owner, she evades capture by sure-
footedly hopping to adjacent boats and scrambling away. The final image of
the scene frames her in a full shot, standing not in a girlishly demure pose,
but defiantly with feet spread wide and arms akimbo. If the Tramp's derangement in the factory scene had induced him into a mock swashbuckling,
masculine posture, the gamin shows how naturally she can assume this attitude.

The next scene makes clear her reasons for her actions: as the oldest of
three daughters of an unemployed, widowed father (Stanley Blystone), the
responsibility of breadwinner has been thrust upon her. The despair that
overtakes her father for failing to provide for his children underscores the
sense of impotence that has undermined the American masculine ideal during
the Depression.[20] By incorporating these dire contemporary social conditions
into the film's plot, Chaplin provides the groundwork for the dynamic relationship that will develop between the Tramp and the gamin. But in doing so,
he risks scuttling the film's comic potential for the sake of the social message. The story doesn't rest with the father's emasculation through unemployment but escalates the family's tragic condition: when "trouble with the
unemployed" erupts, the gamin's father is fatally shot. By including this
profoundly distressing development, as well as the gamin's subsequent grief-
stricken and famished wanderings after escaping from the juvenile officers
who have taken her orphaned sisters into custody, Chaplin's political critique
threatens to overwhelm the comic momentum of the film's narrative. But the
Tramp's absurd dedication to return to jail and the gamin's plucky determination to survive prevent her family tragedy from sinking the humor. Indeed,
fundamental differences between the Tramp and the gamin and their mutual
incompatibility with the gender roles they attempt to inhabit as a newly
formed couple create the necessary comic tension: his attempts to substitute
himself for her before the clutches of the law is not the act of a chivalrous
hero, but the ploy of a social misfit who anxiously desires a return to the
security of prison, nor is this defiantly take-charge girl a feminine victim

awaiting his rescue. When the paddy wagon overturns, presenting them with an opportunity to escape, the gamin's forwardness in insisting that they go on the lam together and his unexpected willingness to follow her lead reflect their inclination to ignore the parameters of conventional gender roles, even as their relationship will encourage them to perform clumsy imitations of them.

Although being part of a couple is enticing to the Tramp, he accepts his masculine role somewhat sheepishly. Projecting ambivalence, he acts like a bashful schoolgirl as they become acquainted curbside before a suburban bungalow. Observing a housewife cheerily waving her husband off to work, the Tramp initially mocks her enthusiasm in parodic mimicry. The bourgeois conventionality of the suburban couple's normative relationship, though, inspires him to fantasize about settling into a middle-class life with the gamin. In his bourgeois daydream, the Tramp exhibits a breadwinner's swagger, an image of masculine confidence and material attainment, in striking contrast to his real-life condition. So, too, does his fantasy image of the gamin's role as happy homemaker diverge from her squalid characterization. The appeal of the fantasy dispels his disdainful ridicule of the suburbanites and motivates him to attain the American Dream for his new partner, vowing to provide them a life of middle-class comfort "even if I have to work for it."[21] The Tramp's vow to attain the fantasy, in utter contradiction to the traits of his character and the serial failures that reinforce those traits, anticipates Butler's observation about the important connection between fantasy and norms: "Norms are not only embodied . . . but embodiment is itself a mode of interpretation, not always conscious, which subjects normativity itself to an iterable temporality. Norms are not static entities, but incorporated and interpreted features of existence that are sustained by the idealizations furnished by fantasy."[22] No sooner does the Tramp's fantasy compel him to forswear his life of vagrancy than he is interrupted, in typical Chaplinesque fashion, by a police officer looming over the two fugitives. And yet, although the threatening police presence deflates the Tramp's rhetorical flourish, it does not dampen his enthusiasm to become the masculine breadwinner and to attain the conventional life as a man of the house.

Of course, as enticing as the lure of middle-class heteronormativity may be to the couple, neither of them is equipped to shift smoothly into the conventional roles that they now desire. The Tramp's vow to work does nothing to alter the fact that he lacks the masculine qualifications of the modern workplace. Even after a lucky break lands him a job as a department store security guard, the couple woefully miscalculates. Rather than utilize the stability of his occupation to strive to make their dream of domestic comfort a future reality, they indulge their appetites for consumer goods that the department store lays before them: gorging on food in the cafe, roller-skating in the toy department, and wrapping the gamin in a fur coat and bedding her down for the night in the luxury of a large and extravagantly sumptuous bed. Although these scenes of carefree conspicuous consumption are pitched to the desires of the Depression-era cinema audience, the comic requirements turn this one night of satisfaction to the Tramp's misfortune. During his security-check rounds, he is confronted by burglars—including one of his former coworkers in the opening factory scene—men who insist that they are not really criminals but simply driven to steal by the desperation of the times. Their alcohol-comforted commiseration ends with the Tramp's firing and arrest the next morning. The transitory luxury that they enjoy in the department store scene reinforces the notion that attaining material security is a fantasy, not a sustainable reality for characters of their class in this environment. While they imitate the roles they desire, Chaplin makes their exclusion from that bourgeois reality an opportunity for laughter.

Upon the Tramp's release from jail, the gamin surprises him with the results of her search for the home of their dreams. In this episode, we see an all-too-real parody of their domestic dreams, experienced fleetingly in the department store. If the Tramp's fantasy home was not sufficiently tangible to gainsay Marshall McLuhan's claim that "pictures of the lonely tramp never take us *inside* an American home," the gamin's new home certainly exists materially.[23] Unfortunately, the domicile is a dilapidated waterfront shack of the sort documented in Dorothea Lange's photography, a comic contrast that could not be a greater counterpoint to the Tramp's middle-class fantasy. Indeed, the humor of this scene is driven by their cracked-mirror reflection of a heteronormative couple. Where his fantasy home was solidly constructed and tastefully furnished, the hovel she has found them plagues him with knocks on the head from unsecured beams and sagging rafters and pratfalls from crumbling makeshift furniture. In his fantasy, he returns home from a satisfying job and plucks an orange from a tree within easy reach of the living room window, and he summons a compliant self-milking cow to the kitchen door. In other words, he rivals Adam's mastery of Eden where he is master of beasts and satisfies his hunger from trees laden with ripe fruit. Within the dream, the gamin too is transformed, though not into Eve; rather, she is a version of Betty Crocker, the marketing invention first introduced in 1921 to epitomize woman as the American homemaker who provides her man with the satisfaction of an exquisite meal. But in the reality of the grim hovel, the Tramp and gamin wrestle with slabs of stolen fried ham between bricks of bread and sip tea from discarded tin cans.

The gamin's shortcomings as a homemaker notwithstanding, her honest ambition redoubles the Tramp's willingness to find work. A reopened factory provides him another opportunity for which he still lacks the required attributes. Yet another misunderstanding with the police lands him back in jail. Left to fend for herself, the gamin finally gets a break when a cabaret owner hires her as a dancer, reintroducing here the figure of the dance hall girl that

Cynthia Miller's essay closely examines. Upon his release from jail, the Tramp finds her transformed by the turn of fortune, signified by the stylishly demure clothing she now wears. Better yet, she has arranged for the Tramp to work as a singing waiter. As a waiter, he's a practical disaster, though a comic success—no different from any of his other failed employments—and he reprises some of Chaplin's earlier comic conventions such as in "The Rink." In *Modern Times*, we are reminded not only of the Tramp's clumsiness, but also of his masculine shortcomings. In one segment of his restaurant service, his attempt to deliver a roasted chicken to a demanding patron is confounded by a quartet of rugged and seemingly drunk football heroes being heralded as celebrities. Snatching the chicken from the Tramp's tray, they proceed to frustrate him by tossing it between themselves just beyond his reach. Chaplin's decision to cast the Tramp's opponents as football players has clear meaning in this era, for the role of sport, and especially football, in the formation of male character in American culture had been widely asserted in institutions of higher learning. Where academic pursuits were hailed as promoting the life of the mind, competitive athletics were seen as crucial in activating the masculine energies that sedentary study failed to tap.[24]

PERFORMANCE, NARRATIVE, AND GENDER IDENTITY

The Tramp's last chance for success arrives when he is called to perform a song. Beyond the rich irony of a silent film character being required to sing, the humor of this episode rests first on his failure to remember the lyrics to the song he's rehearsed, which appears as futile as all of his earlier work stints. As the cabaret audience grows impatient with his stalling tactics, he finally takes the plunge and improvises nonsense lyrics to accompany his pantomimic representation of the song's narrative. Much has been noted about the fact that Chaplin finally allows audiences to hear his voice in this scene. Seven years had elapsed since *The Jazz Singer* (1929) led the revolution from silent film to talking pictures, and for some time the pressure had been mounting on Chaplin to modernize his cinematics.[25] Because his signature humor relied on his skill in pantomime, which also contributed to his appeal to international audiences, Chaplin understandably resisted the new sound technology, a point that Benjamin Click thoroughly develops in his essay on the rhetoric of sound (speech and gibberish) and silence in *The Great Dictator* later in this volume. Even when finally featuring the Tramp's voice, Chaplin mocks the reliance on speech by having him resort to nonsense syllables. The absence of semantic verbal language requires the Tramp to convey his story through Chaplin's signature mode of communication: gesture. Critical readings of the Tramp's long-overdue success in this scene contribute much to how we understand Chaplin's uneasiness about sound film technology. However, the critical emphasis on the form of the Tramp's cabaret triumph over the content obscures an important thematic angle pertinent to the performance of gender.

The Tramp not only performs the song through gestures, he acts out both identities in the heterosexual transaction recounted in the story. In successfully conveying both the masculine and the feminine identities that society has sought to distinctively mark, the film implies that the Tramp's inability to inhabit a lateralized gender identity has found an outlet for performing gender types in an environment where that kind of performance is appreciated and rewarded.[26] To this point, Butler's revelatory point about drag performance provides some traction:

> The performance of gender that the drag queen offers is no less real and no less true than the performance of gender that any ordinary man or woman might perform, that it gives us a kind of allegory of the mundane performance of gender, and that we are all, all the time, as it were, performing gender. The drag show is a moment in which that performance is rendered explicit. It's not an aberration from the norm; it shows us how the norm actually functions, how the norm is instituted through our bodies, through our stylistics, through our bodily gestures.[27]

Granted, Chaplin's Tramp is not a drag performer, but the fluidity of his performances of both gender roles in the cabaret song reveals his ability to adopt gender-coded behaviors when he takes on an explicit performance. In other words, in life the Tramp fails to perform according to the conventions of masculinity, but when consciously performing a role on stage as either a man or a woman, the Tramp is remarkably adept at embodying the physical signs of gender identity. Not coincidentally, the story told through his performance recounts the kind of bad faith bargaining that much heterosexual seduction and marriage-market interplay is predicated upon. The man, who embodies a class identity of wealth, uses the lure of his status to gain access to the sexual property he seeks in the woman. She counters by playing coy in order to extract a jewel in exchange for a kiss as a token of the fuller sexual gratification he desires, only to find out that her own unfulfilled promise of exchange has been undercut by the bauble, which despite its sparkle is worthless. The story, in other words, calls into question the duplicity of conventionalized performances of gender roles in which ulterior objectives are pursued in the false gestures of mutual attraction.

Unlike the scene of the Tramp's machine-induced mania in which he oscillates unpredictably from exaggerated versions of one gender role to the other, or the prison scene in which an unconsciously ingested stimulant fuels his successful performance of masculine honor, his deliberate cabaret performance of gender roles, which, it must be emphasized, serves a narrative purpose itself, provides him the structure to channel his affinity for imitation. The power of this moment in the film stems in no small part from the reflexivity that it projects, uniting the Tramp's and Chaplin's identities in a performance that simultaneously delights audiences both within the film and of the film—that is, the one in the cabaret and the one in the movie theater. [28]

Thus, despite all the attention to this scene as the moment, albeit belated, in which Chaplin accommodated himself to the progress of sound cinema, it is not his speaking that really matters, because aside from the timbre of his voice nothing is revealed in his speech. His pantomimic performance, conversely, signifies a great deal about the performative quality of gender. Enacting the song's story enables the Tramp to tap the two gender identities contained within himself, not only for the sake of the story's closure, but also for the resolution of what had been conflicted attributes into a theatrical asset. The point of this narrative overall and of the cabaret scene particularly bears a complex relationship to the contemporaneous work of sociologists such as Talcott Parsons and Mirra Komarovsky, whose notions of sex roles were crystallizing in the public consciousness of the era. Indeed, their emphasis on sex-role differentiation helped to construct the hegemonic masculinity that Chaplin is clearly challenging in the Tramp's burlesque of manliness. Uncannily, much of Chaplin's characterization of masculinity in the Tramp anticipates the work of contemporary gender theorists and critics who often point to the limitations of the static formulations of early social scientists. [29]

And yet, while he exploited the tensions in gender identity that the Depression brought into sharper focus at a time in his career when he sought to burnish his entertainments with social relevance, we cannot ignore the fact that the structure of the narrative focusing on the heterosexual coupling of the Tramp and the gamin complicates any assumption that Chaplin was consistently moving against the social grain. The Tramp's trajectory of experience in *Modern Times* from misfit to success is catalyzed by his relationship with the gamin. This kind of coupling has functioned most commonly as narrative closure, the hero's final reward, providing the unlikely and comically satisfying triumph by way of a conventional trope of sentimental romance that we find in "The Pawnshop" or as deployed by a rival master of cinematic comedy, Buster Keaton, in *Sherlock, Jr.* (1924) and *The General* (1926). However, the Tramp and the gamin's relationship is the focus of slightly more than half of the film narrative. Their connection provides an alternative to the Tramp's usual solitary meanderings, affording him a sense of purpose that initially questions rigid gender identities but ultimately backs away from the emerging critique to reaffirm the orthodox foundations of heteronormativity. The film's final closure, in the denouement following the cabaret climax, shows us a very different Tramp, one who, in having tasted success, finally asserts leadership in this relationship. On the run from the authorities again, the gamin's usually indomitable spirit begins to flag. But in his newly awakened manliness, the Tramp projects strength and optimism that dissipates her melancholy. As the two take to the road, the camera follows them walking confidently into the future. In this moment, the Tramp not only gets the girl, but also finally achieves his identity as a man. For Depression-era audiences, this image of modest attainment is more than a comic tag—in both the colloquial sense of being humorous and the technical sense of the theatrical genre of comedy, it provides resolution in which others similarly struggling to find a sense of identity could find solace.

NOTES

1. In 1934, Walter Benjamin observed that the Tramp's "feminine touch of the poverty stricken" compared to "Hitler's diminished masculinity," anticipating by six years what Chaplin would achieve in *The Great Dictator* (Quoted in Momme Brodersen, *Walter Benjamin: A Biography*, trans. Malcolm R. Green and Ingrida Ligers [New York: Verso, 1996], 217).

2. R. W. Connell, *Masculinities* (Berkeley: University of California Press, 1995), 77. See also the first two chapters, with particular emphasis on pages 77–81. Judith Butler, *Gender Trouble: Feminism and the Subversion of Identity* (New York: Routledge, 1990), viii.

3. For example, see Harry Brod and Michael Kaufman, eds., *Theorizing Masculinities* (Thousand Oaks, CA: Sage Publications, 1994); R. W. Connell, *Gender* (Cambridge, UK: Polity, 2002); Jeff Hearn, *The Gender of Oppression: Men, Masculinity, and the Critique of Marxism* (New York: St. Martin's Press, 1987); Michael S. Kimmel, *Manhood in America: A Cultural History*, 2nd ed. (New York: Oxford University Press, 2006); Máirtín Mac an Ghaill and Chris Haywood, *Gender, Culture and Society: Contemporary Femininities and Masculinities* (New York: Palgrave/Macmillan, 2007).

4. Kimmel, *Manhood in America*, 8–9.

5. See, for example, Kristin Thompson and David Bordwell, *Film History: An Introduction* (New York: McGraw-Hill, 2003), 11–12, who note the rapid growth of film to the demand "fueled in part by the rising immigrant population and in part by the shorter work hours gained by the increasingly militant labor-union movement. Soon America was far and away the world's largest market for films—a situation that would allow it to increase its selling power abroad as well" (12). World War I would provide the U.S. film industry opportunities for growth without rival competition that would be repeated in the devastation of Europe during World War II less than twenty years later.

6. Max Weber, *The Protestant Ethic and the Spirit of Capitalism* (New York: Scribners, 1958), 41.

7. See Kimmel, *Manhood in America*, 83–84.

8. In *A Connecticut Yankee in King Arthur's Court* (Berkeley: University of California Press, 1979), Mark Twain offers an ironic response to this emerging attitude. Hank Morgan, a late-nineteenth-century mechanic who finds himself transported to sixth-century England, sets out not only to modernize the material of Camelot but to transform social ontology through "man-factories," institutions dedicated to developing a cadre of enlightened individuals who will embody the potential of human agency (114). For Twain, the building of men was a project designed to counteract the effeminacy of the medievalism of the Victorian era—what he terms "girly-girly romance"—clarifying the gender emphasis (*Life on the Mississippi* [New York: Oxford University Press, 1996], 467).

9. Kimmel, *Manhood in America*, 83.

10. George Chauncey, *Gay New York: Gender, Urban Culture, and the Making of the Gay Male World, 1890–1940* (New York: Basic Books, 1994), 320.

11. Kimmel, *Manhood in America*, 100.

12. Butler, *Gender Trouble*, 25.

13. The excellent essays in this volume by A. Bowdoin Van Riper and Randall Gann provide different but complementary angles on the technological and economic vectors of *Modern Times*. See also Lawrence Howe, "Charlie Chaplin in the Age of Mechanical Reproduction: Reflexive Ambiguity in *Modern Times*," *College Literature* 40, no. 1 (January 2013): 45–65, for an analysis of Chaplin's conflicted criticism of technology and the tension between production and consumption at the crisis period of industrial capitalism.

14. See Charles R. Walker and Robert F. Guest, *The Man on the Assembly Line* (Cambridge, MA: Harvard University Press, 1952); and William H. Whyte, *Organization Man* (Philadelphia: University of Pennsylvania Press, 2002).

15. Lewis Terman and Catherine Cox Miles, *Sex and Personality* (New York: Russell and Russell, 1936).

16. Thorstein Veblen, *Theory of the Leisure Class: An Economic Study of Institutions* (New York: Macmillan, 1902), 82. Veblen notes that when practiced in lower-class households, this consumption with respect to articles of taste is an emulation of the leisure class, a pattern that *Modern Times* signals in the shanty that the gamin and Tramp take up as their first home together.

17. Sherwood Anderson, *Perhaps Women* (New York: Boni and Liveright, 1931), 95–96.

18. This emphasis on the positive influence of women corresponds to what sociologist Lester Ward posited as the "gynaecocentric theory" of society, first in his essay "Our Better Halves," *Forum* 7 (May 1888): 258–63, and then more extensively in *Pure Sociology: A Treatise on the Origin and Spontaneous Development of Society* (New York: Macmillan, 1903), 296–350.

19. See Butler, *Gender Trouble*, who discounts the notion of gender as a stable identity founded on anatomical fact, positing it instead as a "signification" that "exists only *in relation* to another, opposing signification" (9). Similarly, the Tramp's identity in *Modern Times* only takes root after he has established his association with a gendered opposite embodied by the gamin.

20. See Mirra Komarovsky, *The Unemployed Man and His Family* (New York: Arno Press, 1971). In the scenes of the gamin's family, *Modern Times* anticipates Komarovsky's illuminating study of the effect of unemployment on men and their families, using interviews with husbands, wives, and children to reveal the kinds of stress that the Depression imposed upon family lives.

21. See Peter G. Filene, *Him/Her/Self: Gender Identities in Modern America* (Baltimore: Johns Hopkins University Press, 1998), especially chapter 3, "Men and Manliness"; and Mac an Ghaill and Haywood, *Gender, Culture and Society*, especially "In and Out of Labour: Beyond the Cult of Domesticity and Breadwinners," for their discussions of the Victorian concept of the breadwinner and the homemaker's civilizing influence over man's "animal nature" (Filene, 75). See also James Truslow Adams, *The Epic of America* (Boston: Little, Brown, and Company, 1931), for what is believed to be the first use of the phrase "The American Dream" (414), just five years before the release of Chaplin's film.

22. Judith Butler, *The Judith Butler Reader*, ed. Sara Salih with Judith Butler (Malden, MA: Blackwell, 2004), 264.

23. Marshall McLuhan, "Canada: The Borderline Case," in *The Canadian Imagination: Dimensions of a Literary Culture*, ed. David Staines (Cambridge, MA: Harvard University Press, 1977), 234.

24. See Joseph Sears, "Foot-Ball: Sport and Training," *North American Review* 121 (1891): 750–53; and Roberta J. Park, "Biological Thought, Athletics and the Formation of a 'Man of Character': 1830–1900," in *Manliness and Morality: Middle-Class Masculinity in Britain and America, 1800–1940*, ed. J. A. Mangan and James Walvin (New York: St. Martin's, 1987), 7–34.

25. Otis Ferguson, writing in the *New Republic*, faulted the film's title as "about the last thing they should have called the Chaplin picture," since there was nothing at all modern about its largely silent mode (quoted in Charles Maland, *Chaplin and American Culture: The Evolution of a Star Image* [Princeton, NJ: Princeton University Press, 1989], 157).

26. Here, it is notable that this successful gender performance takes place on a stage, and thus connects to the crucial, paradoxical use of the stage in the late "trilogy" insightfully

analyzed in Marco Grossoli, "The Paradox of the 'Dictator': Mimesis, Logic of Paradox, and the Reinstatement of Catharsis in *The Great Dictator, Monsieur Verdoux,* and *Limelight*" (152, 157), later in this volume.

27. Butler, *The Judith Butler Reader,* 345.

28. In *The Circus* (1928), Chaplin plays with the related idea of unintentional performance. As a circus stagehand, the Tramp displays incredible comedic gifts, leading the circus owner/ringmaster to recruit him as his next star clown. As a clown, however, the Tramp is a complete flop because he has no facility to learn the stock gags of the trade, let alone master them. But the ringmaster realizes that he can exploit the Tramp's natural comedy by having him delight audiences inadvertently in his role as stagehand. Even better for the ringmaster, he has all the advantages of the Tramp's talent without having to pay him a performer's salary or provide any star billing. In *Modern Times,* it is not the Tramp's "natural" performance that equips him for success but his explicit performance that stands in stark contrast to his inability to perform masculinity in his offstage life.

29. See, for example, Tim Carrigan, Bob Connell, and John Lee, "Toward a New Sociology of Masculinity," in *The Making of Masculinities: The New Men's Studies,* ed. Harry Brod (Boston: Allen & Unwin, 1987), 63–97.

Chapter Five

In the Shadow of Machines

Modern Times *and the Iconography of Technology*

A. Bowdoin Van Riper

The factory sequence that opens Charlie Chaplin's *Modern Times* compresses the ultimate "bad day at work" into twenty chaotic minutes. Chaplin, in his final screen appearance as the Little Tramp, first feeds the machines with the component parts of an unseen product, then is chosen to be fed *by* machines in a test of a new invention that goes comically awry, and finally is fed *to* the machines when, unable to keep up with the quickening pace of the assembly line, he throws himself onto its moving conveyer belt. Sucked into the machinery like one more piece of raw material, he is—in the film's most iconic sequence—passed through the gears forward, then backward along the same path, until he is spit back onto the conveyer belt unharmed. Unhinged by the experience, he runs through the factory—gleeful, almost dancing, yet teetering on the edge of a complete breakdown—throwing its carefully ordered world into chaos with squirts from his oilcan. The action of the factory scenes is overtly fantastic: a preposterous burlesque of real assembly line work.[1] The factory within which it is staged seems, especially to modern viewers, more subtly fantastic: too sleek, too bright, too clean . . . too obviously a stage set. The contrast between those fantasies—wildly chaotic action amid the sleek orderliness of the factory—lies at the heart of the film's critique of technology.

Two sets of images—equally familiar, but so different from one another that they are barely reconcilable—define modern machinery in the Western imagination. One set celebrates the wonders that technology makes possible and the godlike powers it confers on its users. It depicts structures that defy gravity, vehicles that annihilate time and space, and manufacturing systems that create goods of every shape and size in any quantity desired. It is expressed in advertisements' promises that machines can change lives and was given form in stories—like Garrett Serviss's *Edison's Conquest of Mars* (1898) and Rudyard Kipling's *With the Night Mail* (1900)—where heroic engineers transform the world. The other set condemns the costs that technology exacts: blackened skies and poisoned water, dazed survivors wandering amid twisted metal after a train wreck or building collapse, cities crumbling and burning beneath the power of modern weapons. It took fictional form in stories where powerful machines run amok (as in Mary Shelley's *Franken-stein*) or fall into the hands of madmen (as in Jules Verne's *20,000 Leagues under the Sea*) or despotic rulers (as in H. G. Wells's *The Sleeper Awakes*). Science fiction—a genre for which Serviss, Shelley, Verne, and Wells all served as antecedents—embraced both strands and, as it matured, increasingly featured works that interwove them.

Both visions of technology were interwoven, as well, with the image of industrial capitalism. Manufacturers used words and images, decontextualized displays and entire model factories, to evoke images of plants in which line after perfectly ordered line of machines hummed beneath the hands of vigilant workers filled with energy and pride. Journalists, social reformers, and labor organizers countered with bleak tales of workers as young as ten trapped in a world of gray light, deafening noise, and unguarded machines that could kill or maim in an instant. The same technological innovations that enabled factory owners to display their latest wonders to the masses—cheap wood-pulp paper, offset printing, and steam-powered presses—also spread grim images of hollow-eyed workers bent to their machines in dust-choked rooms. Far from resolving the tension between these conflicting images of industrial technology, the onset of the Great Depression intensified both. Images of "Hooverville" shanty towns, endless breadlines, and crowds of desperate men clustered around chained factory gates suggested that industrial capitalism might be not merely flawed, but doomed to complete and irrevocable collapse. To those whose belief in industrial capitalism remained unshaken, however, the shuttered factories were sleeping giants: still powerful and capable—once awakened by sound government policies—of pushing the nation toward prosperity again.

Whether *Modern Times* was part of the intensified critique of industrial capitalism that emerged during the Depression has divided commentators since its release. Critics on the political right, Charles Maland concludes, "affirmed the humor and denied the social significance" of *Modern Times*, while those on the political left found the film "both funny and socially aware."[2] A similar division, though perhaps along aesthetic rather than political lines, was still visible among film historians in the mid-1970s. Roger Manvell writes, in *Chaplin*, that *Modern Times* "had little social comment and no political party implications whatsoever," a stance that Garrett Stewart compares to "dying of thirst in a rainstorm."[3] Walter Kerr, in *The Silent*

Clowns, argues that the factory scenes offered "at least two dazzling opportunities for ironic social comment," but that they (implicitly) went un- (or at least under-) utilized, since "Chaplin's true theme lies elsewhere, and is more personal."[4] The factory scenes in *Modern Times* are the story of the Little Tramp trying, and spectacularly failing, to find a place in the "modern" world of 1930s industrial capitalism. The question is whether the failure lies with the flawed system (as the Left would contend) or the Tramp's personality (as the Right implicitly assumes).

The factories in *Modern Times* are, for commentators from both the Left and Right, significant primarily as sites for the labor that sustains industrial capitalism. Their references to the factory scenes say little or nothing about the machines themselves, focusing instead on the Little Tramp's interactions with them—first as a dutiful and dedicated worker and then as a twitching, oil-squirting casualty of "progress." To see the factory *solely* as a stage on which the drama of labor is played out is, however, to miss a critical element in the film's critique of industrial society: Chaplin's interwoven depictions of technology-as-wonder and technology-as-curse.

Modern Times embraces both sets of images at once. It celebrates the unexpected beauty and the limitless power of modern machinery, inviting the audience to admire the ingenuity of those who operate it, even as it lampoons the ways in which manufacturers use it. The factory scenes are filled with technological marvels that are capable of amazing things, but the same inventions can and do cause chaos without warning. The straight-faced supporting cast enacts the idea that control of technology gives man control of nature, but the Little Tramp's own actions call even the possibility of such control into question. The visual language of the factory scenes—the film's iconography of technology—draws on ideas about the relationship between humans and their machines that pervaded the culture of the interwar United States, manifest in the memoirs of Henry Ford, the photography of Lewis Hine, the industrial exhibits of world's fairs, and the latest newsreel footage from Hoover Dam. *Modern Times* dramatizes, with uncanny precision, both the hopes and the fears that Depression-era Americans projected onto the machines around them. The background celebrates the American ideal of technology-driven progress, even as the foreground satirizes the excesses committed in the name of progress.

Critics who see Chaplin's vision of the factory as a denunciation of industrial capitalism's excesses are, like those who see the apolitical antics of a comic misfit, tugging loose a single thematic strand from a tightly braided skein. *Modern Times* was part of a complex dialogue about science, technology, and progress that unfolded in the United States between the world wars, and, within that dialogue, Chaplin's film played an unusually complex role.

AMERICANS AND TECHNOLOGY BETWEEN THE WORLD WARS

Americans have been fascinated since the 1840s by what historian David Nye calls the "technological sublime": the feeling, somewhere between awe and terror, that massive structures and powerful machines evoke in those who view them at close range.[5] The American vision of the technological sublime began in the nineteenth century as part of the nation's declaration of cultural independence from Europe and continued in the early twentieth as an expression of American imperialism.[6] Its meaning shifted again between the world wars, tied to notions of progress and (more explicitly than before) mastery over the physical material world. The great engineering projects of the late 1920s and 1930s—giant airships and ocean liners, the great dams of the far West, and the skyscrapers of midtown Manhattan, the Golden Gate Bridge, and Ford Motor Company's mile-and-a-half-long River Rouge assembly plant—added still another cultural dimension.[7] They "stunned the soul" with their sheer size and their defiance of natural forces, but they also provided thousands of jobs and a tangible symbol of the country's faith that the alliance of science and business could "lead the country out of the depression to a new . . . promised land of material abundance."[8]

The mass media—emerging as a technological marvel in its own right—engendered fascination with other marvels and facilitated appreciation of them. The movies documented the latest engineering achievements in weekly newsreels and documentary shorts like *Power and the Land* (1940), which documented the electrification of the rural South.[9] Photojournalists such as Alfred Stieglitz, Margaret Bourke-White, and Lewis Hine documented machines and the men who built and ran them. Their work, with few exceptions, ignored precision industries—instrument making, electronics, tool-and-die making—in favor of construction and heavy manufacturing: shipbuilding, ironworking, steelmaking, and automobile assembly. Still and moving images alike featured construction sites and factories where nature—whether in the form of undisturbed earth and trees or in the form of raw material—was reshaped, on a massive scale, to meet human needs and fulfill human desires. Hine, in particular, turned machine-age laborers into idealized heroes: not Marx's downtrodden proletariat, but individuals full of vigor, industry, and skill. His 1932 book *Men at Work*, a collection of the best in a series of "work portraits" shot over the preceding decade, showed boilermakers, mechanics, and the construction gangs on the Empire State Building posed and lit like Greek gods.[10] Diego Rivera (in his twenty-seven-panel mural *Detroit Industry*, painted in 1932–33) and the artists funded by the Works Progress Administration undertook similar idealizations in works displayed across the United States.[11] Compositions in which men were dwarfed by the technology around them—or by the natural world that they were using technology to subdue—became a familiar visual trope in such images, both still and moving. They replicated, within the boundaries of a frame, the feeling of standing in the shadow of immense machines. (See figure 5.1.) A trip to a major city was, by the mid-1930s, no longer a necessary prerequisite for experiencing the technological sublime; it was available to anyone with a dime for a movie ticket or the latest copy of *Life* magazine.

The new media of the 1920s and 1930s also, however, highlighted the potential of technology to go awry. There had always been accidents in which the massive size and unstoppable power of modern machinery—unleashed by misjudgment or mechanical failure—brought death and destruction to those they were supposed to serve. The new media (and a new hunger for spectacle) made those accidents more visible in interwar America, however, than they had ever been before. The airship *Shenandoah*, pride of the U.S. Navy's lighter-than-air fleet, tore itself apart in a summer storm over Ohio in 1925; its successors *Akron* and *Macon* fell into the sea in 1930 and 1935. The St. Francis Dam, built by William Mulholland to provide water for the booming city of Los Angeles, collapsed in 1928, drowning 450 people in the valley below. Ten passengers, including Notre Dame football coach Knute Rockne, died when a TWA airliner—its wooden wing spar weakened by rot and broken by turbulence—plunged into a Kansas field in 1930. The nine hundred–foot ocean liner *Olympic*, running at 20 knots when visibility was less than 500 feet, ran down and sank the Nantucket Lightship on a foggy night in May 1934. Four months later, fire swept through the luxury liner *Morro Castle* off the coast of New Jersey, consuming her wooden wall paneling and rich draperies and killing 135 of the 549 onboard. The great civil engineering projects of the era also claimed lives, though usually in ones and twos rather than dozens and scores. Eleven men died working on the Golden Gate Bridge, fourteen on the Empire State Building, seventy-two on Grand Coulee Dam, ninety-six on Hoover Dam. The latter, according to tales circulated at the time, included men who fell into the wet concrete and were buried, entombed forever because the work could not be stopped in order to retrieve their bodies.

The tales from Hoover Dam, though not true, reflected a deeper anxiety: that the needs and demands of machines would trump those of the humans they supposedly served and that the future new technology ushered in would indiscriminately sweep away cherished aspects of the present along with undesirable ones. Massive building projects created jobs and stirred national pride, but skyscrapers turned city streets into shadowed canyons, bridge approach ramps loomed over two- and three-story neighborhoods, modern freeways obliterated some neighborhoods and cut others in two, and entire towns disappeared beneath the lakes created by new dams. The automobiles that rolled out the doors at River Rouge and other Detroit assembly plants were, by 1930, already altering everything from grocery stores to teenage courtship

Figure 5.1.   Human figures dwarfed by massive works of engineering were staples of Depression-era images of technology. Fort Loudon Dam, Tennessee, Library of Congress Collection.

rituals. Anecdotal reports of Detroit assembly line workers suffering nervous breakdowns, or coming home at night too tired to even eat added another layer of ambivalence about the unintended human costs of modern machinery.[12] Photographs of mill workers with hollow eyes and expressionless faces, such as those that Lewis Hine took in the 1910s and early 1920s for the National Child Labor Committee, reinforced it.[13]

The ambivalence that Americans of the interwar era felt about technology—fascination with the power it represented, mingled with fear of the consequences of that power turned against them—was apparent in the technology-themed films of the era. Some feature films envisioned technological wonders even more spectacular than those in the newsreels—all-skyscraper cities in *Just Imagine* (1929), mid-ocean airports in *F. P. 1 Does Not Reply* (1932), a transatlantic tunnel in *The Tunnel* (1932)—and invited audiences to marvel at them. Others placed their characters in the path of machines they could neither control nor defeat—cannon and machine guns in *All Quiet on the Western Front* (1930), a manmade monster in *Frankenstein* (1932), or a deadly energy beam in *The Invisible Ray* (1935)—and invited audiences to cringe. *Modern Times*, released in 1936, was part of that ongoing cinematic dialogue and of Americans' ongoing wrestling with the social costs of modern technology. Like another 1936 release, Alexander Korda's *Things to Come*, it simultaneously reflected the hopes and the fears of the era.[14]

MASTERS OF MACHINES: *MODERN TIMES'* EMBRACE OF TECHNOLOGY

The factory in *Modern Times*—the battlefield on which the Little Tramp struggles with machines and regimentation—is as idealized as those in a Lewis Hine photograph, a Works Progress Administration (WPA) mural, or a world's fair industrial exhibit. The building is clean and bright, the machines sleekly beautiful, and the workers full of competence, vigor, and purpose. It is a place of wonders, where men bend machines to their will and remake nature to suit their needs: a dreamworld defined by hope and confidence rather than fear and anxiety.

The factory itself is a vast, open, airy space, flooded with light from unseen skylights or bulbs. The shop floor, uncluttered by cables, tracks, or boxes of parts, gleams with polish, as clean and sterile as that of a hospital operating room. There are no oil spots on the floor, no drifting motes of dust in the air, and (because of Chaplin's decision to make *Modern Times* a silent film) no rattle and hum of machinery. The auditory stillness of the factory is matched by its visual stillness. Even when full of activity, it is defined by unbroken planes and smooth curves rendered in deep, cool grays made familiar in Hine's silver gelatin prints. It is, in other words, an idealized version of the showplace factories made possible, after 1900, by the advent of electric motors, electric lighting, and new forms of architecture made possible by the mass production (and thus widespread use) of steel and glass. Factories, once shunned by the genteel middle classes as dirty and unhealthy, became tourist attractions. The Ford assembly plant at Highland Park drew an average of three thousand visitors a day for tours conducted by twenty-five full-time guides by 1920, and the River Rouge plant drew even more. For manufacturers, factory tours were an invaluable promotional opportunity; for tourists, they were a chance to watch one of the wonders of the age.[15] Machines had been displayed at fairs and expositions for decades, but factory tours offered the opportunity to see them in context and in operation: machines and workers join in the elaborate dance that turns raw materials into finished goods. The factory scenes in *Modern Times* offer viewers the same opportunities and, like factory tours and world's fair exhibits, present the (fictitious) Electro-Steel Corporation in the best possible light.

The factory in *Modern Times*, in addition to being a technological wonder, also contains wonders. The most striking is the television system that allows the boss, seated in his luxurious office, to monitor conditions and communicate with workers through the factory. Television was, in 1936, brand new and wholly experimental: the first public demonstration took place in Britain in 1925, and the first primitive broadcasts in the United States occurred in 1928. The system in the film—with its large, crystal-clear screens, its two-way video broadcasts, and its capability to transmit live sound—was infinitely more sophisticated. When similar systems appeared in other films of the period, first in *Metropolis* (1927) and then in the 1932 feature *The Tunnel* and the 1935 serial *The Phantom Empire*, they did so in an explicitly science-fictional context.[16] Its presence in the Electro-Steel factory—integrated into the structure of the plant like a telephone system—exemplifies the Century of Progress Exhibition's dream of scientific breakthroughs put, quickly and reliably, to practical use.

The machines that do the work of production are, though less exotic, also more conspicuously beautiful: embodiments of the idea that machines could be aesthetically pleasing as well as efficient. Belief in that idea was manifest in the halls of the New York Crystal Palace Exhibition in 1853 (where one observer described a walking beam steam engine as "the most perfect product of Venus and Vulcan"), the Centennial Exposition of 1876, and the Columbian Exposition of 1893–1894. It was evident in the organically curved housings of early sewing machines, the mingling of black-painted iron and polished brass in microscopes and surveyor's instruments, and (beginning in the mid-1920s) the art deco sleekness of everything from toasters to locomotives.[17] It is also apparent in the control room of the Electro-Steel factory: the most technology-filled set in *Modern Times*. The massive electric motor that stretches into the middle distance is hidden—like a streamlined locomotive—inside a metal shroud that masks the complexity of its ceaselessly moving parts. Polished steel wheels, brass-handled levers, and dials with broad white faces stand out crisply against the dark-enameled control panel like elements in a beautifully composed collage of technological elements: circles and lines, instruments and controls, electrical and mechanical. (See figure 5.2.)

The worker (Sam Stein) who mans the controls is, himself, part of the composition. Handsome, muscular, and shirtless, he could be one of Hine's nameless subjects, fresh from work in some branch of heavy industry or on the Empire State Building. His bare chest makes little sense, in fact, *except* as an homage to the shirtless laborers in Hine photographs and WPA murals; the workers on the assembly line at least wear undershirts, and his clearly less-strenuous job (throwing levers and turning wheels) is unlikely to raise a sweat. The juxtaposition of sculpted muscle and sleek machinery is central to Hine's still images and WPA paintings, however, and central to the control room scene.[18] The shirtless man represents Hine's idealized view of the modern American worker—a machine-age Adonis, made strong and (impli-

Figure 5.2.   The control room epitomizes the gleaming, idealized beauty of the factory in *Modern Times*. Courtesy of Photofest.

citly) beautiful by his labor—and *Modern Times* presents him, without apparent irony, in the same approving way.

The shirtless man is—like similar figures in Hine's carefully posed and lit photographs and in Depression-era public art projects—an idealized representation of the character, as well as the body, of the American worker. Like them, he displays complete mastery of his machine-filled workspace and utter confidence in his ability to control it. His ability to do the work competently and efficiently is simply assumed. Turning the frozen motion of Hine's photographs fluid, *Modern Times* makes that efficiency manifest. The shirtless man strides boldly from the television screen where he receives orders from the boss (Allan Garcia) to the levers and wheels he uses to execute them. The orders are simple and the controls are, by 1930s standards, complex, but he executes the orders—and implements the required control settings—without hesitation. Even when the Little Tramp—in his anarchic, whirlwind passage through the control room—manipulates the controls at random and throws the factory into confusion, the shirtless man is never in doubt about what he has to do and how to do it.

The men who work on the factory floor possess the same qualities, though in a more muted way. They are conspicuously ordinary looking—a variety of heights and body types, neither especially handsome nor notably homely—and dressed in ordinary work clothes. They are, in that respect, virtually identical to the figures in newsreels from the Empire State Building, Hoover Dam, and the River Rouge plant. Nothing about them suggests a Greek statue come to life, but they are vigorous, competent, and hard working. Their work requires speed and rhythm more than judgment, but they do it smoothly and efficiently. Many turn-of-the century industrialists embraced Frederick Winslow Taylor's theories of "scientific management," hiring outside experts to carry out "time-motion studies" of their workers and teach them the "one best way" (that is, the most efficient way) of performing a particular task. The line workers in *Modern Times* (save for the Little Tramp) are embodiments of Taylorite principles: they waste neither time nor motion as they carry out their jobs. Foremen in white, collared shirts attend them as the boss attends the shirtless man in the control room—monitoring progress and giving occasional orders—but they know what to do and how to do it and carry out their work without direct, ongoing oversight from anyone.

The Electro-Steel factory is thus a world in which men, individually and collectively, exercise firm control over the machines that surround them and, through those machines, over the material world. The boss, issuing orders through his television system, controls the rhythms of production. The shirtless man controls the machines themselves. The line workers' control over *their* technological environment is more subtle but still apparent. When the Little Tramp falls behind in his bolt tightening, he is reprimanded first by his fellow workers and only later by the white-shirted foreman. When he throws himself onto the moving belt of the assembly line and disappears into the machinery, it is his fellow workers who call for the line to be stopped. When he runs through the factory, introducing anarchy into its otherwise supremely orderly world, it is his fellow workers who attempt to contain his anarchy and restore order. The workers' actions suggest that their immediate concern is for the machines rather than the Tramp as an individual and that their commitment to the integrity of the sociotechnical system that is the factory is paramount. There is, as far as the Little Tramp is concerned, no working-class solidarity on the shop floor of the Electro-Steel factory.

The Depression-era setting of *Modern Times* makes it possible to read the line workers' actions as the product of simple self-interest and ruthless determination to keep their jobs in an economy where work is hard to come by. The factory-as-prison and worker-as-automaton imagery established in earlier films such as Lang's *Metropolis* and Rene Clair's *A Nous la Liberté* makes it possible to read their actions as the result of relentless social conditioning. Neither explanation, however, fits comfortably with the film's depiction of the workers or the workspace. The staging of the factory sequences suggests, instead, that *Modern Times* sees the workers—excepting, always, the Little Tramp—as willing participants in the celebration of modernity and efficiency that the factory represents.

The factories in *Metropolis* are Blake's "dark, satanic mills" brought to terrifying life. Scenes in the subterranean manufacturing districts not only suggest the darkness and fires of hell, but present the machines as demons whom the workers struggle to appease, lest they be devoured.[19] The factory in *Modern Times*, in contrast, is as luminous and orderly as those showcased in the corporate-run factory tours and world's fair exhibits of the 1930s. It is so clean, in fact, that the dirt and oil stains on some (but not all) of the workers' clothes seem oddly out of place. The instruments of social and physical coercion present in real-world factories of the era—familiar to mid-1930s audiences from published mill worker narratives, journalistic exposés, and documentary photography, if not from personal experience—are as absent as grime. There are no warning signs, no hovering line bosses, no bellowing foremen, and no threats of pay docking or firing. The only use of the two-way television system to monitor and admonish (centered, inevitably, on the Tramp) involves a genuine—albeit trivial—violation of company policy: using what is ostensibly a toilet break to smoke a clandestine cigarette. By the standards of an era when oppressive and dangerous working conditions were commonplace and companies kept paid thugs on staff to beat labor organizers unconscious and intimidate "troublesome" employees, the factory in *Modern Times* is strikingly progressive.[20]

The individuality of the workers in *Modern Times* is part of this picture and sets them apart from their counterparts in Lang's and Clair's visions of the factory. The workers in both earlier films exhibit a dourness, a uniformity of appearance, and a slow, trudging motion that mark them as men who have long since lost all hope of autonomous action. Particularly in *Metropolis*, they are (like coal, iron, or electricity) a resource to be ordered up in the desired quantity by those in charge then manipulated to achieve a desired end. They act as servants to the machines that surround them, scurrying frantically and desperately to meet their never-satisfied hunger. The workers in *Modern Times*, by contrast, retain their humanity. They are low-ranking members of an enormous hierarchical organization, taking their orders from others, but—like the workers in celebratory images from 1930s newsreels and magazine photographs—they wear their own clothes, eat food prepared in their own homes. They move with a briskness and vigor alien to the prisoner-slaves of *Metropolis* or, for that matter, to the characters in contemporary songs like Bruce Springsteen's "Factory," who trudge off to work "with death in their eyes."

The assembly line work in *Modern Times*, whether the Little Tramp's nut tightening or his linemates' striking of the bolt ends with a hammer and punch, consists of actions too simple to give the workers who perform them any intrinsic satisfaction. Nor is it apparent—perhaps not to the workers and certainly not to the audience—how the parts on which they work will fit into a larger finished product. Yet, even in the absence of such intrinsic satisfaction in the act itself or visible coercion from their supervisors, the workers go about their tasks with a brisk efficiency that suggests some degree of emotional investment in the process (rather than simply in the paycheck that it brings them). None of the workers *except* the Little Tramp is shown engaging in minor acts of resistance and rebellion to break the monotony of the work.[21] They appear—again, like the workers that populated idealized depictions of 1930s industry—to find meaning in their ability to be part of the system and to mesh their actions with that of the machines to achieve a common end.

The factory and virtually all the factory workers in *Modern Times* are a seamless extension of those in other Depression-era images of modern machinery. The factory is breathtaking, the machines beautiful, and the workers (though a scruffy, individualistic group) are vigorous and competent. The film functions, incidental to the main action, as a kind of virtual factory tour, but one touched with the glamour of a Hine photograph and (in the two-way television screens) the science-fictional trappings of *Just Imagine*. Nothing in the factory setting *itself*—the production design, the staging, or the supporting characters—presents a critique of modern technology or of industrial mass production as it was practiced in the 1930s. The film's critique of industrialism—or, more precisely, of the attitudes toward technology and "modernity" on which industrialism depends—is vested entirely within the figure of the Little Tramp and in the antics that are played out against that richly detailed and carefully constructed backdrop.

CONFORMITY AND CONTROL: *MODERN TIMES'* DUAL CRITIQUE OF TECHNOLOGY

The factory scenes of *Modern Times* derive most of their humor from the interactions between the Little Tramp and the (literal and figurative) machinery of the industrial workplace. It is the comedy of failure taken to an epic level: failure to keep pace with the line, failure to control his body after stepping away from the line at lunchtime, failure in his attempts to break the monotony of the work, and—at last—failure to maintain his sanity. Alongside the Tramp's string of personal failures, however, runs a parallel set of institutional failures: the system itself sputtering and tottering around him, if not breaking down outright. In those dual, intertwined strings of failure lies *Modern Times'* critique of the vision of gleaming, polished modernity it so expertly re-creates.

The Little Tramp is not incompetent in the sense of lacking the manual skills required by the assembly line. His assignment—tightening a pair of nuts on a steel plate—is not difficult, and at the beginning of the sequence he performs it efficiently enough. Nor does he lack energy, ambition, initiative, or ingenuity: he displays all those qualities in abundance later in the film. The Tramp is, finally, no principled opponent of the modern, machine-driven world that so baffles and bedevils him. He neither opposes the excesses of industrial capitalism on political grounds, like the Luddites in the nineteenth century and the Wobblies in the twentieth, nor absents himself from the clamor of the factory and the city in search of inner peace, like Henry David Thoreau or John Muir. He willingly engages with the latest technological marvels (doing his best to "cooperate" with the feeding machine) and seeks work in a factory even after his breakdown. Even the fantasy in which he seeks escape from the stresses of "modern times"—a comfortable, middle-class life shared with the gamin—immerses them in, and indeed depends on, the cornucopia of modestly priced consumer goods that industrial mass production makes possible.

Rather, the Tramp fails at his factory jobs because his personality renders him utterly unsuited to the demands of the work. Throughout the film, he is a pronounced outlier among the workers: the only one who fails to find and maintain a stable working rhythm, the only one who cannot economically mesh his actions with the actions of the machine, and the only one who twitches uncontrollably after setting down his tools. He is the only worker to grow bored, the only one to be distracted, the only one to linger in the bathroom, and the only one to be admonished by a superior. He is the only worker (from the boss to the bolt hammerers) whose actions are driven by considerations *other* than efficiency, and—not coincidentally—the only one driven mad by the ever-quickening pace of the assembly line. Factory work, in *Modern Times*, does not break the bodies or spirits of men in general, but it does, quite decisively, break the Little Tramp.

A character's complete, abject failure to cope with the demands of a familiar environment becomes, under most circumstances, a reflection on the person rather than the setting.[22] The audience's established sympathy for the Little Tramp—carried over from previous films but burnished anew in *Modern Times*—allowed Chaplin, however, to do just the opposite. The Tramp, because he brings his history with him, enters the film already established as a gentle, humane everyman figure. His inability to integrate himself into the life of the factory thus becomes an implied critique of the factory world's privileging of speed and efficiency over comfort and contemplation and of the uniform and predictable over the unique and unexpected. The aspects of the Tramp's character that are most apparent in the factory scenes—his desire to be useful, his exuberant playfulness, his longing for a moment's relaxation—are so elemental, so modest, and so familiar that the factory's inability to accommodate them is immediately rendered suspect. That all the *other* workers are seemingly well-adapted to factory life becomes an invitation to reflect on why and to see them as somehow less human—or at least more willing than the Tramp to accept, adapt to, and even embrace a system that treats them inhumanely.

Even as it breaks the Little Tramp's sanity, however, the system itself is breaking around him. A large part of Americans' anxieties about technology in the 1920s and the 1930s centered on the possibility that—whether by mechanical failure, human error, or deliberate mischief—control of it might be lost and chaos might ensue.[23] The factory scenes in *Modern Times* dramatize all three of those possibilities, each time with the Little Tramp as instigator, victim, or both. Chaplin's actions are comic and the resulting chaos ultimately harmless, but the underlying message is serious: the control we exert over our machines is fragile, and our serene confidence in that control is misguided. Even seemingly ineffectual figures like the Tramp can, by the simplest of actions, reduce our machine-age world to chaos.

Mechanical failure enters the story when the Tramp is drafted to serve as a test subject for a new feeding machine designed to allow workers to eat without putting down their tools. Once turned on, the feeding machine also proceeds to fail on an operational level, not simply failing to execute its narrow assigned tasks, but running out of control and becoming simultaneously uncontrollable and unstoppable. The bowl of hot soup is dumped down the Tramp's shirt front, the spinning ear of corn is ground against his mouth, and the sponge-like device meant to wipe his face repeatedly slaps it instead. The feeding machine scene is, significantly, staged as the most controlled and scripted of all technological activities: the sales pitch demonstration. The machine is put through its paces under ideal conditions: there is no outside interference, the user is gamely cooperative, and the inventors themselves carefully monitor its every motion. The camera's close attention to each of the feeding devices in turn draws viewers into the demonstration and invites admiration of the ingenuity of the mechanisms and the precise choreography of the movements. The polished smoothness with which the first half of the scene plays out heightens the comic effect of the machine's eventual break-down but also underscores its utter randomness. The failure occurs without warning and for no apparent reason; the machine runs amok—assaulting rather than serving the user—because, the film suggests, it is simply the nature of machines to do so. [24]

The feeding machine also fails on a more subtle level: it is designed to increase efficiency by feeding the worker as he does his job, but its design works against that goal at every turn. The machine as a whole is far too large and intrusive for even one—much less one for every worker—to be used on a crowded assembly line. Its table blocks the worker's forward and downward view, and its support structure (though Chaplin's camera angles hide it from the audience's view) inhibits the worker's use of his hands. It also requires a technician to wheel the machine into and out of position, to pour soup into the bowl, and to load corn onto the rotary rack. The machine's reliance on a highly specialized, absurdly overcomplicated mechanism to achieve a simple task is echoed by the sales pitch itself, which is delivered by a recording (a mechanical salesman) even though flesh-and-blood salesmen are present in the room. Like the whimsical devices drawn in the 1930s by British cartoon-ist William Heath Robinson and his American counterpart Rube Goldberg, it satirizes engineers' privileging of ingenuity over common sense and techno-crats' imposition of technological "fixes" in realms where nothing was brok-en. The engineers and salesmen who promote the machine, seeing it as a triumph, exhibit both delusions. The managers of the factory do so as well, but more subtly. They are intrigued by the concept of the machine—oblivi-ous, as the audience is not, to its absurdity—and reject it only when it fails to live up to its promise.

The machines with which the Little Tramp interacts as he works suffer from neither conceptual flaws nor mechanical breakdowns. They are well designed and robust to a fault, demanding only that skilled workers keep them adjusted and supplied with raw materials and partially assembled com-ponents. The workers on the assembly line are clearly equal to this task; the Tramp, however, is not. When the line is sped up on the orders of the boss, the other workers adjust smoothly, quickening their pace but retaining a steady, rhythmic motion without wasted effort. The Tramp—less attentive, perhaps, to the prescription of some Taylorite efficiency expert teaching the "one best way" to tighten bolts—is pushed to, and then past, the limits of his bolt-tightening skills. Like a wobbling top as it slows, his motions become steadily more eccentric, less coordinated, and more wasteful of time and energy; no longer able to stand still and let the machines bring parts to him, he lunges down the line and then scuttles back, caroming off his coworkers in a desperate attempt to keep up. His last deliberate motion is to fling himself bodily onto the passing belt and be sucked, in an instant, into the machine.

All that separates the Tramp from his fellow workers is a slight deficit in speed, efficiency, and calmness under pressure. But the power and speed of modern machinery means that even those slight deficiencies can bring about catastrophe. The theme was already familiar to audiences from the real world. News accounts of workers who erected Depression-era bridges and skyscrapers emphasized their need for absolute sure-footedness, leaving the consequences of a misstep unspoken. A quarter-century before *Modern Times*, Rudyard Kipling's poem "The Secret of the Machines" has the machines caution their human masters that machines can neither love, pity, nor forgive—and if humans don't handle them correctly, they'll die. Just as significantly, they were primed, by the Little Tramp's earlier appearances on film, to see him as a character for whom missteps were the stuff of everyday life, and whose passage through the world was a string of small, comic catastrophes. Once the hapless Tramp comes into contact with the pitiless machines, disaster is inevitable. The audience is primed to expect it and also to expect that the Tramp will emerge—as he does from all his other collisions with the world—startled but unscathed. Sucked into the giant gears of the machine, he is passed through them like a strip of film through the sprockets and rollers of a projector until—his fellow workers having stopped then reversed the machine—he is ejected from it again.

The film's third technological catastrophe involves the Little Tramp's deliberate, albeit playful, attempts at sabotage. Driven past the breaking point by his experiences with the assembly line and the feeding machine, he descends into insanity. Dancing through the factory in a magnificently choreographed freak-out, he squirts his fellow assembly line workers with his oilcan and turns their conveyer belt off and on without warning, quickly reducing them to the same state of befuddled, arm-waving confusion that he experienced. Entering the control room, he pulls levers, throws switches, and spins wheels at random, creating chaos faster than the shirtless man can restore order. Overwhelmed by conflicting inputs from the controls, the machines surrounding the control room spin out of control, belching smoke and flame and frustrating the boss's attempts to keep electronic watch over the factory. The Little Tramp's burst of gleeful anarchy is simultaneously a parody of the purposeful actions carried out by the shirtless man—the anti-Tramp—at the beginning of the workday and a reminder that, in the human-created world of machines as well as in the natural world, disorder is the norm and organization a state that must be imposed and constantly maintained.

The myth, as Chaplin sees it, of humans' firm control over their machines is given one final thumping in the scene, late in the film, where the Little Tramp is hired at another factory (the Jetson Works) as a helper to an experienced mechanic (Chester Conklin). The Tramp's responsibilities extend only to carrying the older man's toolbox and handing him what he needs, but as on the assembly line his skills are not equal to the task. Three times in quick succession, he is surprised by the machine's motions: placing the mechanic's heirloom pocket watch between two moving parts that smash it flat, allowing the toolbox to be drawn into the machine's complex train of gears, and perching atop a piston that suddenly lifts him skyward, arms and legs flailing. The mechanic himself, however, fares no better. Despite his extensive knowledge, he, too, is surprised by the machine's movements and knocked into the gears. Like the Tramp in the earlier scene, he remains physically unscathed, but unlike him, he remains there. "Caught in the machinery"—a nineteenth-century phrase that drew a veil of euphemistic vagueness over horrific industrial accidents[25]—becomes, in the film, the stuff of comedy as the mechanic's head emerges from between the gears. Like the episode of the feeding machine, however, the comedy hints at a nightmare: he remains stuck in the gears throughout his lunch break, fed by the Little Tramp, and emerges again only when the factory returns to life. He is—for all his knowledge and experience—humbled by the machine of which he is ostensibly the master.

The factory scenes in *Modern Times* begin with the humbling of the Little Tramp himself by the great machines. Over the course of the film, however, everyone who claims (and who the audience expects) to exert control over the machines has been humbled as well. The inventors of the feeding machine—whose dress and manner suggest that they are scientists, engineers, or some other type of learned expert—stand helplessly by as their brainchild turns against them (and against the Tramp). The shirtless man in the control room, who seemed master of his domain when the day began, is shown by early afternoon to be powerless against the Tramp's lighthearted fiddling with the controls. The boss, isolated in his office when the fiddling causes his television surveillance system to fail, loses control of his factory as a result. Even the mechanic—the individual who can take any machine in the factory apart, piece by piece, and reassemble it again—can and does become the captive of the machine he is servicing. Stuck among the gears, with his head protruding like an errant flywheel, he is forced to remain there, even while eating his lunch and drinking his tea, until the machine can be coaxed into releasing him.

Over the course of *Modern Times*, then, every scene that Chaplin stages in the factory comes to the same conclusion. We may believe that we are masters of our machines, and on our best days, under ideal conditions, we may be exactly that. Even so, the Little Tramp reminds us, it takes very little to turn the tables, creating a situation where our machines are masters of us.

CONCLUSION

The factory scenes in *Modern Times* play differently for audiences in the 2010s than they did for audiences in the 1930s. The film's images of machines and machine operators belong to that earlier age, not ours, and the very specific cultural resonances those images would have had then are lost on casual viewers today. The sight of the shirtless man working his levers no longer immediately calls to mind Lewis Hine's work portraits; the huge, sleekly beautiful machines of the control room no longer spur memories of world's fair displays and factory tours; the visual connections of the shop floor scenes to WPA murals are no longer obvious. Technology has changed, and our sense of the technological sublime has changed with it—not lost, but recalibrated for an age whose signature technological achievements are electronic rather than mechanical. Immense machines driven by complex trains of gears and run from control rooms filled with levers, dials, and wheels no longer read as shining examples of human ingenuity: humans' power over nature made manifest in steel, brass, and steam. Muscular workers wielding hammers and wrenches no longer seem as heroic.

The larger meanings that the images would have carried for 1930s audiences have, similarly, been obscured—if not altogether lost—with the passage of time. Factories are no longer equated, as a matter of course, with prosperity and economic opportunity. Technological change is no longer seen as inherently progressive, and the regulation of human activity to match the findings of the latest scientific research no longer seems like an inherently good idea. The hallmarks of technological modernity have also shifted. The cutting edge of technology is now defined by ever-smaller electronic devices rather than ever-larger structures. "Speed" and "power," desiderata pursued as fervently as ever, are now invisible, manifested in the movement of electrons through microprocessors and measured not in miles per hour or revolutions per minute but in computations per second. Efficiency is still valued—directly, by corporations enamored of the profits it produces; indirectly, by consumers entranced by the inexpensive goods and services it yields—but its pursuit is no longer regarded as a self-evident, self-justifying good. Finally, our aesthetic expectations of modernity have changed: we no longer expect the inner workings of our machines to be visible, much less available for us to touch and manipulate, and we no longer expect the surfaces that enclose them to please the eye.[26]

Postwar audiences and critics alike thus come to the film far more primed to "see" its commentary on the dehumanizing effects of modern technology and the treatment of workers as interchangeable parts than its depiction of the sense of wonder and possibility that the Industrial Age once evoked. The Little Tramp's comic struggles with the relentless pace of the assembly line sticks in modern viewers' minds. The beauty and power of great machines, the thrill of watching them at work, and their association with prosperity and progress pass by, largely unnoticed. When they do register, it is without the deeper emotional resonances that 1930s audiences would have seen in them. Lost, along with the latter, is the tension between the two, on which the film's critique of industrial society depends and with which the opposing critical views of the film can be at least partially reconciled. To ask whether the Little Tramp's comic collisions with the machinery of the Industrial Age are a critique of modern technology or simply an extended essay on the character's misfit status is to miss the point. The critique of technology is present, but it exists in tension with a thoroughly unironic celebration.

Modern Times is not about the inherent evils of industrialization, but rather a film about the tension between the pleasures we derive and the costs we impose on ourselves in embracing industrial capitalism and its defining values of speed, efficiency, and power over nature.[27] The figure of the Little Tramp serves as the focus and the agent of that critique. His struggles to avoid sacrificing his individuality on the altar of efficiency dramatize the costs of modern technology, and his endless, fruitless struggles with the machines raise questions about its benefits by underscoring the fragility of our control over our machines. Apprehending the full meaning of *Modern Times* means seeing it as 1930s audiences might have seen it, through the eyes of an age when great machines could still instill a sense of awe, and factories could still seem beautiful.

NOTES

1. Presented realistically, it would be horrifying: even without the Little Tramp's (invariably fatal) passage through the gears, the sequence is—at its core—a depiction of a man suffering a debilitating work-related injury and undergoing a complete mental breakdown.

2. Charles J. Maland, *Chaplin and American Culture: The Evolution of a Star Image* (Princeton, NJ: Princeton University Press, 1989), 155.

3. Roger Manvell, *Chaplin* (Boston: Little, Brown, 1974), 143; Garrett Stewart, "Modern Hard Times: Chaplin and the Cinema of Self-Reflection," *Critical Inquiry* 3, no. 2 (winter 1976): 296.

4. Walter Kerr, *The Silent Clowns* (New York: Knopf, 1975), 357.

5. David E. Nye, *American Technological Sublime* (Cambridge, MA: MIT Press, 1994).

6. Nye, *American Technological Sublime*, 34–43 (cultural independence); Michael Adas, *Machines as Measures of Men: Science, Technology, and Ideologies of Western Dominance* (Ithaca, NY: Cornell University Press, 1992), 348–64 passim (imperialism).

7. Nye, *American Technological Sublime*, chapter 4 ("Bridges and Skyscrapers") and chapter 5 ("The Factory"); David P. Billington, *Power, Speed, and Form: Engineers and the Making of the Twentieth Century* (Princeton, NJ: Princeton University Press, 2006); David P. Billington and Donald C. Jackson, *Big Dams of the New Deal Era: A Confluence of Engineering and Politics* (Norman: University of Oklahoma Press, 2006); John Lienhard, *Inventing Modern: Growing Up with X-Rays, Skyscrapers, and Tail Fins* (Oxford: Oxford University Press, 2006).

8. Robert Rydell, *World of Fairs: The Century-of-Progress Expositions* (Chicago: University of Chicago Press, 1993), 9.

9. Jack C. Ellis and Betsy A. McLane, *A New History of the Documentary Film* (New York: Continuum, 2005), 80–91; Raymond Fielding, *The American Newsreel: A Complete History*, 2nd ed. (Jefferson, NC: McFarland, 2004); Ronald R. Kline, "Ideology and the New Deal 'Fact Film' *Power and the Land*," *Public Understanding of Science* 6, no. 1 (January 1997): 19–30.

10. Alan Trachtenberg, *Reading American Photographs: Images as History, Matthew Brady to Walker Evans* (New York: Hill and Wang, 1989), 164–230; Sean Callahan, *Margaret Bourke-White: Photographer* (New York: Bulfinch, 1998); Kate Sampsell-Willmann, *Lewis Hine as Social Critic* (Jackson: University Press of Mississippi, 2009); Lewis Hine, *Men at Work* (New York: Dover, 1977); Lewis Hine, *Empire State Building* (Munich: Prestel-Verlag, 1998).

11. Erika Doss, "Toward an Iconography of American Labor: Work, Workers, and the Work Ethic in American Art, 1930–1945," *Design Issues* 13, no. 1 (spring 1997): 53–65.

12. Chaplin writes, in *My Autobiography* (New York: Simon and Schuster, 1978), that such reports were one of the inspirations for *Modern Times* (383).

13. Russell Freedman, *Kids at Work: Lewis Hine and the Crusade against Child Labor* (London: Sandpiper, 1998).

14. Frederik Pohl and Frederik Pohl IV, *Science Fiction: Studies in Film* (New York: Ace, 1981), 51–90.

15. Nye, *American Technological Sublime*, 129–31.

16. J. P. Telotte, "Lost in Space: Television as Science Fiction Icon," in *The Essential Science Fiction Television Reader*, ed. J. P. Telotte (Lexington: University Press of Kentucky, 2008), 37–53.

17. Quoted in John Kasson, *Civilizing the Machine: Technology and Republican Values in America, 1776–1900* (New York: Grossman, 1976), 139–80; on 147.

18. Doss, "Toward an Iconography of American Labor," 62–65.

19. Sol Gittelman, "Fritz Lang's *Metropolis* and Georg Kaiser's *Gas I*: Film, Literature, and the Crisis of Technology," *Teaching German* 12, no. 2 (autumn 1979): 27–30.

20. Ford Motor Company's "internal security" department was the most notorious of these organizations, but far from the first. Led by Harry Bennett, an ex-prizefighter and ex-sailor who became Henry Ford's right-hand man, its members used mob-style intimidation tactics, brutal beatings with clubs and brass knuckles, and occasionally gunfire against enemies of the company: labor organizers and employees alike. On Bennett and conditions at Ford, see, for example, Steven Watts, *The People's Tycoon: Henry Ford and the American Century* (New York: Random House, 2006), 446–65. On the use of hired thugs in general, see Stephen H. Norwood, *Strikebreaking and Intimidation: Mercenaries and Masculinity in Twentieth Century America* (Chapel Hill: University of North Carolina Press, 2001).

21. For one worker's account of coercion and rebellion, see Ben Hamper, *Rivethead: Tales from the Assembly Line* (New York: Warner Books, 1992), 109–16.

22. The "Private Snafu" series of cartoon shorts (1943–1945), for example, featured a hapless soldier whose lethal errors were designed to reinforce the importance of following standard U.S. Army operating procedures. See Michael S. Shull and David E. Wilts, *Doing Their Bit: American Wartime Animated Shorts, 1939–1945* (Jefferson, NC: McFarland, 2004), 80–89. Walt Disney Studios used the "negative exemplar" formula in educational shorts such as "Motormania" (1948) and "Freewayphobia" (1965) and the "How to Have an Accident . . ." and "I'm No Fool . . ." series. On the former, see A. Bowdoin Van Riper, "A Nation on Wheels: Films about Cars and Driving, 1948–1970," in *Learning from Mickey, Donald and Walt: Essays on Disney's Edutainment Films*, ed. A. Bowdoin Van Riper (Jefferson, NC: McFarland, 2011), 103–11.

23. Anxieties about loss of control over technology intensified sharply after 1945, with nuclear weapons, computers, and biotechnology as successive foci for them. *Fail-Safe* and *Jurassic Park* are among the best known of the hundreds of short stories, novels, films, television programs, and songs that dramatized such anxieties.

24. Decades later, sociologist Charles Perrow argued that in complex, "tightly coupled" technological systems in which a large number of critical components must interact in a specified way in order for the machine to operate, failure becomes an inevitable feature of the

system—one that can be mitigated but never eliminated. See *Normal Accidents* (New York: Simon and Schuster, 1984), 3–4.

25. The frisson of horror evoked by the climax of W. W. Jacobs' 1902 short story "The Monkey's Paw," for example, depends in large part on the reader's understanding of the gruesome reality behind the euphemism.

26. The shift toward a utilitarian visual aesthetic is so pronounced that striking exceptions—like Apple's multi-hued "gumdrop" iMac computer and iPod portable media player—are the stuff of marketing legend. For a fuller discussion, see Donald A. Norman, *Emotional Design: Why We Love (or Hate) Everyday Things* (New York: Basic Books, 2003), and the "Cool" chapter of Stephen Levy, *The Perfect Thing: How the iPod Shuffles Commerce, Culture, and Coolness* (New York: Simon and Schuster, 2006).

27. On the concept of "modern" and its relationship to technology in the first half of the twentieth century, see Lienhard, *Inventing Modern*.

Chapter Six

Deconstruction and the Tramp

Marxism, Capitalism, and the Trace

Randall L. Gann

There is profit in a Marxist reading of Charlie Chaplin's 1936 film *Modern Times* insofar as the casual observer can recognize the basic tenets of Marx's critique of capitalism at work. The division of labor, a binary opposition of capitalist and worker, is sketched so completely that the clarity of the critique in the film might serve to explain the absence of a Marxist reading of *Modern Times* in scholarly writing. The profit of a Marxist reading, however, doesn't come from simply filling a gap in the scholarship; it comes from exploiting the opening provided by the Tramp when his comic machinations unravel the carefully constructed Marxist scenario. In other words, taking a closer look at the Marxist critique in *Modern Times* allows us to see the Tramp as a deconstructive force. Marxism and deconstruction both have a penchant for a radical critique of the rootedness of discourse and the institutional frame in which it occurs. But is also important to note that Marxism is founded in an historical dialectic, whereas deconstruction is explicitly ahistorical, predicated on a persistent condition of discursive failure. The two do not work in tandem, but neither are they mutually exclusive; nevertheless, the opening they provide destabilizes the capitalist/worker binary through the deconstructive force of Chaplin's Tramp character. The Tramp acts to decenter the authority of the Marxist binary and the mechanized order of the factory system to achieve good ends. Although his disruption on the factory line is a comic performance, it achieves more than simply making us laugh; through the humor we see the Tramp destabilize capitalist practice in a way that shows the profit of reading *Modern Times* deconstructively.

In late 1929, the stock market began to fall and the American economy crumbled into the prolonged and profound Great Depression. Cycles of eco-

nomic instability had been common through the nineteenth century and occurred about every twenty years or so after the Civil War. The panics of 1893
and 1907 were not short-lived phenomena, but the Great Depression was
certainly the worst and most sustained one. Economic uncertainty and stag-
gering unemployment replaced the prosperity and industrial growth of the
Roaring Twenties that had shaped American culture into one of affluence and
materialism. In the early years of the 1930s, American capitalism was showing signs of instability. In 1933, Congress passed the National Industrial
Recovery Act (NIRA), which forced capitalist businessmen to make conces-
sions to unions representing skilled workers. However, big business dominated the regulation writing process called for by the act, and in 1935, the
Supreme Court invalidated NIRA and, along with it, the guarantee that workers could bargain collectively.[1] So even though capitalism was struggling
and showing signs of instability, the worker was struggling more, and there
was no cessation in the class warfare inherent in the capitalist/worker binary.
In fact, the unions representing skilled workers were losing influence because unskilled workers now made up most of the industrial labor force.[2]

Capitalism's ideal model consists of a highly disciplined and interchangeable workforce, which, in turn, would enable the global spread of Taylorism
and Fordism. Named after theoretician Frederick Winslow Taylor, Taylorism
is a production model based on the scientific management of the workforce
that subdivides tasks and gives management more control over the workplace. Instead of individual craftsmen making products, workers manage
labor-saving machinery, greatly increasing output. Fordism, named after
Henry Ford, refers to mass production work on an assembly line. Basically
Taylorism in practice, Henry Ford introduced this type of labor in his automobile plants in 1914. In *The Unfinished Nation: A Concise History of the
American People*, historian Alan Brinkley notes that the assembly line was
both an actual place and a concept that "stressed the inter-changeability of
parts,"[3] both mechanical and human. But precisely because of the philosophy
of interchangeability, the Fordist model robs the worker of all human dignity.

Modern Times shows how the Fordist model replaces the idea of worker
as craftsman with the idea of worker as expendable commodity. The worker
sells his labor power for a specific wage but produces an amount of goods
worth more than his wage. The margin between the worker's wage and the
goods he produced for that wage is surplus value, and it is precisely this
surplus value from which the capitalist extracts profit. A worker's wages are
obviously an important part of this equation; however, *Modern Times* seems
more concerned with a common understanding of labor insecurity within its
historical moment. By the Depression, there was much less concern for the
exploitation of wage slavery than there was for the unemployment caused by
technological automation and, worse, overproduction.[4] Thus, *Modern Times*

exploits the class divisions that exist within the capitalist system in an explicitly comedic way.

After the title cards, the movie opens on a screen filled with sheep moving quickly through a pen, then fades to workers streaming out of the subway and swarming toward the factory gates for their shift. The viewer immediately confronts the metaphor of the common man as a herd animal blindly following the rest of the herd. This series of images is what Sergei Eisenstein would have called "an 'intellectual montage': two shots that create a third meaning through their juxtaposition."[5] The sheep, which graze until the grass disappears and are then sold to slaughter, are betrayed by their own instinct to survive; their mere survival is the basis of profit for the stockman. In "The German Ideology," Marx, too, compared man to sheep, and the difference that he saw was the presence of consciousness: "Man is only distinguished from sheep by the fact that with him consciousness takes the place of instinct or that his instinct is a conscious one."[6] In other words, although both sheep and man have survival instincts, only man is conscious of that instinct, and he can make choices concerning his survival. But capitalism exploits the conscious human instinct because the worker is forced to choose between capitalist wage-labor and the inability to survive. The natural instinct to survive, then, becomes a *forced choice*[7] to enter the capitalist system and its strictures. The opening montage of *Modern Times* aligns its sympathies with the plight of the worker and then offers an unsympathetic picture of a capitalist boss that will stand in binary opposition to the worker.

After the herd of workers enters the factory, the scene cuts to the glass-plated door of the president of the Electro-Steel Corporation. The next shot shows the factory boss sitting behind an enormous wooden desk; he is immaculately dressed in a fine three-piece suit with a bowtie and is well groomed. Every detail of the mise-en-scène shows the capitalist as a stereotypical member of the bourgeois class and underscores the idea that he works not for survival, but for profit. It is obvious that he has too much time on his hands; a half-finished jigsaw puzzle occupies him for a moment before he absently moves to the comics in the newspaper. He is only rescued from his boredom when his secretary enters to bring him a glass of water and a small box containing a pill.[8] The viewer is meant to read these frivolous activities in a way that underscores the amount of leisure time that is enjoyed by the privileged class, even when they are at work. The factory boss represents a vulgar form of capitalism because it is clear that his basic needs are more than adequately met, and so his time is now spent extracting capital/profit from the labor of others who are less fortunate. This succinctly bleak portrait of the factory boss conveys Chaplin's characteristic lack of sympathy for figures of power; it also provides a foil for the upcoming comedy of the Little Tramp. With the capitalist side of the Marxist binary adequately constructed for Chaplin's comedic ends, *Modern Times* returns to the worker.

The establishing shots of the factory immediately stand in juxtaposition to the leisurely pace of the capitalist boss's office. Wide shots show a large industrial space filled with complex machinery and bustling with men hard at work. When the camera pans to reveal the Tramp and his immediate coworkers, their appearance contrasts starkly with that of the capitalist. Their hair is mussed and their countenance dirty, their clothes are shabby and smeared with grease. It is immediately clear that these men do not belong to the privileged bourgeois class based on their appearance alone. They stand in front of an assembly line with a conveyor belt that quickly rolls by an unending line of steel plates. The scene further emphasizes the difference between capitalist and worker by demonstrating that there is no time for leisure on the factory floor.

When the Tramp momentarily pauses to scratch an itch, both his coworkers and the line foreman remonstrate him and dramatically insist that he keep up with the pace. This moment is a setup for the following comedy bit, where the Tramp lampoons how tightly each worker's time is controlled in the factory setting. A cut to a medium shot shows the Tramp on pace and focused on his job, when suddenly a large insect begins buzzing around his face. He wildly swipes at it with both hands but again falls behind and has to concentrate on catching up. As soon as he catches up, however, the insect returns. The Tramp nervously eyes the insect and tries to blow it away while still working. The comic payoff comes in the following wide shot when a passing worker sees his troubles and smashes the bug on the Tramp's face with a rolled-up newspaper. The Tramp's clowning around in response to the insect shows that not only is there no leisure time in contrast to the factory boss, but there is not even a moment for the elementary and normally trivial gesture of protecting oneself from an insect. Chaplin uses the comedic moment to demonstrate how capitalism robs the worker of his dignity.

The depiction of the Tramp and his fellow workers on the factory line superbly illustrates the Marxist critique of the capitalist system by showing how the Fordist division of labor moves away from the ideal of man's natural industry. He no longer owns the fruits of his labor, nor does he own the surplus value of his industry beyond that which he requires to survive. As Marx explains in "Wage Labour and Capital," the division of labor works to remove the worker from the finished product: "What he produces for himself is not the silk that he weaves, not the gold that he draws from the mine, not the palace that he builds. What he produces for himself is wages."[9] In the factory setting, the idea of worker as craftsman disappears because he is removed from the final product and any sense of completion and pride. He is reduced to a small mechanical role in a complex process, moving away from natural industry and toward commodification. The film is very clear in its imagery that standing on a factory line, engaged in a repetitive motion that any worker can do, is alienating.

The Fordist assembly line practices portrayed in *Modern Times* demonstrate how the division of labor separates the worker from his natural industry. The Tramp's job is to tighten two nuts on each plate as it goes by. Subsequently, the two workers to his left pound each of the tightened nuts with a hammer. Their labor seems absurdly out of context because it remains unclear how it fits into any finished product or even what that finished product might possibly be. In "Wage Labour and Capital," Marx insists that the more complex the machinery becomes, the less complex the role of the worker: "Workers employed in the machine factories, confronted by highly elaborate machines, can only play the part of highly unelaborate machines."[10] Their labor requires no thought or skill and thus transforms them into simple automatons doing a job that anyone could perform. In other words, the worker becomes a commodity, an interchangeable part within the machinery of capitalist industry. Thus, *Modern Times* uses the factory setting to portray Depression-era capitalism as exploitation of the class inequity inherent in the capitalist/worker binary.

Chaplin's critique of the industrial and sociohistorical context of *Modern Times* responds to the class inequalities of capitalism that are made more acute by the social, political, and economic woes of the Great Depression. According to Charles Maland, Chaplin's previous comic features established a convention that contrasted a moral polarity within which those on the social margins struggle to survive. In fact, *Modern Times* is not the first time Chaplin implied a critique of capitalism and Fordism. In an early two-reeler titled "Work," Chaplin portrays an assistant wallpaper hanger working for a bourgeois-class family named Ford. Maland argues that with "this basic contrast, [*Modern Times*] evinces sympathy for the have-nots of society, particularly their dreams of getting by, and hostility for the haves in society who desire profit and control of others at whatever cost."[11] The hierarchy that is inherent in the capitalist/worker binary, according to Marx, turns the worker's labor against his own self-interest. The capitalist will never labor out of a pure need of survival, and the worker will never command his own labor power. In other words, the film's plot engages the impermeability of class divisions inherent in capitalism and made even more problematic by the Great Depression.

At the beginning of the economically disastrous 1930s, many American artists and intellectuals were drawn to more socially conscious art. One change noted by Maland in his article "The Depression, Technology, and the Tramp," was "a weakening of what Malcolm Cowley called the 'religion of art' so widespread among American expatriate artists of the 1920s and its replacement with the conviction that art should acknowledge and grapple with the social and political conflicts of the age."[12] After the success of his early films, Chaplin was recognized as an important film artist, but some critics suggested that he was too sentimental and failed to deal with important social issues. [13] These critiques weighed on Chaplin as he toured Europe for eighteen months after the release of *City Lights* (1931). In his autobiography, Chaplin states that he avoided work on a new project, in part, because of a sense of guilt: "I was depressed by the remark of a young critic who said that *City Lights* was very good, but that it verged on the sentimental and that in my future films I should try to approximate realism. I found myself agreeing with him." [14] As a result of his agreement with the critics, Chaplin was preparing his Tramp for a more socially conscious exploration into the cultural and economic unrest of the 1930s. And the portrayal of the economic situation of the Depression as the main trope in *Modern Times* seems to be the result of that exploration. But even though Chaplin was a comic genius, he wasn't overly sophisticated as an intellectual thinker.

While traveling, Chaplin met with world leaders and artists and discussed economic and social affairs. Chaplin's meeting with Mahatma Gandhi demonstrates his naïveté concerning the power of industrial capitalism just four short years before he began shooting *Modern Times*. Gandhi explained to Chaplin that it was through machinery that India had become dependent on England and mass-produced goods. But Chaplin insisted that he did not understand Gandhi's aversion to machinery because it should, if used with an unselfish concern for others, "help to release man from the bondage of slavery, and give him shorter hours of labor and time to improve his mind and enjoy life." [15] Chaplin's inability to foresee the potential abuses of industrial capitalism and his penchant for sentimentality help explain why the narrative of *Modern Times* cannot sustain the Marxist critique it so brilliantly initiates.

Just as *Modern Times* finishes constructing the framework of the capitalist/worker binary, we are reminded that Chaplin is a slapstick comedian, not a political philosopher. But that does not suggest that the slapstick comedy lacks theoretical import, quite the contrary. The comedic disruptions of the Tramp work as a funny, disruptive force that unravels the Marxist critique so carefully constructed up to this point. If we return to the factory line where the Tramp and his coworkers toil in front of the conveyor belt, we can see clearly that the Tramp stands apart from the workers, and his difference from them destabilizes the capitalist/worker binary. The Tramp's struggles to keep up with the conveyor belt become even more pronounced when the factory boss orders an acceleration of the pace. The frustration with the day's monotonous labor has reached a fevered pitch for the Tramp; when he falls behind yet again, he acts on that frustration. Desperately trying to keep up, he jumps onto the belt and follows the plates into the machine. The following shot shows the Tramp moving through the inside of the machine, still trying to tighten the bolts. A surface reading, and one consistent with a straight Marxist critique, might interpret the Tramp's fate as symbolic of becoming part of the capitalist machine. But the astute viewer will note that the Tramp does not remain a part of the machine of industry; rather, his coworkers stop and then reverse the factory mechanism and extract him. He then works to disrupt the work of the factory. The Tramp's disruption of the factory line highlights the danger that would ensue were Taylorism and Fordism allowed to stand unchallenged and become the norm. But his comic disruption holds revolutionary potential because it represents the possibility for any worker to remove labor power. The revolutionary potential lies in the challenge to the authority of Taylorism and Fordism. In other words, the Tramp's explicit challenge to the factory system exposes the capitalist theories that Jacques Derrida would call "a regulating and trans-historical ideal."[16] The Tramp is disrupting the desired increase in production and that disruption is the trace of the potential to subtract labor power and begins to hint at what Derrida calls *différance*.[17]

The Tramp's refusal to surrender to the repetitive motion of the factory line suggests his decision to be Other and shows the possibility of a previously unrecognized third space within the structure of the binary. But a binary by definition cannot account for a third element, thus the previously unrecognized space shows a slippage in the very structure of the capitalist/worker binary. Significantly, then, the structure of the binary contains a revolutionary potential. It is important to note here that the revolutionary potential of this slippage also denotes a gap between the theories of Marxism and deconstruction. Revolution in the Marxist sense refers to a synthesis from the two contesting terms of the binary, or what Marxism would call the dialectic, thesis versus antithesis. In this sense, revolution requires a replacement of a rejected hierarchy with an improved structure, presumably one that is more efficient and more equitable. But the dialectic process is cyclical because the synthesis from one dialectic simply becomes part of another, higher-order dialectic; it reproduces and reinforces the Western tradition of producing meaning through binary opposition. In a deconstructive sense, the previously unrecognized third space within the binary absolutely does not work toward synthesis; rather, it disrupts the order of operations that might lead to any synthesis by invalidating the viability of the either/or structure of binary opposition. In other words, the slippage shown by the appearance of the previously unrecognized space compromises the integrity of the binary. Furthermore, it belies a profound revolutionary potential not because it seeks to broker a synthesis between the thesis and antithesis, but because it invalidates any claim of authority from either. For Derrida, the standard practice for understanding the world through binary opposition is entangled with metaphysics. In a binary opposition, the first term is assumed to be superior and the second term derivative. According to Michael Ryan, Derrida's argument is that "the second term in each case usually connotes something that endangers the values that the first term assures, values that connote presence, proximity, ownership, property, identity, truth conceived as conscious mastery."[18] Because of the revolutionary potential contained within the binary, the controlling side—in the case of *Modern Times*, the capitalist—must master the secondary term, the worker. The capitalist must make sure that he remains on the controlling side of the binary and emasculates the revolutionary potential in the worker's side by maintaining a distinct separation between the two; the capitalist must not allow the Tramp to blur the boundaries of the binary. But it has already become clear that the Tramp does not belong on either side of the binary.

It goes without saying that the Tramp is not a capitalist, but it is important to note that his disruption exercises a form of control over production, specifically the revolutionary potential that the other workers fail to recognize at this point in the film.[19] An example from earlier in the film demonstrates the point. When a relief worker comes by to offer a short bathroom break, the Tramp goes into the bathroom to enjoy a leisurely smoke. He clocks out before entering the bathroom, but that does not prevent the capitalist boss from appearing on a giant video monitor in the bathroom and scolding him to get back to work. Upon returning to his workstation, the Tramp manicures his nails while the relief worker continues doing the Tramp's job. One may, at this point, accuse the Tramp of simply being a recalcitrant worker, for the relief worker does do the work of the Tramp while he subversively stalls. But a close reading shows that the Tramp also skillfully reenacts the role of the foreman when the relief worker attempts to hand back his tools. As the relief worker turns, the Tramp animatedly points to the next plate needing attention on the swiftly moving conveyor belt. Suddenly the relief worker is behind and the Tramp exercises authority by insisting that the worker get back on pace. This does buy the Tramp a few more seconds of leisure while the relief worker catches up and provides the viewer with another laugh, but it also expropriates a trace of the responsibility of authority. The Tramp successfully assumes the role of a line supervisor when he admonishes the relief worker for getting behind when he tries to give the tools back to him. He also keeps a close eye on the relief worker as he hustles to catch back up with the pace. Even though the Tramp's ascension in the hierarchy of labor lasts only a brief moment, it shows at least a trace of a work ethic inconsistent with recalcitrance. Despite what the boss may think, the spare moments the Tramp attempts to carve out of the hustle and bustle of the factory are not laziness but an equivocation of/over authority.

Leisure time is a luxury that is denied to the working class, but somehow the idea is not foreign to the Tramp even though he does not possess the necessary means for a fully funded life of leisure. By definition, the term "tramp" suggests the term "leisure." Leisure is defined as time not occupied with work and, thus, working puzzles and reading the funnies as the president of Electro-Steel does or manicuring one's nails as the Tramp does upon returning to his workstation is leisure time.[20] Only the capitalist and, ironically, the Tramp experience leisure within the confines of the factory, thus disrupting the Marxist binary. Obviously, the Tramp does not fit into the capitalist side of the binary, but he retains a trace of the privilege enjoyed by the bourgeois class through his subversive ability to make time, however brief, for leisure. A worker who contracts his labor for a wage doesn't have the ability to "make time"—the capitalist purchases his time. And in the factory setting of *Modern Times*, it is the Tramp's time/labor that is purchased. He's not paid for piecework, but for his hours on the job. The accelerated assembly line is the capitalist's way of getting more labor out of his time-waged employee. The failure of the Tramp to adhere to this Fordist work ethic makes us laugh, and this laughter signals a disruption of the capitalist's desire because he is not profiting from his employees' labor power when they are not laboring.

The revolutionary potential within the binary threatens the capitalist, but it also threatens the workers' side of the binary. In the context of the Great Depression, it would be devastating to lose a job. If the factory produces no goods, if the workers do not work, then the exchange value system the worker relies on for subsistence is disrupted. Moreover, failure to actively oppose any disruption could be construed as revolution itself. In other words, if a worker is not looking out for the interest of the capitalist, he may be thought to be a part of the Depression-era struggle to organize labor. The film demonstrates the consequences of any association with organized labor when the Tramp is arrested after being mistaken as the leader of a workers' rights march. Although that particular scene is outside the scope of this argument, it helps explain why the disruptive and revolutionary potential of the Tramp also endangers the workers.

The disruptive nature of the Tramp's presence on the factory line excludes him from being neatly categorized as worker. When the Tramp's clowning around forces the workers to stop working by taunting them and squirting them with oil, they must first stop the equipment before they can trap him. He is working counter to the productivity of the workers and is in clear contradiction to them; he is Other. An intertitle confirms his Otherness when it announces, "He's Crazy!" requiring the workers to subdue this disruptive Other. It obviously makes him different, or Other, from the workers if he is crazy; moreover, the diagnosis of the Tramp's Otherness as a psychological difference is significant linguistically on an ontological level. Appearing as Other, the Tramp is quite different from the workers; here, though, his Otherness is more pronounced because it is officially diagnosed. A parallel example of his Otherness occurs later in the film when he is officially sentenced to jail. After serving his time and returning to society, he longs for the security of jail, again suggesting his Otherness. It would seem that no matter what environment he finds himself in, he is always the Other. As Michael Ryan puts it, "The law of identity, which is the law of sovereignty, be it of meaning or of the state, is broken. Such transformations of supposedly self-identical things into different things are irrational; hence they trouble the rationalism of fixed, legitimate, proper meaning."[21] Working from Jacques Lacan's description of schizophrenia as a linguistic disorder that disrupts the signifying chain of meaning, Frederic Jameson suggests that when this signifying chain snaps, "we have schizophrenia in the form of a rubble of distinct and unrelated signifiers."[22] If we define who we are through "a certain temporal unification of the past and future with the present before [us]," we realize the possibility in ourselves of the inability to "unify the past, present and future of our own biographical experience or psychic life" when we come face-to-face with the Other.[23] In the terms of *Modern Times*, when the workers are forced to confront the Tramp's radical alterity, they essentially confront the idea that the Other is not only a possibility within each and every one of them, but that possibility also erodes the very stability of the chain of signification within which they understand reality. Through his "craziness" the Tramp has lost the ability to unify, or anchor, himself within the reality represented by the factory and the capitalist/worker binary. The normal referents—past, future, and present—no longer work cohesively and allow him to abide with the forced choice of labor. What it means to *be* is called into question, and all who confront the Tramp in this state must face the possibility of themselves as Other. Furthermore, the Tramp's deviance from normativity is also measured economically.

When the workers nearly have the Tramp trapped, he turns the machines back on. The power switch invokes the herd mentality of those whose instinct to survive has compelled them to sell their labor power, which defines the worker's side of the Marxist binary. The machines roar back to life and the workers obediently—instinctively—return to work, minus the Tramp. "Charlie" as worker regresses to being the Tramp, who signals not just the absence of work, but its comic disruption. The Tramp, minus the "*m*," has become the trap of the workers. But what is the "*m*" that is taken from "tramp" to make the trap? If the workers are not working, they run the risk of becoming minus money (-*m*) and, therefore, work in opposition to their forced choice to sell their labor for survival; in other words, they risk realizing the revolutionary potential. In essence then, in "trapping" the Tramp, they become "trapped." The Tramp "traps" them. The Tramp, like the capitalist, has exploited the threat of being minus money to turn the workers' own labor against them. The workers, like the sheep in the opening montage, cannot ignore their forced obedience to work, however conscious it might be, to trap the Tramp, so they are trapped between two extremes of capitalism. Thus, by making the forced choice to labor for money, the worker is trapped by capitalism. In effect, the workers are equivalent to their wages, or capitalized labor, in the system of the factory. The Tramp's resistance to work helps to provide a clearer sketch of the dilemma. On one side of the trap, the capitalist will pay the workers only enough money to survive but not to get ahead. On the other side of the trap, the Tramp when he disrupts stands as an example of what can happen when one is minus money. The workers are caught in the trap of capitalism, only this time their capitulation to exploitation is exposed by the disruption of the Tramp. They will have to displace the disruption until the machines can be turned off again. What the Tramp's disruption shows is that the workers are part of the capitalist machine, literally unthinking gears in the works. If the machine is running, the workers are working, and vice versa. The workers, like the machines, are operated by the power switch and, from the perspective of capitalism and the factory system, retain only a trace of their humanity. The Tramp, who is now radical alterity precisely because of his madness, retains only a trace of worker and no definite inclusion in the machinations of capitalism.

The once-clear definitions implied by the capitalist/worker binary begin to show their weakness through the work of what Derrida calls *différance*.[24] There is a punning significance inherent in *différance* because Derrida bases the idea on the French infinitive *différer*, which means both to differ and to defer. In *Course on General Linguistics*, Ferdinand de Saussure acknowledged that the principle by which signification occurs is based on the play of differences within that system.[25] Derrida notes that what the principle then prohibits is any chance that "a simple element be present in and of itself, referring only to itself."[26] So, from the very beginning of human language the unity of the sign is undermined because of the play of differences as the ground of signification. As Derrida puts it, "no element can function as a sign without referring to another element which itself is not simply present."[27] In the context of *Modern Times*, the Tramp is without work, but he has worked before and been a part of the collective known as workers. The term "tramp" retains a trace of work by definition. A tramp differs from a worker, but also defers to the term worker in its own definition, "in search of employment."[28] The trace works to show spacing, or a gap, between the two spheres of the capitalist/worker binary, a weakness that allows it to be destabilized. So the Tramp, previously a worker, is very much separate from (the) worker(s). He is not a worker and, therefore, he is not a part of the collective known as the workers; he does not fit into either side of the worker/capitalist binary. The Tramp occupies a previously unrecognized space within the binary and, as a result, is working as a deconstructive force against the binary's stability.

The Tramp as Other, as deconstructive force, threatens the binary and those who are defined by it because he is a specter who forces us to confront the possibility of another existence. In *Specters of Marx* Derrida asks, "What is the being-there of a specter? What is the mode of presence of a specter?"[29] For Derrida, the specter puts into question what it means to exist—what it means to be—because it problematizes the Western tradition of understanding the world through binary opposition. It instead indicates a third possibility, which in turn suggests the existence of multiple other possibilities. The need to label and trap this disruptive force ("He *is* crazy!") cannot close off that risk because the workers have metaphorically seen a ghost. The Tramp that the workers knew is only physically present, but he is no longer the person they knew; he is a ghost of his former self. The Tramp now represents a previously unacknowledged alternative to the binary of capitalist/worker. Once the audience confronts the impossibility of choosing between certainty and uncertainty, there is little hope for returning to the illusion of a past where everything fit neatly on either side of the opposition between capitalist and worker or even capitalism and communism. From inside the Marxist binary, inside the crack in the façade that the Tramp occupies as Other, we can begin to see the unreliability of any notion of a simple either/or. The definitions of capitalist and worker that *Modern Times* so neatly constructed are in flux because they must acknowledge a third space, the radical alterity of the Tramp. Because of the disruptions of the Tramp, who is neither capitalist nor worker, the entire production of the factory comes to a standstill. There is instability in these definitions because the workers are not working, and yet they are still defined by the term worker; the capitalist is not making a profit, but still he is a capitalist. In fact, at the height of the Tramp's disruption, the workers and the capitalist combine their efforts in order to trap him because only when they contain his disruption can they resume their roles in the binary. Previous to the Tramp's disruption, the interaction between the workers and the capitalist is mediated through a video monitor. The separation between worker and capitalist is not imaginary, but concrete because the two rarely meet face-to-face.[30] The capitalist controls the speed of his machines by appearing on a video screen and arbitrarily barking orders. Likewise, we see him scold the Tramp in the bathroom via another of these screens. But at the height of the Tramp's disruptions, the capitalist is on the factory floor with the workers, working to trap the Tramp. Capitalism is working in contradiction to itself here because worker and capitalist have a common task that appears to be of equal priority to both. Their work is the same—they chase the Tramp together. As they come together as one, however briefly, with a common task, the binary becomes even more unstable. The unity of the simple capitalist/worker binary cannot withstand the pressure of something that is not recognized within the binary but that is also inseparable from it. So while the Tramp makes us laugh, his shenanigans are also profound—the Other is the clown who creates disruption that is signaled by laughter. The inability to define the Tramp by either term in the capitalist/worker binary laughably deconstructs the possibility of that binary. Thus, the controlling side of the binary is no longer in control. The Other will have as much to say about capitalism as either of the privileged sides of the capitalist/worker binary.

In response to the threat of the Other in deconstructing the binary, the controlling agency of capital seeks to reinforce the binary, to restore its

clarity and predictability, because it provides an illusion of clarity and predictability, a comfortable space for the workers and the capitalist to ignore
the Other. The workers, and to an equal degree the capitalist, need to get the
crazy Tramp out of the factory because of the disruptive nature of confronting the possibility of the Other. But because of the play of differential meanings, ignoring the Other and adhering to strict, unmoving definitions will
prove to be flimsy shelter against the work of the trace. Throughout his entire
corpus, Derrida argues that if there is never any point at which meanings
could leave behind the play of differing and deferring and come into presence, then no meaning is ever fixed or final. Because the Tramp complicates
what it means to be capitalist and worker, in fact hints at the impossibility of
a definite meaning of either term, he questions not just the authority of the
binary but its essential validity.

The deconstruction of the binary is important because the loveable Little
Tramp comically demonstrates the inability of capitalism or Marxism to
stand as Truth. There is no longer any solid purchase on what it means to *be*
worker or to *be* capitalist because, as Ryan argues, "Deconstruction, operating from within the outlines of bourgeois philosophy, shows how what that
philosophy excludes is in fact internal to its makeup."[31] In the terms of
Modern Times, the Tramp is neither capitalist nor worker, but his slapstick
disruptions cannot be excluded or ignored in an effort to prop up the Western
tradition's desire to understand being via binary opposition. The terms
"worker" and "capitalist" rely on each other for definition; therefore, the
roles of either and the absolute authority of the rules of capitalism are caught
in crisis, all because of the Tramp's hilarious inability to conform to either
term in the binary. It is easier for the worker and the capitalist to make the
best of their current situation by banishing/containing the Other. If the capitalist and the workers can put down the Tramp's disruption of the factory
line, they can perhaps return to the illusion of authority provided by capitalism and the capitalist/worker binary. But as Derrida suggests, ignoring only
provides the perception that they are shielded from the danger of the Other:
"by hiding from themselves all these failures and all these threats, people
would like to hide from the potential . . . of what we will call the principle
and even, still in the figure of irony, the spirit of the Marxist critique."[32] The
figure of the Tramp as Other, as specter, works because it demonstrates the
inability to choose between being and non-being, or any other binary opposition for that matter; he exceeds any simple either/or. So, while the Tramp as
deconstructive force serves to flout the authority of the capitalist/worker
binary and displaces its order and productivity with chaos, this does not
disarm the Marxist critique of capitalism. The Tramp's actions demonstrate
the discursive failure of the binary of capitalist/worker to stand as truth. But
he also still stands as Other to any stable idea of Marxism as truth. The trap
that must be avoided here is simply replacing the old binary with a new one.

And *Modern Times* avoids that trap precisely because it does not offer a solution to the woes of capitalism, Marxism, or even the Great Depression. It simply makes us laugh as the Tramp does his thing within these historical contexts.

Laughter is the legacy of the Little Tramp. To be disappointed that *Modern Times* cannot sustain the Marxist critique it begins is to misunderstand the genius of Chaplin. He was ambivalent at best about entering the realm of social critique.[33] He only wanted to make us laugh despite the fact that his Tramp is often found in situations with political import. Anyone who has seen a Chaplin film knows in advance that he will disrupt the factory's order and productivity. The only question is how he will make us laugh as he does it. But it remains significant that the laughter is very much about disruption. The comic disruptions of the Tramp are profound because of their deconstructive force that, in the end, makes light of and questions the seriousness with which we approach the "-isms"—Taylorism, Fordism, Marxism, capitalism, and so on. His jaunty walk into the sunrise at the end of *Modern Times* implies a promise of a future even though we cannot know where or what that future will be. It is simply the promise of a new day and a new life elsewhere. We must read the deconstructive force of the Tramp as not only overflowing with possibility, but also with unpredictability and, most importantly, the disruptive force of laughter.

NOTES

1. Alan Brinkley, *The Unfinished Nation: A Concise History of the American People*, vol 2, *From 1865*, 4th ed. (Boston: McGraw Hill, 2004), 681–87.

2. Brinkley, *The Unfinished Nation*, 688.

3. Brinkley, *The Unfinished Nation*, 462.

4. This aspect of economic vulnerability, however, doesn't appear in the film until later, with the Communist demonstration and the gamin's father out of work and unable to provide for his family of daughters.

5. Charles J. Maland, "The Depression, Technology, and the Tramp," in *Film Analysis: A Norton Reader*, ed. Jeffrey Geiger and R. L. Rutsky (New York: Norton, 2005), 244.

6. Karl Marx, "The German Ideology: Part I," in *The Marx-Engels Reader*, ed. Robert C. Tucker, 2nd ed. (New York: Norton, 1978), 158.

7. I have italicized the term "forced choice" to indicate its ironic usage.

8. This pill could be some sort of medication signaling a need to regulate his health; it could also be a vitamin or some other form of dietary supplement.

9. Karl Marx, "Wage Labour and Capital," in *The Marx-Engels Reader*, ed. Tucker 205.

10. Marx, "Wage Labour and Capital," 216.

11. Maland, "The Depression, Technology, and the Tramp," 253.

12. Maland, "The Depression, Technology, and the Tramp," 244.

13. Maland notes in his article that Harry Alan Potamkin and Lorenzo Turrent Rozas, both writing in the early 1930s, "urged Chaplin to focus on serious social concerns instead of the wish fulfillment of romance and the emotional balm of pathos" (245).

14. Charles Chaplin, *My Autobiography* (New York: Simon and Schuster, 1964), 382.

15. Chaplin, *My Autobiography*, 344.

16. Jacques Derrida, *Specters of Marx: The State of the Debt, the Work of Mourning, and the New International*, trans. Peggy Kamuf (New York: Routledge, 1994), 62.

17. Jacques Derrida, "Différance," in *Deconstruction in Context: Literature and Philosophy*, ed. Mark C. Taylor (Chicago: University of Chicago Press, 1986), 396–420.

18. Michael Ryan, *Marxism and Deconstruction: A Critical Articulation* (Baltimore: Johns Hopkins University Press, 1982), 9.

19. Later, however, his onetime antagonist in the factory wants to be his friend when they confront each other after hours in the department store where the Tramp is a security guard. The former factory worker identifies himself as the Tramp's old pal and explains that he's been driven to burglary of the department store due to unemployment. This onetime industrial adversary has now joined the side of disruption of the capitalist system—taking the goods that from a revolutionary perspective would have been the theft of labor by capital.

20. This definition comes from the Oxford English Dictionary online.

21. Ryan, *Marxism and Deconstruction*, 4.

22. Frederic Jameson, *Postmodernism, or the Cultural Logic of Late Capitalism* (Durham, NC: Duke University Press, 1991), 56.

23. Jameson, *Postmodernism, or the Cultural Logic of Late Capitalism*, 58.

24. Derrida, "Différance," 396–420.

25. Ferdinand de Saussure, *Course on General Linguistics*, ed. Charles Bally, Albert Sechehaye, and Albert Riedlinger (New York: McGraw-Hill, 1966).

26. Jacques Derrida, *Positions*, trans. Alan Bass (Chicago: University of Chicago Press, 1981), 26.

27. Derrida, *Positions*, 26.

28. One of many variants to the noun "tramp" as it appears in the Oxford English Dictionary.

29. Derrida, *Specters of Marx*, 38.

30. The boss does go to the factory floor during the feeding machine demonstration, but this is arguably a time-out from the work period.

31. Ryan, *Marxism and Deconstruction*, 63.

32. Derrida, *Specters of Marx*, 68.

33. See Charles J. Maland, *Chaplin and American Culture: The Evolution of a Star Image* (Princeton, NJ: Princeton University Press, 1989), 143–49.

Chapter Seven

Chaplin's Presence

Rachel Joseph

Early in Charles Chaplin's *The Circus* (1928), the Tramp ducks into a mirror maze trying to avoid the pursuing police. Once inside, he sees himself magnified and duplicated into infinity.[1] The Tramp's duplication within the film is also duplicated in the replication of Chaplin's cinematic image. The replication of both Chaplin and the Tramp mirrors the replication of film itself. The sheer immenseness of the reproducible universe becomes a trap in which the Tramp loses a sense of himself in time or space—not knowing the real from the image. He searches for a way out of the maze only to be thwarted by reflections, making his bodily presence invisible even to himself. Shortly thereafter, the scene is repeated with the addition of the pickpocket and policeman. Both characters attempt to capture the Tramp, but continually miss coming into contact with him and instead find themselves tackling reflections and bumping into the flat surfaces of the glass mirrors.

The maze represents the quandary of the body of the performer in relation to the cinematic image. Embodied presence, seemingly impossible for film, triggers a comic quest in the mirror maze. The Tramp loses himself in the reflections, yet (comically) achieves a kind of cinematic presence. The reflections of the Tramp mirror the reflections of Chaplin across the cinematic landscape. Chaplin straddles the worlds of reproducibility and embodiment, constantly vacillating between the two as he both transcends and becomes one with his mechanical image. This collision between presence and reproducibility is staged upon the character of the Tramp. Chaplin's body exists in a liminal space that invites the presence of the live within the cinematic that transcends the absence that defines the ontology of film. The theatricality of Chaplin's Tramp along with the situations he finds himself in provides a kind of screened stage wherein a singular cinematic presence surfaces.

For example, during the same chase scene, Chaplin both performs and transforms into the mechanical. The Tramp and the pickpocket are both being chased through a funhouse by the police. In an attempt to escape, first the Tramp and then the pickpocket pose as mechanical dolls at the entrance to the funhouse, fooling the audience watching the automaton "performance." The "show" of the automaton sequence is an important structuring device of the entire section and becomes a kind of microcosm for the film as a whole. The rhythm of the automaton's show is punctuated by a staccato jerkiness that vacillates between stillness and movement. The Tramp and pickpocket's performance must adhere to the mechanical motion of the automata around them to fool the audience into seeing them as mechanical beings. This image inverts what cinematic creators must do in taking live performances transformed into the mechanical world of film and giving them the illusion of presence. The automata become a collision point between the theatricality of a live performance and the world of reproducibility. Although they are mechanized, the automata's "show" occurs in front of an audience, which makes them inherently theatrical. The mechanized nature of their performance brings to mind cinema and the world of mechanical reproduction, yet the outcome of this collision is a liminal space somewhere between presence and reproducibility.

In his theory of laughter, philosopher Henri Bergson points out that the comic comes from us seeing human beings behave like machines, inflexibly and without regard to the contingencies of the present.[2] Laura Mulvey has said of the above scene: "Chaplin's screen persona celebrates the cinema as an apotheosis of the human as machine and as a realization of the fascinating, ancient ambivalence between movement and stillness as ambivalence between the animate and the inanimate, from automata to the rhythmic movement and pose of the dancers."[3] Mulvey goes on to point out, "As a personification of the cinema's fusion of human and machine, he also points constantly to its vulnerability, the threat of breakdown, an ultimate ephemerality."[4] Bergson highlights the machine's inflexible nature when attached to the human, whereas Mulvey gestures to the fragility, the humanness, of the machine. Chaplin dances between the two positions, positing the cinematic as a place wherein the fragility of the machine and sometimes machine-like behavior of humans collide. The aftermath of these collisions are moments of a kind of flickering cinematic presence that creates a liminal oscillation between human and machine. The fixation in Chaplin's work on issues of the human and machine can also be seen as an extended meditation on mechanical reproducibility and presence. Encapsulated in Chaplin's oscillating attention between reproducibility and presence, the collision between the theatrical and the cinematic emerges as a space wherein the divide between theater and cinema collapses and becomes a singular presence. This essay suggests that Chaplin's representations of the theatrical within the cinematic offer moments of presence within reproducibility. These moments occupy a space somewhere between theater and cinema and highlight the dependence of presence on absence and absence on presence; what seems to be a binary opposition between presence and absence is in fact ontologically connected. Bergson's and Mulvey's theories, when looked at together, show the interdependence of the mechanical and human. The relationship between theater and cinema is one that bridges the apparent divide between mechanical re-producibility and presence.

Chaplin's films *The Circus* and *Limelight* (1952) are seemingly obsessed with ways in which presence and absence emerge, miss one another, and disappear. This missing artistically re-creates what psychoanalytic philosopher Jacques Lacan refers to as the traumatic Real. The traumatic Real is that which the subject cannot directly experience because its very presence over-whelms reality in an inassimilable shock to the system. Lacan divides psychic experience within a subject among the orders of the Symbolic, Imag-inary, and the Real. The Symbolic deals on the level of language whereas the Imaginary occurs on the level of fantasy. The Real is that which the subject cannot directly experience and as such is always traumatic. The other orders help the subject find a sense of reality and narrative continuity without di-rectly experiencing the Real.

In the work of Chaplin, performance emerges as a longing for an encoun-ter with an impossible and traumatic Real. In the live event, performance is necessarily "missed" in the way the Real is always missed because of the inability of the spectator to take the performance all in. In the cinematic, the Real is impossible because of the ontology of absence at the heart of cinema. When performance is represented onscreen, it causes a paradox between absence and presence. As Marco Grosoli points out in this volume, "Cathar-sis consists thus in the encounter with the void at the core of identity—that is, with the 'productiveness of nothingness' aligning art to nature in what has been so far called second-order. In order to be effective, this second-order needs a stage: some kind of representational distance so that the subject can recognize him/herself as nothing and come to terms through practice outside the theater with this unpleasant fact."[5] A scene within cinema wherein a live performance is presented to an audience within the film's narrative, what I refer to as a screened stage, allows a kind of cinematic presence to assert itself. Presence emerges during moments of theatricality onscreen and offers both the possibility of encountering the Real and its traumatic impossibility. As Grosoli points out about Chaplin's *Limelight*, "In other words, *through* the screen, he looks for a stage, a place where he can settle a frontal eye contact with the audience. A stage-like representational distance beyond the-ater and the theatrical apparatus, like in the final scene of *The Great Dictator*, where, as many critics have noticed, Chaplin himself seems to be addressing us and not just the barber."[6] This essay suggests that the traumatic Real

within Chaplin's films is a presence that becomes twisted into the frame of
the cinematic and asserts itself through performance and representations of
the stage.

The Real reveals itself within reproducibility through images of theater
within the cinematic. These representations are revealed within the concept
of the Lacanian stain—that which blurs reality and resists narrative integration. The theater when viewed onscreen gives an appearance of depth that
could also be said to trap the gaze. The spectator becomes trapped within this
depth of the theatrical. The actor's form within the stage onscreen further
functions as an aspect of this revelatory annihilation that allows the full force
of the traumatic register of the Real to enter into the picture. The Real,
through the figures of Chaplin and the Tramp, exists onscreen as a heightened theatricality that vacillates somewhere between presence and absence.

CHAPLIN AND THE STAIN OF THEATRICALITY

Slavoj Žižek points to Chaplin's presence onscreen as one of a Lacanian
stain, a "perturbance in reality."[7] The stain is a deliberate distortion that can
best be apprehended from the side.[8] Lacan uses Holbein's painting *The Am-
bassadors* and its white "stain" to explain the concept of the anamorphic.[9]
This seeming blemish on the painting reveals itself as a skull when the
viewer shifts positions to the side, rendering the relationship between trauma,
the Real, and the gaze. According to Lacan, "Holbein makes visible for us
here something that is simply the subject as annihilated."[10] Lacan goes on to
distinguish the annihilated subject from a symbol of castration, which also
figures into the concept of the gaze, and instead relates it to a symbol for
vision itself: "But it is further still that we must seek the function of vision.
We shall see emerging on the basis of vision, not the phallic symbol, the
anamorphic ghost, but the gaze as such, in its pulsatile, dazzling and spread
out, function, as it is in the picture."[11] In this way, the stain operates both to
annihilate and to reveal. The stain, in essence, traps the viewer in its gaze:
"This picture is simply what any picture is, a trap for the gaze. In any picture,
it is precisely in seeking the gaze in each of its points that you will see it
disappear."[12] This stain is the object's gaze itself. Lacan defines the gaze as
the object that looks back.[13] Chaplin's theatrical appearance—his body comically unveiled in front of a crowd of people at the beginning of *City Lights*
(1931)—invites the spectator's gaze to look at the Tramp while at the same
time the very presence of the Tramp and his theatricality suggests an object
that not only can be seen, but that also can look back. The gaze originates
from both the spectators viewing the object and from the object itself returning the gaze. The Tramp becomes the theatrical stain that operates as excess

that cannot be fully incorporated into the narrative and therefore becomes something other than the reproducible universe.

Theatricality invites the film spectator's gaze into the screen and through the very reflexivity of its presence cannot help but look back at the viewer. This reciprocity brings to mind Tom Gunning's theory of the "cinema of attractions," which posits that early cinema was characterized by performers' theatrical gesturing at the camera, which invited the audience to look, but also clearly showed the performer looking into the camera and out into an imagined audience.[14] This version of theatricality marks the relationship of performer and spectator as one of both a gaze that looks and one that looks back. Theatricality then becomes excess in addition to the narrative of the film. But when the Tramp looks back, what does the spectator see? A kind of theatrical blur in the field of vision, a presence that is unable to be smoothly placed within the context of narrative reality and instead becomes a place where the Real emerges. The Lacanian stain functions as excess that is present, though not initially apprehended. The theatrical becomes a kind of excess within the cinematic, metaphorically staining the surface of the film.

The stain manifests the gaze by interrupting the normal schema of the visual field and cannot be integrated smoothly into view. In this way, the Tramp operates as this excess in the world as represented by the film and is therefore impossible to assimilate—he sticks out like a sore thumb wherever he goes, and, as Žižek contends, he is constantly misapprehended, mis-seen. These moments leap out because theatricality confers a moment of presence on film that connects to the Real. It is the initial collision between theater and film that brings the Real to the fore, if just for a moment, as if a stain.

Žižek uses the opening scene from *City Lights* to illustrate the Tramp's relationship to the world when he is trying in vain to disappear from the other's gaze. The Tramp is revealed in front of a large crowd gathered for a dedication of a statue. A large white cloth is lifted, like a curtain, and the Tramp is found lying across the newly unveiled grand statue like some sort of blemish. The Tramp's disheveled appearance contrasts with the classical beauty of the statue. We see the Tramp thrust unwittingly into a performance. The Tramp becomes an actor who doesn't know he's acting. The crowd reacts with shock and surprise. The Tramp scrambles to exit but increasingly in a scene of rapidly escalating comic ridiculousness finds himself unable to leave. The seat of his pants is impaled upon the statue's sword, and he later slides upon the sculpture's face, quickly diminishing the newly unveiled statue's place in the community as a marker of civic pride and order. According to Žižek, "The tramp is thus an object of a gaze aimed at something or somebody else: he is mistaken for somebody else and accepted as such, or else—as soon as the audience becomes aware of the mistake—he turns into a disturbing stain one tries to get rid of as quickly as possible."[15] The Tramp's costume, bowler hat, white face reminiscent of a clown, bent cane, and exaggerated walk are all aspects of Chaplin's performance that operate as theatrical excess that sticks out from the reproducibility of film.[16] The theatricality of the Tramp, especially in scenes like the one from *City Lights*, *The Circus*, and, as we shall see later, *Limelight*, invites and traps the audience's gaze much like Lacan suggests the Holbein painting operates to catch the observer's. Theatricality becomes the lure and because of its particular presence onscreen, not only lures the gaze to it, but also looks back.

Presence, therefore, is the stain that Žižek speaks of as being represented in the character of the Tramp. As Walter Benjamin points out, the actor within cinema becomes merely "a prop within the frame," used as an object and lacking the subjectivity of an actor onstage.[17] This means that the figure of the actor on film perhaps gains its presence from its lack of subjectivity. The screened actor, by becoming a thing, is given the illusion of presence by being placed within a narrative that creates a sense of reality.[18] Chaplin, through his theatricality that clearly stands out from the other performers onscreen, confronts the viewer with his excess—impossible to assimilate, difficult to apprehend, thus achieving an "embodied" cinematic presence somewhere between absence and presence.

The most striking aspect of performance, as Peggy Phelan has theorized, resides in its singularity. This singularity makes its essential ontology one that "becomes itself through disappearance."[19] A performance is unrepeatable: once it is gone, it is gone for good and therefore, according to Phelan, escapes the economy of reproduction.[20] Although a performance is constructed specifically so that it can repeat, as in a play or circus performance, no two performances ever can be reproduced exactly. Cinema, although the performance aspect is absent, persists through absence because of its reproducibility. As a performance disappears, the audience necessarily misses its essential nature because the Real of the event can never be completely processed. Psychoanalysis teaches that the present moment always emerges with whole fragments unperceived. These missed moments, particularly the ways in which they are reenacted, contain the roots of trauma. That theater's presence irrevocably entwines with the Real has been shown in the critical literature, particularly in the work of Phelan.[21] Trauma's emergence during moments of theatricality creates a Real that Chaplin's Tramp traverses and performs as an absent present that gains presence.

THE CIRCUS OR THE UNKNOWING PERFORMANCE

The plot of *The Circus* revolves around a small, particularly unhappy circus. The ringmaster and owner of the circus berates performers for unsuccessful routines. He is the quintessential bad director materialized, even hitting his daughter and withholding meals as punishment for mistakes made during her act. This all changes when the Tramp unwittingly emerges as a star in the circus.

The Circus fundamentally operates as a film about the "rules" of performance. The fact that performance, in cinematic terms, disappears doesn't change the fact that the goal of much of performance is to prevent disappearance through repetition and repeatability. The circus as a form is particularly ruled by customs and rules so that the very repeatability it achieves results in a dulling of presence and what Peter Brook termed "deadly theatre." In the film, Chaplin's Tramp continually and unknowingly finds himself onstage, delightfully being perceived (by the movie-house audience) as performing in an inspired way. When the movie-house audience sees the Tramp "failing" to perform, the film's audience sees a successful and wildly funny act. Despite the conflicting audience expectations (between film audience and movie-house audience), Chaplin's Tramp emerges as cinematically successful. Later in the film, when the Tramp discovers that he is a performer and is hired to do his "act," suddenly the performance becomes dull and uninspired. The Tramp is unable adequately to master the conventions of clowning (while all the while Chaplin is slyly exhibiting his mastery of the form through the Tramp). Why is it that in *The Circus* Chaplin highlights the dichotomy between successful performances and unsuccessful ones? Why does the film do this by focusing on the difference between the performer's own awareness or lack of awareness as a performer? How might this apply to the spectator— both the onscreen and movie-house audience? The fact that the movie-house spectator perceives the fact that the Tramp is outside of the act and that the film audience thinks that he is part of the act also creates a kind of liminal presence. The audiences both house the same vacillation between presence and absence that Chaplin's Tramp also embodies.

The questions posed by *The Circus* seem strange in that Chaplin himself was known for the amount of time he spent planning and rehearsing for his films. Moreover, *The Circus* itself ran well over its schedule and was beset by problems in production.[22] The rigor of the stunts that Chaplin himself personally performed in the film remains legendary, yet the entire narrative revolves around notions of spontaneous virtuosic feats contrasted with the dullness of rehearsal and stale performance. This distinction could be said to draw attention to reproducibility in film contrasted with live performance. For example, Chaplin's Tramp operates as a liminal figure in between the two media highlighted most strikingly in the differences between the actor Chaplin and the character of the Tramp. Chaplin's body, as the performer, showcases an absolute discipline and rehearsed (mechanical) precision. Chaplin's discipline is contrasted with the character's virtuosic spontaneity and pure clownish expressions when he is unable to master the Tramp's live routines. The Tramp amuses audiences with his clumsiness that just so happens (through the effort and discipline of Chaplin) to have a comic genius to it.

In 1928, the year *The Circus* was released, cinema was going through the transformation of sound. This lends the quality of Chaplin somehow working through the relationship between his body, voice, and performance in *The Circus*. This process is particularly relevant, considering that *The Circus* was released the year *after* one of the first sound films, *The Jazz Singer*.[23] The technological upheaval of the era generated particularly potent theatrical imagery and themes as filmmakers struggled to define the medium's ontological status.

The silent film has been said to draw attention to the body in performance, displacing the role of language and the voice.[24] Music and intertitles accompanying the silent film serve to highlight and fill in the emotional realm of the narrative. The narrative itself, however, comes from the movements of the bodies onscreen. *The Circus* actively attempts to solve various dilemmas concerning the complex demands within the narrative and performance. The actor onstage must "know" his performance. Once the film is cut and made into a whole narrative, the screen actor is absent and therefore repeats the same performance to the masses.

KNOWING UNKNOWING AS PERFORMANCE

Before the chase sequence in which the Tramp ends up unknowingly performing in the circus, the film audience is unmoved by the more traditional circus acts. The clowns in particular are not funny, as their act once again seems over-rehearsed and performed as if by rote. Before the Tramp's entrance we see him being chased by a police officer until he is pursued into the big top, smack-dab in the midst of a performance. This moment echoes Chaplin's start in Mack Sennett's Keystone Kops films. The first moment of the Tramp's "performance" in the circus repeats Chaplin's earliest performances onscreen. The audience watching the circus mistakes the chase for a slapstick clown routine. The Tramp's bumbling attempts to escape the police officer are met by laughter and applause from the audience. This is ironic in that Chaplin's unknowingly performing Tramp becomes the quintessential iconic clown image on film.

The performances seen before the Tramp's entrance seem to be a collection of acts that have been repeated (insofar as any performance can be truly repeated) for years, and the overall effect is one of a dead form emptied of any spontaneity or surprise. Despite the fact that performance is, as Phelan has suggested, unrepeatable—meaning the exact moment of performance can never be replicated—the clowns' performance takes on all the qualities that make performance seem repeatable, almost reproducible. The same performance movements are seemingly enacted and, perhaps, call into question the very definition of performance itself as that which cannot be repeated. If reproducibility can produce a sense of presence, it would therefore make sense that presence could house the repeatability that is characteristic of reproducibility.

Chaplin's Tramp infuses new life into the circus by interrupting the routines, and soon it becomes apparent that part of his success is rooted in his own ignorance of being a performer in a show. The unfolding chase amuses the audience because it offers a surprising yet seemingly planned interruption of the clowns' dead act. However, for the Tramp, the police officer's pursuit is very real; the stakes for Chaplin's character couldn't be higher.

The fact that the acts of the circus are seen as stale before the Tramp's unknowing entrance points to something particular to many forms of theater: performance requires the illusion that the events onstage are happening for the first time in order to lend believability and suspense to the narrative. This need for planned spontaneity may be even more pronounced in circus acts. The circus, with its emphasis on the body engaged in spectacular acts, particularly needs this quality of both newness and danger. If an act is simply old hat, then the sense of astonishment for the audience is diminished. Variety acts need to continually raise the stakes in order to generate the excitement of audiences. In the performance of a play, this quality of the first time is necessary for the audience to "believe" in both the narrative and characters in the play. Staleness leads to "deadly" performances, which the Tramp's flight into the circus ring shatters when it becomes a performance, albeit one comically unknown to the performer who is simply trying to flee from the police.[25]

Contrast the idea of the first time with the fact that a film is, of course, never occurring for the first time. The mere mechanics of its production require that the flow of running something from beginning to end rarely occurs in the course of production. The narrative flow is created by assemblage; it only occurs after piecing together all of the different fragments of film in the editing room. The flat repetition of the clown's routines could be seen as the endless running of the film through the projection machine, always repeated, never for the first time. Aligning the clowns with the reproducibility of film points to the irony of their lack of presence: within the narrative of the film they represent a tradition of live performance that seems to defy the definition of performance as unrepeatable, and yet the Tramp, the iconic cinematic clown, seems to bring performance back to a state of unrepeatability. Their version of live performance illustrates Peter Brook's characterization of "deadly" theater, which can be defined as performances that have been emptied of any inherent spontaneity and liveliness. Yes, such performances are represented onscreen as aspects of live performance, yet they feel and appear dead. The clowns provide a clear contrast to the Tramp's presence as a stain on film because the theatricality of his presence that defines him is emptied out and hollowed out in the clowns. Their actions seem mechanical despite their representation of theatricality. Chaplin's Tramp, again the iconic *cinematic* clown, infuses the screen with a kind of presence that the representatives of the theatrical tradition, in the figures of the clowns, lack. Liveness, as postulated by *The Circus*, is best represented on film through the figure of the Tramp. The repetition of the clowns' routines flattens the visual field into the sameness of reproducibility. The Tramp, by contrast, exists as a singular presence unable to be assimilated and therefore in the realm of the Lacanian Real, that which cannot be taken in and comprehended fully at the moment of its inception.

Shortly after this first scene, the Tramp is hired as a performer but finds he is unable to learn the traditional acts. The ringmaster then devises ways of replicating the Tramp's original performance, but that goes stale as well once the Tramp becomes aware that it is merely a repetition. The film continually draws a distinction between old and new forms and between the stale, almost robotic clown sketches and the Tramp's inability to perform those same sketches as demanded of him. "Live" performance continually repeats itself throughout the film, showing the degradation that occurs after the spontaneous act. For example, the policeman chasing the Tramp onstage becomes contrasted with the necessary repetition and set nature of the spontaneous act encased into a repeatable performance night after night. The fear that drove the first "performance" when the Tramp stumbled in front of an audience cannot be manufactured through the meaninglessness of the clown's act. As a performer, Chaplin seems limitless in his skill, discipline, and precision. Chaplin's performance of ineptitude achieves a comedic narrative that privileges the spontaneous over the rote and liveness over reproducibility. Yet, it is reproducibility that allows Chaplin to create the illusion of liveness and both carries and complicates the film's exploration of the limits of performance. This intersection is where Chaplin's ontology of the liminal spaces between human and machine, theater and film, rests. Both the comedy and the traumatic come from the tension between illusion and the Real. Nowhere is this highlighted more than during the magic show scene in *The Circus*.

THE "TRICK" EXPOSED

If illusion supplies the seeming presence of filmic narrative, a disastrous magic show in which illusion itself is exposed offers a moment in which presence is revealed as absence. The unfolding of this exposure begins when the Tramp is told to bring the magician's table into the center ring. As he brings it out, he accidentally pushes buttons that reveal the secret compartments. Suddenly, balloons, doves, rabbits, and all the rest of the tricks fly out of the table as the Tramp frantically tries to force them back into the compartments. The harder he tries, the more he exposes the illusion promised by his magic act. (Of course, in the context of the film as a comedy, the scene succeeds in upping the comedic ante.) The audience laughs. Eventually, the magician storms onstage, astonished and outraged by the Tramp's revelation of his secrets. Everything about his act has been exposed, and the magician is left helpless without his gadgets of illusion.

The scene shows the fundamental fragility of the magic show and its reliance upon a hidden mechanics that enable the trick to create the outer illusion. Piercing the magician's illusion of wonder, the Tramp negates the suspension of disbelief on which the magician's trick relies and converts the magician's aura of seriousness to Chaplin's humorous purpose. The trick itself loses all of its power when the magician's performance is punctured by the Tramp's collision with the mechanics of the magic show. Chaplin's Tramp mercilessly exposes this mechanism unknowingly. The bumbling revelation of the magic trick stains the illusion that the magician hoped to evoke for his act. The Tramp's accidental revelation of the magician's tricks serves as an example of the Lacanian stain that, in this particular case, highlights the separation between the live and mechanical reproducibility.[26] This separation between the two is traumatic because, as we have seen, they are (instead of split binaries of one another) irrevocably bound up and entwined. Cinema's obsession with representations of theater betrays its inability to display the live event as anything but a trace.[27] Psychoanalytic thought has also tried to account for excess in the form of affect, and one way is through this concept of the stain. The stain appears in the leftover trace of the live that cinema attempts to reproduce.

The difference between the cinematic and the live act resides in the cinema's purely mechanical nature. Like the clowns rehearsing endlessly how to move their bodies onstage, the cinematic image also repeats. Yet the clowns are represented as live in their performances but are still somehow bound up in the reproducible, whereas the ultra-cinematic Tramp revels in the illusion of spontaneity and through this illusion reveals a presence that the live cannot reproduce. The live as represented by the Tramp's unknowing performance appears as unpredictable and singular. *The Circus* stages a collision between the cinematic and the live, making the distinction between the two complicated and wrapped up in one another rather than appearing as a simple binary. Although in the live act the magician's tricks rely on the mechanical, his hands must move with skill to hide this fact. The magic trick in cinema can be handled in the editing room, without the body at all. The actor in live performance must memorize the continuity of a performance from beginning to end, whereas the actor in a film need only know the particular scene he is shooting. The actor onstage must have a cognitive map of the performance, which must be performed in one sweep, whereas the actor onscreen is unable to do this in such a systematic way since the requirements of film acting fragment the performance over time. Although the actor onscreen knows the overarching path of the narrative through a knowledge of the screenplay, the actual performance, in most cases, is out of order and broken up into small pieces. Stage actors have a certain agency in creating the all-at-onceness of the live, since they make the journey through a narrative housed within the running time of the performance. The necessities of production within cinema require a certain fragmentation both in the method of creation and in the audience's reception, where editing radically changes the experience of continuity that is observed in live performance. This fragmented method of creation brings us to the other level at which this scene operates: the process of the actor.

The relationship between the interior processes of the actor in cinematic and theatrical traditions is acutely different, yet aspects of both are used in both the live and recorded media. The magician's trick and any special effect onstage require the actor to break with the psychological realm of the character to physically make sure the technical requirements for the effect are achieved. Despite the fragmentary nature of filmmaking, the actor still must appear to achieve continuity in the performances even though the technical requirements of shooting are acute. The psychological aspect of performance also remains important. This difference is highlighted in *The Circus* with the odd juxtaposition of the boring performance of the clowns with the Tramp's spontaneous acts that are unknowingly transformed into a performance by virtue of him being thrust onto the circus stage. The clowns know they are performing; therefore they represent live performance, and yet their performances are repetitive, almost recorded. Yet, the Tramp, Chaplin's virtuosic film clown, represents a triumph of the filmic through the seeming liveness and theatricality of his acts. This collision between the cinematic and the theatrical creates a complicated relationship between the live and reproducible and presence and absence. They are both tangled and bound up in the other. It is this entanglement that makes Chaplin's cinematic Tramp achieve a kind of heightened presence on the screen that, perhaps, only the cinematic can provide. If performance is a form of disappearance, then film is a dance of absence that reveals presence. When the screened stage, through the venue of the circus, appears within the film, it could be that presence itself, through the figure of Chaplin, asserts itself despite its absence.

In the scene with the magician's table, Chaplin's comment on appearance and disappearance plays with both aspects of performance: the necessary technical underside of any actor's performance, as well as the absolute reliance of the film actor on the technical aspects of reproduction. The actor in both live and reproduced performance needs to keep these processes of production hidden. The comedy of the scene comes from the exposure of methods of production alongside the Tramp's blithe unknowing of the chaos that he brings wherever he goes during the "live" event. The repetition throughout the film of other such unveilings suggests that Chaplin was actively playing with the differences in production between the two media. These connections bring us to the third scene, in which the virtuosity of the performer becomes highlighted next to the necessary separation between the body and voice in the cinematic.

THE ABSENT VOICE OR CINEMATIC SPLIT

The Tramp once again tries to impress the girl he loves. He ends up performing a series of hair-raising feats on the high wire. These feats include doing handstands while wearing a harness, losing the harness, and trying to save himself while walking with a monkey balanced on his head as other monkeys scamper up his body and pull down his pants, until he slips on a banana peel and ends the performance by riding a bike down the wire. This amazing performance highlights the absolute skill and fearlessness of Chaplin as a performer in relation to the unknowing performance of the Tramp. Chaplin the performer uses repetition, discipline, and virtuosic skill, whereas the Tramp needs to appear to have none of these traits. Although Chaplin's antics as the Tramp are silent, this scene provides an interesting vacillation between a virtuosic performance of the body and the absent voice. In the few instances when we see a cutaway from the Tramp, it is to the horrified and astonished faces of the crowd. They are screaming, pointing, applauding, gasping, and laughing throughout the scene. All of this action plays out purely on the visual level, with the occasional insertion of text. The split between the body and the voice in this scene is especially pronounced because of the silence from an audience giving vocal expressions and applause.

This split points to cinema's absolute separation between the body and the voice. The silent film necessarily highlights the body because of the absent voice, yet, in its absence, one could say it becomes all the more present. The appearance of mouths open with gasping screams or laughter creates a startling effect. Chaplin's inclusion of the open mouths and applause of his spectators again points to the fact that he was playing with both the limitations and possibilities of reproducibility and its contrast with the live. Chaplin's clown offers the cinematic representation of the theatrical as a space for the performer to play with the possibilities and limitations of a new medium.

The relationship between Chaplin as stain on film and performance as a space of play and trauma expresses itself clearly in the ending of *The Circus*. The Tramp watches the circus pull away and leave him behind in the dust. We see him with his distinctive walk disappearing into the distance, twirling his cane, split between presence and absence. Thirty years later, Chaplin's

Limelight allows Chaplin's voice to be heard through the character of Calvero, and what we hear is a melancholy meditation on love, death, and the stage. The voice is now present, but the split and then collision between presence and absence still remains. What is different in *Limelight* is the narrative's focus on the traumatic and how the stage is implicated as a place of both love and death. In *The Circus*, the Tramp appears as a stain; in *Limelight* that stain is clearly visible as a skull through the direct focus on death and mortality (through performance) that is the subject of the film. The stain of the Tramp's "presence" onscreen (for presence onscreen asserts itself despite its absence) offers not so much a meditation on the nature of play, but rather a direct link to disappearance, which connects the Tramp to both trauma and death.

LIMELIGHT—PERFORMANCE TO DEATH

Chaplin's *Limelight* tells the "story of a ballerina and a clown."[28] This description that appears at the beginning of the film immediately highlights performance as a major component of the film. Set in 1914, *Limelight* tells the story of a suicidal ballerina who is saved when Calvero, a washed-up, once-famous clown, discovers her unconscious in her room with the gas on. From the very beginning of the film, trauma and performance are inseparable. Phelan has alluded to a link between performance and trauma when she observed, "it may well be that theatre and performance respond to a psychic need to rehearse for loss, and especially for death."[29] *Limelight* is a film expressly about the link between death and being onstage. Calvero rehearses his eventual disappearance, and the stage in the film becomes a place of both presence and absence. Performance and death are also connected in the film to ideas of love—the love between Calvero and the ballerina, which develops into a particular kind of love through their sharing of their plights and helping one another, obtaining resolution through the reliving of trauma. The relationship could be said to mirror the love found between analyst and analysand when working toward a psychoanalytic cure. The need for the cure fuses performance, love, the eventuality of aging and death. The connection of the "talking cure" juxtaposed next to the "talking clown" points to the relationship between the voice and the body explored in *The Circus*, but in *Limelight* the body and voice are fused together, not split as they are in a silent film. For this reason, *Limelight* works toward a performance of the psychoanalytic cure connected to body and voice, which then are connected to absence and death.

Indeed, both of the main characters are portrayed as hovering on the edge between life and death. Terry, the ballerina, has been, according to the landlady, "sick since she came here."[30] Calvero recently had a heart attack from which he nearly died. The relationship between the painfulness of life, the "life" of performance, and the finality of death plays out in almost every scene of the film. As Calvero eloquently states: "Are you in pain? That's all that matters. The rest is fantasy."[31] Fantasy seems to be the register that *Limelight* highlights—more particularly, the failure of fantasy. The Lacanian Real asserts itself in the midst of the fantasy, preventing any kind of resolution between desire and satisfaction. Calvero's dream sequences provide the perfect stages for the conflict (and intermingling) between fantasy and the Real to play out. Dreams, as psychoanalysis has established, become a stage in which the longings and anxieties of the subject are rehearsed.

In the first dream, Calvero performs his flea circus act. He stands onstage in front of a painted backdrop and cracks his whip at Phyllis and Henry, the invisible flea performers. The audience is unseen throughout the act and is dead silent except at the very end, when there is the sound of applause and, just as suddenly, silence. The scene ends with a shot of an empty theater and Calvero peering into the void. The void where the audience should be, the failure of the fantasy, makes clear Benjamin's distinction of the difference between acting on film and onstage. The loss of presence that is at the heart of the difference between theater and cinema comes to the fore in the dream sequences in the film. The stage becomes a prominent aspect of the fantasy that Calvero seems to long for—although he often laments his age, his fantasies show him at the same age he is throughout the film. His dreams of performing don't restore his youth; instead, they compensate for his ebbing presence, vitality, and liveness in the world. There are two levels of the film that speak to the resonance of the dream: the narrative and the ontological. It is worth pointing out here that the cinema has long been thought of as a kind of "dream factory" wherein the spectators "dream" themselves onto the screen and live out their fantasy world through fantasy selves. The dream allows the subject to live through the fantasy and, at the same time, disappoints in its intangible presence. Calvero's dreams point to the two-sidedness of fantasy: First, Calvero is searching for a sense of presence in the world, which fails in the dream because his very presence is slipping away as his body grows sick and weak. Second, ontologically, this presence that Calvero searches for is impossible on film, and, for this reason, it fails. He is performing "live" onstage and yet this liveness is fake and screened instead of lived. Through these failures of both Calvero's body and the ontological status of the stage within the cinematic, the traumatic Real asserts itself in the void where the audience should be and the silence during the act itself. The silence and nonresponsive fantasy of an audience fail to connect Calvero to the world and to any hope for a cure for his situation.

In Calvero's second dream, the audience can be heard cheering, but the camera never reveals them. Once again, they are disembodied phantoms on the screen. The dream begins with him onstage, dressed in a modified version of his Tramp costume, picking a flower and eating it. He then sings a song about love. He eyes the camera flirtatiously as he dances and sings. Terry joins him in the dream as it continues its theme of love. She declares, "All life is motivated by love."[32] The loneliness of the flea circus dream clashes with the warmth and connection found in the relationship between the clown and ballerina. Still lurking in the background is the missing audience, which gives a very isolated feeling to the dream that highlights it as an unreal Real. The first dream shows Calvero alone onstage watched by no one. In the second dream, the audience is present (heard, but not seen) but fragmented. This mirrors and foreshadows the fragmented state of Terry's hysteria later in the film (her body is separate from her voice, which narrates her psychic illness). Her call to love brings a new element of fantasy to the screen. Rather than a fantasy of a singular performance, Calvero begins to dream of connection, sharing the stage, and substitutes the imaginary flea circus for the real figure of Terry. This dream of connection is tempered by the isolation of the stage from the world. The audience is closer, they can be heard, but they are still absent, leaving the stage as a space at a remove, clearly fantasy.

DISAPPEARING PRESENCE

The transition from dream to life is one that Calvero struggles to come to terms with and fails to completely apprehend. In a later scene, while explaining his evolution as a performer, Calvero says that he "lost contact with the audience. Couldn't warm up to them."[33] The terror of the missing dream audience and the reality of his lost ability to connect transform the audience for him into "a monster without a head."[34] When he performs in a show reluctantly arranged by his agent, the reality of the situation becomes clear. First, Terry, rather than dancing, is confined to bed with hysteria that prevents her from moving her legs. Calvero decides to listen, enacting the analyst/analysand relationship, and through talking and reliving traumatic moments, Terry gradually regains the use of her legs. These moments of loving compassion show a growing relationship that is based on Calvero's and Terry's presence for one another—it is through this presence that a cure is eventually enacted. In sharp contrast to this presence is Calvero's performance in front of a restless audience that walks out. The end of the scene shows Calvero slowly removing his makeup, revealing his age, and commenting, "Trouble was I was sober. I should have been drunk before going on."[35] When he comes home drunk, Terry tries to convince him of his worth as a performer. She speaks with such passion that suddenly she stands and from then on she can walk and dance once again. This moment is key in connecting the voice and the body as separate in a fragmented and diseased state, yet connected in a material way to one another, which can be seen fully integrated when a subject is healthy. Terry's moment of connection to her body links to Calvero's dreams, which feature the missing or disembodied audience that is fragmented instead of whole. The integration and connection of spectator and performer, ballerina and clown, promises a cure to what ails the characters in the film, a lack of presence in a world that has seemingly forgotten them or left them behind, leaving them sick, weak, and at the brink of both physical and psychic death.

Scene after scene in *Limelight*, the film links the body and presence together with mortality and dreams. For instance, Calvero is given a small role of a clown in a ballet in which Terry has been given the role of Columbine. The story revolves around a young woman on her deathbed. Calvero and the other clowns take her bed to the window for one last look outside. After Columbine dies, she dances in the cemetery with her lover. Before the scene, Terry once again is struck with her hysterical paralysis. Calvero strikes her to get her to perform—she does to thunderous applause. Terry's movement from illness to healing is enacted once again, only this time onstage. As almost all of the crucial moments of the film suggest, repetition through enactment onstage presents a way to work through psychic pain and illness. The stage becomes a fantasy dream space in which the psychic pain and trauma can be relived with the promise of being worked through.

Reality, again and again, intrudes upon the fantasy, dream, or stage. After Calvero disappears in order to set Terry free to love the composer Neville, she tours the world performing. Neville discovers Calvero playing violin with a ragtag band. Terry arranges a benefit performance for Calvero. Perhaps in the most famous scenes of the film, Calvero teams up with his old partner (played by Buster Keaton). We see the two famous actors at the end of their careers preparing to go onstage, putting on makeup in the dressing room. This scene is complicated by the history of cinematic performance that Keaton and Chaplin represent within *Limelight*. The past, the whole history of film through their careers, is on display. So, not only are the characters preparing to perform once again at the end of their careers, the audience also is aware that the actors who are enacting this scene are performing near the end of their careers. The narrative suddenly is punctured with reflexivity; the actual historical presence of the aging performers Keaton and Chaplin complicate the relationship between narrative reality and fantasy that has been highlighted throughout the film. The world outside of the film intrudes and we see Chaplin's relationship to Calvero highlighted as one of two aging performers with failing careers. Instead of a story about an aging performer, the real aging performer interrupts and asserts a kind of presence. The way that theatrical presence operates in the film as a yearned-for fantasy of integration and cure for the characters, a fantasy that fails onstage but succeeds through characters connecting in reality with one another, is seen to be something that not only is enacted within narrative reality, but in reality itself. This underscoring of the actual situation of the artist along with the intermingling of narrative and history is disconcerting yet enacts the destabilizing force of fantasy's collision with reality that infuses the film. Chaplin himself is fighting for his life, just as we watch Calvero, in a kind of cinematic dream, do the same.

Once again, what is highlighted onstage is disappearance. This time, however, it is done by fusing the audience reaction to the fantasy. During the benefit performance, the audience laughs and claps for the flea circus routine. During the main act, Calvero's partner sits at the piano, endlessly preparing to play, but the sheet music keeps falling down around him. Calvero keeps adjusting his violin while he is held up by one leg bunching up shorter than the other and needing to be stretched back to normal. During the whole of the Keaton/Chaplin act the audience is silent—once again giving the scene a dreamlike feel until the end, when the applause is deafening. Calvero tumbles off the stage into a drum. He has a heart attack. As Terry dances in the second act, Calvero is moved to the wings where he watches her and dies.

With *Limelight*'s narrative of lost presence, concluding with Calvero's death while the ballerina spins on an empty stage, Chaplin links performance to the traumatic Real expressed through a yearning for presence. Not coincidentally, this desired presence conflicts directly with the cinematic process upon which Chaplin's own performing success was based. The uniqueness of Chaplin's performances onscreen relates directly to both theatrical presence that keeps revealing itself in the narrative of his films and his appearance that refuses to blend neatly into the flatness of the screen. *The Circus* features the Tramp trapped in unknowing performances that delight and amaze the crowds with his joyful ignorance. *Limelight* highlights the melancholy of performance as a passage to death. Chaplin's presence makes the audience aware of this split between absence and presence in cinema. Performance, as alluded to in *Limelight,* offers not just this split, but rather the unique possibility of a healing as Calvero's talking cure with Terry demonstrates.

Through his performance, Chaplin prepares us not just for his presence, but also for his eventual disappearance. The stain of his presence onscreen becomes an anamorphic blur and a defined skull, an obfuscation of mortality and its incarnation. The collision between presence and absence is staged through his character's repeated encounters between the cinematic and theatrical. The interaction between them occupies a liminal space somewhere between illusion and reality, laughter and trauma, fantasy and the Real. Screened stages within Chaplin's oeuvre offer moments within the cinematic in which reproducibility and liveness bump up against one another and find a cinematic presence, a glimpse of the Real. The traumatic nature of Chaplin's absence sticks out like a stain as a result of his continual and poignant assertions of presence.

NOTES

1. *The Circus*, two-disc special edition DVD, directed by Charles Chaplin (1928; Burbank, CA: Warner Home Video, 2004).

2. Henri Bergson, *Laughter: An Essay on the Meaning of the Comic*, trans. Cloudesley Brereton and Fred Rothwell (New York: Macmillan Company, 1911).

3. Laura Mulvey, *Death 24x a Second: Stillness and the Moving Image* (London: Reaktion Books, 2006), 178.

4. Mulvey, *Death 24x a Second*, 178.

5. See Marco Grosoli, "The Paradox of the 'Dictator': Mimesis, Logic of Paradox, and Catharsis in *The Great Dictator, Monsieur Verdoux*, and *Limelight*," 146 in this volume.

6. Grosoli, "The Paradox of the 'Dictator,'" 153.

7. See Slavoj Žižek, *Enjoy Your Symptom! Jacques Lacan in Hollywood and Out*, 2nd ed. (New York: Routledge, 2001); and *The Pervert's Guide to Cinema: Parts 1, 2, 3*, DVD, directed by Sophia Fiennes, presented by Slavoj Žižek (A Lone Star, Mischief Films Amoeba Film Production, 2006; P Guide, 2006).

8. See Jacques Lacan, *The Four Fundamental Concepts of Psychoanalysis*, ed. Jacques-Alain Miller, trans. Alan Sheridan (New York: W.W. Norton, 1978), 79–90.

9. Lacan, *The Four Fundamental Concepts of Psychoanalysis*, 79–90.

10. Lacan, *The Four Fundamental Concepts of Psychoanalysis*, 88.

11. Lacan, *The Four Fundamental Concepts of Psychoanalysis*, 88–89.

12. Lacan, *The Four Fundamental Concepts of Psychoanalysis*, 88–89.

13. Lacan, *The Four Fundamental Concepts of Psychoanalysis*, 95–96.

14. See Tom Gunning, "The Cinema of Attraction: Early Film, Its Spectator and the Avant-Garde," *Wide Angle* 8, no. 3/4 (1986): 229–35.

15. Žižek, *Enjoy Your Symptom!* 4–5.

16. The Tramp both in *The Circus* and *City Lights* becomes a performer despite his most earnest attempts to exit the stage. Ira S. Jaffe, in "Chaplin's Labor of Performance: *The Circus* and *Limelight*," *Literature Film Quarterly* 12, no. 3 (1984): 202–10, argues that Chaplin's Tramp "seeks at critical moments to assert or recreate himself directly before an audience, and who often comes to depend on the opinion of an audience."

17. Walter Benjamin quoting Rudolf Arnheim in "The Work of Art in the Age of Its Mechanical Reproducibility," in *The Work of Art in the Age of Its Technological Reproducibility and Other Writings on Media*, ed. Michael W. Jennings, Brigid Doherty, and Thomas Y. Levin (Cambridge, MA: Harvard University Press, 2008), 32.

18. See Lacan, *The Four Fundamental Concepts of Psychoanalysis*, 53.

19. Peggy Phelan, "The Ontology of Performance: Representation without Reproduction," in *Unmarked: The Politics of Performance* (London: Routledge, 1993), 146.

20. Several other scholars have offered different analyses of the relationship between liveness and reproducibility. For a detailed example, see Philip Auslander, *Liveness: Performance in a Mediatized Culture* (London: Routledge, 1999).

21. See Peggy Phelan, *Unmarked*; and *Mourning Sex: Performing Public Memories* (London: Routledge, 1997).

22. *The Circus* was beset with problems in production, so much so that it was the only film Chaplin didn't reference in *My Autobiography*. This was despite the fact that Chaplin won his first Academy Award for the film in 1929, a special award for "versatility and genius in writing, acting, directing, and producing." The film was shot during the breakup of his marriage to Lita Grey, one of the most sensational divorces in 1920s Hollywood. Production was brought to a halt for eight months when lawyers sought to seize Chaplin's studio assets. Chaplin smuggled the uncompleted film out of the studio and hid it for safekeeping. The production itself had difficulties: the circus tent was destroyed by wind, four weeks of filming were lost because the negatives were unusable, and a fire destroyed the studio where they were shooting the film. (*The Circus*, DVD, Special Features.)

23. *The Jazz Singer*, directed by Alan Crosland (Warner Bros., 1927).

24. See Žižek's commentary on Chaplin in *The Pervert's Guide to Cinema*.

25. For more on the concept of "deadly" theater, see Peter Brook's *The Empty Space: A Book about the Theatre: Deadly, Holy, Rough, Immediate* (London: Touchstone, 1995).

26. Žižek defines the Lacanian stain as the portion of the gaze that appears as "a remainder of the real that 'sticks out'" in *Looking Awry: An Introduction to Jacques Lacan through Popular Culture* (Cambridge, MA: OCTOBER Books/MIT Press, 1992), 93.

27. Phelan, "The Ontology of Performance," 146.

28. *Limelight*, DVD, directed by Charles Chaplin (United Artists, 1952; Burbank, CA: Warner Home Video, 2004).

29. Phelan, *Mourning Sex*, 3.

30. Chaplin, *Limelight*.

31. Chaplin, *Limelight*.

32. Chaplin, *Limelight*.

33. Chaplin, *Limelight*.

34. Chaplin, *Limelight*.

35. Chaplin, *Limelight*.

Chapter Eight

The Paradox of the "Dictator"

Mimesis, the Logic of Paradox, and the Reinstatement of Catharsis in The Great Dictator, Monsieur Verdoux, *and* Limelight

Marco Grosoli

In the now-crowded Olympus of renowned auteurs, a handful of them also performed as actors. Among the most notable who played the double role—Erich von Stroheim, Orson Welles, and Jean Renoir—none reached the legendary success that Charlie Chaplin gained; indeed, Chaplin is arguably the auteur-actor par excellence. His Tramp is a unique case of an imaginary construction known and appreciated literally all over the world, making him a universal figure—a "mythical figure," according to André Bazin. [1]

For him, speaking of myth in a cinematic context meant first and foremost referring to Chaplin. Although Bazin never really gives a stable definition of what he means by "myth," he employs the term often in his writings. Ironically, it is while writing about the films celebrating Stalin that he comes closest to a possible definition of myth: something that is simultaneously "a social essence" and a "vehicle for transcendence." [2] For Bazin, a myth is an imaginary figure that condenses collective and social impulses so powerfully that, albeit as a mere appearance, gains a peculiar kind of "transcendent" existence of its own. Bazin refers to Chaplin "as myth" in the subtle reflections he dedicates to the British filmmaker; his use of the term constitutes the starting point of this analysis. [3]

In "Pastiche or Postiche?" Bazin identifies the "mythological confusion of the persona and the person." [4] Notoriously, the relationship between Charlie Chaplin and his Tramp was tight, complicated, almost symbiotic—the mask and the face seemingly blur into one another. This relationship between

persona and person creates the kind of paradox that Philippe Lacoue-Labarthe defines as a movement "by which the equivalence of contraries [here,
the actual face and the fake mask] is established."[5] Three late films by
Chaplin—*The Great Dictator* (1940), *Monsieur Verdoux* (1947), *Limelight*
(1952)—each in a different way indirectly involve the myth of Charlie Chaplin and his Tramp, and this essay explores the similarities and differences
between actor and character.[6] Recognizing the persona/person paradox at the
core of all three films, this essay particularly focuses on the way in which
myth and paradox in the late Chaplin are solidly bound together by mimesis—the Greek term translated literally as "the imitation of what exists."
However, the original formulation of the term, dating back to Plato and
Aristotle, conceptually presents ambiguities and complexities that prove useful in analyzing the paradox of the Chaplin myth.

When examined through the lens of mimesis, these films may be viewed
as a trilogy. Specifically, *Monsieur Verdoux* functions as a bridge leading
from *The Great Dictator* to *Limelight* in that its subplot about a young
unfortunate girl turning her fate upside down by means of marriage with a
gun trader (a *Limelight*-like rags-to-riches parable) posits its twist in the
years when Verdoux's fortune goes down the drain—that is, when Mussolini
and Hitler (who appear in some archive footage during this film, after they
were caricatured in *The Great Dictator*) seemed to be destined to rule over an
economically devastated Europe.

For all three of these films, the most recognizable mimetic element is
resemblance: between Chaplin and the Tramp as well as Hitler, between the
Tramp and Verdoux, between Calvero and the biographical Charles Spencer
Chaplin. Each of these examples of mimesis leads directly to opposing terms,
such as the good barber vs. the evil dictator or the harmless Tramp vs.
Verdoux the serial killer—that is, they point to what Philippe Lacoue-Labarthe calls the "hyperbologic." For Lacoue-Labarthe, this word identifies
the inherent logic of paradox, not contemplating any possible conciliation for
the opposite terms. Similarly, the ethical extent of classical tragedy's catharsis (that is, acquiring some distance toward a paradox that one cannot really
solve) relies on the impossibility of such a conciliation. A notion whose
traces significantly mark the "trilogy," catharsis has been at the core of the
concept of democracy in classical Greece. These films involve and recuperate catharsis in the classical sense; they reinstate theatricality inside cinema
while dealing precisely with democracy as opposed to totalitarianism, at least
in *The Great Dictator* and *Monsieur Verdoux*. Thus by pushing the inherent
link between mimesis and paradox to the extreme, these three films assert the
ethical value of a representational (theatrical, cathartic) distance.

But mimesis is involved in the establishment of a democratic community
not only in that it provides the kind of theatrical distance whereby the audience can face the contradictions it cannot solve. Indeed, it is involved in

another sense as well, which has to do with the deep connection between mimesis and myth. Admittedly following the Heideggerian legacy, Lacoue-Labarthe's *Typography* presupposes that the origin of a community, rooted in Western civilization's origins in ancient Greece and is strictly connected to the theatrical representation of its own myths, which is thus also a kind of self-representation.[7] In other words, a community comes into existence only when it theatrically represents itself in the very way that it self-represents its own myths. It exists as a community only through a paradoxical, "bootstrap-like" act of self-copying: how can one copy something that exists only *after* being copied? As such, besides clearly being a matter of mimesis, this act is also an inevitably *fictional* one, hence the structural connection between myth and mimesis for our argument, overtly inspired by *Typography*. Most notably in *Monsieur Verdoux*, as this essay shows, Chaplin's intertwining of myth and mimesis demonstrates, through the reversal of a myth created by society (that is, Verdoux as the exact reversal of the Tramp), that society is *nothing* but its own self-representation, nothing but its own myth. This is perhaps the ultimate form of what I will shortly be defining as "second-order mimesis," the structural affinity between mimesis and paradox, which is at the very core of all three films examined in this essay.

NOTHING BUT A MOUSTACHE

Quite obviously, Chaplin's Tramp has a lot to do with mimesis, for he is constantly imitating. He often camouflages and indifferently changes his identity: in "A Woman" (1915), he assumes the identity of the title character; in *Shoulder Arms* (1918), he disguises himself as a tree; and in *The Pilgrim* (1923), he poses as a parson. Chaplin was always able to emphasize a substantial correspondence between the world he had seen in his childhood and the Tramp's adventures, which have often been reputed to be "drawing on all his memories of his harsh Lambeth life."[8] So a possible general inquiry into the relationship between Chaplin's films and mimesis (a critical exercise that will not be performed in detail here) is certainly justifiable. *The Great Dictator* will be of particular interest because for the first time mimesis is explicitly at the very heart of the operation set forth by Chaplin. Much of the fame of this movie comes from its very peculiar link to the political reality of its times: Chaplin plays a character (Adenoid Hynkel) who unmistakably recalls Adolf Hitler. Therefore, imitation is very much the point of the film. However, as André Bazin points out, Chaplin's Hynkel is not Hitler's caricature; it is rather Benzino Napaloni (Jack Oakie) who is supposed to be Mussolini's caricature.[9] Rather, Hitler is himself an imitation because he "stole" from the Tramp his unmistakable moustache. Of course, Bazin does not "suggest, however, that Hitler did it on purpose."[10] In other words, such a claim does not pertain to the level of personal biography, but rather to the level of myth, which Bazin defines, as mentioned in the beginning of this essay, precisely as a form of "social transcendence" with regard to actual biography. It is at this nonbiographical level, the level of social mythologies, that the real match between Chaplin and Hitler takes place. And at that level, Hitler was certainly exercising significant influence when the film came out—only a year and a half after he was named "man of the year" by *Time* magazine. By portraying a ridiculous image of what in the geopolitical narrative of the day was a mythic figure, Chaplin not only ridicules Hitler's standing but also shows that the reversal of mimesis had already occurred.

So when Chaplin seemingly imitates Hitler, he actually imitates himself, since the moustache was already his own. Quite a paradox indeed. In order to disentangle it, it would be helpful to refer to Lacoue-Labarthe's "Diderot: Paradox and Mimesis." Commenting on Diderot's "The Paradox of the Actor," Lacoue-Labarthe detects within the fictional dialogue accurate references to two kinds of mimesis, both coming from Aristotle. The first one is the plainly imitative one: art imitates nature. [11] The second is more complex: it is a form of supplementing nature's inevitable faults (an attribution of the "limits" of nature based on the fact that nature is not at man's full disposal but, on the contrary, limits his action through finitude, mortality and so on). In other words, there are fundamental inconsistencies within nature (the inescapable incompleteness of what nature produces and offers to men—including the very gifts that an actor has been given by nature) that art has to "repair." It is a kind of "productive" mimesis that essentially blurs the borders between nature and art, because art "steals" from nature its productiveness, on the basis of the "nothingness" (absence of identity) at the core of nature now regained by art. [12] More precisely, the point of repairing the faults of nature is not so much to make nature adhere to a certain notion of "how nature should be"—which would still be first-order mimesis—as the copying of a model that is somewhere outside nature, in "the mind of the artist/ creator/repairer," as it were. The point of the repairing is rather that art *replaces* nature in what Lacoue-Labarthe calls the "productiveness of nothingness."

According to Diderot's analysis of Aristotle's two kinds of mimesis, a subtle, perceptive actor perfectly capable of seizing and reproducing his character's emotional universe is condemned to follow the first, inferior kind of mimesis: he is condemned to be a copy "running after" a model in relation to which there would always be a difference. On the contrary, the natural actor is the one who assumes the nothingness at the core of nature and who is "natural" by virtue of that core of no identity. In other words, he or she is a completely insensitive actor, who precisely by being nothing at all in him- or herself is capable of playing anyone. [13] "In order to do everything, to imitate everything—in order to (re)present or (re)produce everything, in the strongest sense of these terms—one must oneself be nothing, have nothing *proper* to oneself except an 'equal aptitude' for all sorts of things, roles, characters, functions, and so on."[14] This second kind of actor is clearly connected with the second kind of mimesis:

> It is nature, Diderot said at the start, that gives the qualities of the person; it is art that perfects the gift of nature. But what do we find at the conclusion? This: the *gift of nature* is the *gift of impropriety*, the *gift of being nothing*, even, we might say, the *gift of nothing*. I would add, to bring out what lies in this "nothing," the gift *of the thing itself*. By this I mean nature's gift of itself, not as something already there or already present—"natured," as one would have said at the time—but more essentially as pure and ungraspable poiesis (in withdrawal, and always withdrawn in its presence): a productive or formative force, energy in the strict sense, the perpetual movement of presentation. [15]

By stealing back his own moustache, Chaplin discards the first mimesis in favor of the second. It is no longer a matter of resemblance, but of the void at the intersection between nature and art. Hynkel is not the copy, and Hitler is not the model ("a bad imitation of me, with its absurd moustache," wrote Charlie Chaplin in his autobiography[16]) because, as a model, Hitler is already Chaplin's copy. According to Bazin, "It was necessary for Hynkel to behave no less like Little Charles than Hitler, that he become at once as much one as the other—to be nothing. It is the very clash of the two myths that annihilates both beings."[17] The moustache is the little "nothing" that marks the ponderous yet inconsistent reality of myths, the myth of the Tramp as much as Hitler's. Both the Tramp and Hitler owe their existence to their own respective myths, and the moustache is the symbol of this convergence; in both cases their myth does not as such belong to nature or to art but is placed precisely at the intersection between the two. This intersection directly implies a thorough, but nonetheless problematic, affinity between myth and second-order mimesis, the latter being the point where the distinction between art and nature falls apart. I will address this important feature later in the essay. For the moment, we should focus on the fact that the paradox of mimesis, as portrayed by Diderot and Lacoue-Labarthe, makes it clear that this intersection is empty: art and nature are aligned when the former endorses the "productiveness of nothingness" of the latter. Bazin's conception of myth is indeed an imaginary construction that proves to be "productive" because it has a certain effective "weight" and active influence within reality. Hynkel inhabits this intersection instead of simply being a caricature, and Hynkel's role in this productive nothingness suggests that Hitler does not belong to Hitler, but to the "empty" myth of himself, just like Chaplin owes everything to the myth of the Tramp, of which the moustache is a highly recognizable signifier. As such, he is no more real than the Tramp is. "The small amount of existence that he took from the little Jew's [the barber's] lips would allow the little Jew to take back from him much more, that is, to drain him entirely of his biography for the benefit of, not exactly Little Charles, but an intermediate being, a being of pure nothingness."[18] Thus, Hitler is reduced to being nothing but an appearance. "For what is Hynkel but Hitler reduced to his essence and deprived of his existence?"[19] He is nothing but his own myth—which is not even his own, because the moustache is not his.

Lacoue-Labarthe calls the logic behind this paradox of being nothing as the best way to embody someone: "hyperbologic." In order to clarify this term further, it is important to fix what "paradox" means in the first place:

> A hyperbolic movement by which the equivalence of contraries is established (probably without ever *establishing* itself)—the contraries themselves pushed to the extreme, in principle infinite, of contrariety. This is why the formula for the paradox is always that of the double superlative: the more mad it is, the more wise it is; the maddest is the wisest. Paradox is defined by the infinite exchange, or the hyperbolic identity, of contraries.[20]

The hyperbologic is (as Derrida confirms in his preface to the volume) "the law of the paradox,"[21] the inherent logic of the paradox. It is the logic of pushing two contrary terms to the extreme, that is, up to the point of their equivalence. It is important to point out that Lacoue-Labarthe clearly distinguishes this logic from the speculative logic of dialectic, although the former lies at the innermost core of the latter: the hyperbologic contemplates no resolution but the pure maximization of the paradox as such.[22]

Lacoue-Labarthe reclaims the logic of Diderot's second order as the ultimate manifestation of the hyperbologic. The logic of mimesis is overtly paradoxical: imitation best succeeds when nobody imitates no one—that is, when there is no more imitation. Not in the sense that no one could tell the difference between the original and the copy, because it is not for the copy a matter of adhering to the model (first order), but rather of adhering to that zero point on behalf of which the identity with any model is granted per se (second order, that is, hyperbologic proper). Here the paradox is thus that the perfection of first order is achieved, and any difference between the copy and the model is eliminated, precisely when this first order and its premises are most fully discarded, that is, when the focus on the correspondence the final copy has to reach in relation to the original model is replaced by the focus on the initial attitude by the copy in the first place (that is, adhering to that zero point), regardless the model. In other words, the first order, for which nature is a model to be copied, must be distinguished from the second order, for which nature is precisely that zero point, in a properly Aristotelian fashion. What second order does by means of achieving first order the very moment it discards it, is to make art rejoin that zero point, which means to rejoin nature, which means to rejoin its opposite. As such, second order is the ultimate manifestation of hyperbologic—that is, of the inherent logic of paradox: "the 'logic' of the open-ended exchange of the excess of presence and of the excess of loss, the alternation of appropriation and disappropriation."[23] What makes second order "ultimate" is that it involves a zero point, which is also at the core of hyperbologic: it is that point in relation to which the contraries are recognized as equivalent. The contraries have nothing in common, and yet they have everything in common. Lacoue-Labarthe calls this "zero point" straightforwardly "*the gift of mimesis*: in effect, a gift of nothing (in any case, of nothing that is already present or already given). A gift of nothing, or of nothing other than the 'aptitude' for presenting, that is, for substituting for nature itself; a gift for 'doing' nature, in order to supplement its incapacity and carry out or effect, with the aid of its force and the power proper to it, what it cannot implement—that for which its energy alone cannot suffice."[24] Hence,

> the logic of paradox is always a logic of *semblance*, articulated around the division between appearance and reality, presence and absence, the same and the other, or identity and difference. This is the division that grounds (and that constantly unsteadies) mimesis. At whatever level one takes it—in the copy or the reproduction, the art of the actor, mimetism, disguise, dialogic writing— the rule is always the same: the more it resembles, the more it differs. The same, in its sameness, is the other itself—which in turn cannot be called "itself," and so on infinitely.[25]

The Great Dictator shows that "where the question concerns the actor, this hyperbologic regularly converts the gift of everything into the gift of nothing, and this latter into the gift of the thing itself."[26] Chaplin does not need to imitate Hitler in the first-order fashion: he already has him all, because he has that "nothing" marking the second order, that is, those moustaches that make the two opposite myths (his own and the führer) potentially convergent, as the barber's final speech confirms. This is the hyperbologic: by means of "nothing," the contraries are made equivalent, including those absolute contraries, which are nature and art. This way he reaches Hitler while by- passing imitation—just like the barber in the film, as we see shortly, ends up being easily mistaken for Hynkel without any need to imitate him at all. No wonder, according to William F. Fry Jr., Chaplin "must be regarded as a human embodiment of paradox."[27]

TWO SIDES OF THE SAME COIN

An obviously mimetic figure as an outstanding case of symbiotic inextri- cability between actor and character, nature and art, Chaplin conceived *The Great Dictator* as a huge, troubling paradox. The two contraries, Hynkel the evil dictator and the meek Tramp-like Jewish barber, are strangely convergent: when one of them is placed in a certain context, such as when one wears the other's uniform, he can be easily mistaken for the other. In this case, Hynkel and the barber share "first orderly" the same physical appearance, and, when the latter happens to substitute the former, nobody realizes the swap, even if one affirms something incompatibly out of character from the other. Hynkel's words burst with violent rage, while the Jewish barber gives humanity a touching speech about the importance of peace, solidarity, loving each other, and the like (and it is easy to realize how this scene is conceived so that there is a substantial conflation in the eyes of the audience between the barber and the myth Chaplin: the latter is *also* making a speech to his audience). Lately, some thinkers—among which Mladen Dolar[28] and Slavoj Žižek (in Sophie Fiennes's 2006 film *The Pervert's Guide to Cinema*)—have tried to push the paradox further: the final speech by the Jewish barber is less a redemption of the aggressive one by his Nazi-like doppelganger and more a confirmation that totalitarian and democratic discourses are two sides of the same coin. Such an analysis would suggest second order of the highest order: clearly this is the logic of pushing two contrary terms to the extreme. Dolar and Žižek especially emphasize the fact that the notes from Wagner's *Lohengrin* grace equally that final speech and the famous scene where Hynkel plays with the globe. In other words, good and heartfelt feelings are as powerful and potentially as dangerous as ruthless dictatorships, especially in that they both potentially have the power to be so extreme.

Several texts support this hypothesis. To name but one: one of the recurring "humanitarian" sentimental speeches by Hannah (Paulette Goddard) is suddenly interrupted by an insert showing Hynkel passionately playing the piano before returning to Hannah; no possible narrative or thematic explanation justifies this insert. So there really could be just one explanation:[29] music, and all that is generally associated with it (nobleness, tenderness, emotional warmth), can also be a sincere inspiration for the most loathsome individuals and acts. Hannah's speech ("Look at that star: isn't it beautiful? One thing Hynkel with all his power could never touch that.") and Hynkel's warmhearted music are aligned by montage on the same level: there is nothing inherently redeeming in nice feelings.

Ultimately, this daringly paradoxical interpretation looks convincing—on one condition: one should not infer that totalitarianism and democracy are one and the same. In this respect, the sequence of the final speech contains a key detail. Hannah, in her Osterlich farmhouse, stands up and listens to the gentle words pronounced by the barber qua dictator. This scene must be compared to an earlier one, when Hynkel's voice was broadcast by megaphones during a pogrom in the ghetto. The Osterlich mansion shots lack only the megaphones. There is no possible physical explanation why Hannah should be able to hear a speech being pronounced presumably miles away, addressing *her in particular*, and by her own name on top of that. And yet she hears it. As we see in detail shortly, the difference between a totalitarian discourse and a democratic one is to be located less at the level of their content than at their formal level—that is, at the level of the ways in which these discourses take shape and are conveyed, enacted, and communicated.

Once again, Lacoue-Labarthe's definitions of mimesis shed light. His interpretation of two kinds of mimesis corresponds to two different manners of imitation that the subject can assume. There is a mimesis consisting of being "possessed" by some external force or identity; in this case, a subject is possessed by another subject according to a standard copy-model relationship, while not ceasing to be a subject in its own right.[30] It is the irrational outburst of the orgiastic confusions of identities that needs precise identities to properly work as a dissolution of them. To confuse identities, initially there must be stable identities to be then blurred: the point here is the mutual necessity between this "possession" and the regular ownership of the identities in the first place, which eventually get confused but only to be in turn reconfirmed thereby. Such a possession "presupposes . . . the matrix or malleable matter in which the imprint is stamped."[31] In the film, the irrational outburst is the pogrom scene, where the crowd is "possessed" by Hynkel's voice pushing them to violence, while at the same time fully embracing a consolidation of one's identity; the pogrom reinforces the alterity of xenophobia, where the Other is beaten to reinforce the self.

The other mimesis corresponds to what Aristotle called catharsis: a subject finds him- or herself deprived of his or her own identity and reduced to that "nothing" that marks the coincidence of the productive force of nature and art alike by experiencing from a certain (representational) distance the identity of contraries—that is, the hyperbologic of classical tragedy, the logic of paradox at its very core.[32] Catharsis consists, thus, in the encounter with the void at the core of identity, with the "productiveness of nothingness" aligning art to nature in what has been so far called second order. In order to be effective, this second order needs a stage, some kind of representational distance so that the subject can recognize him- or herself as nothing and come to terms through practice outside the theater with this unpleasant fact. In the film, the last sequence involves a stage, namely the one from which the barber—the embodiment of the hyperbological coincidence between opposites—speaks. This stage formally emphasizes the distance: Hannah hears the barber's words while being too far away for it to be true. It is a strictly theatrical mimesis, one that relies on a myth through which a collective audience enacts a cathartic representation of itself. This also explains why, in an earlier step of our argument, we stumbled upon a singular coincidence between myth and second-order mimesis, which is precisely the kind of mimesis, a "proper" mimesis, at stake here. While the first example (as corresponding to first-order mimesis) is a wild practice usually ending in irrational riots, the second one possesses a highly ethical, civic, and political value.

In the film, the megaphone scene ends with a pogrom, while Hannah can hear the final hymn to civilization without any megaphone. The first case represents an abolition of the theatrical distance, as Hynkel's voice is immediately right there in the massacred ghetto, while in the second case the Jewish barber and Hannah seem to look at each other thanks to a simple editing trick (shot and countershot) that reinvents the theatrical distribution between speaker and audiences beyond theater itself. So, if other parts of the movie questioned the difference between the totalitarian discourse and the democratic one, now this difference can be reaffirmed through a subtle insight on what actually distinguishes them beyond any platitude and hasty judgments. The barber's inspired elegy to love and humanity and Hynkel's barely comprehensible bestial babble, albeit obviously very different, engender the same kind of passively enthusiastic reaction in the audience in front of the speaker; what distinguishes the democratic approach from the totalitarian one is thus not the content of the words spoken by the leader, but the underlying mimetic structure. In the first and first-order case, we have the "authoritarian" conservation of the theatrical distances distinguishing the stage/copy from the world/model, along with their violent dissolution: during Hynkel's first speech, after a close-up of him, there is a 180 degree countershot showing a fictional clapping crowd, while later in the film the riot in the ghetto is directly "assisted" by Hynkel's megaphoned voice. In the other, second-order case, the theatrical structure is broken from within only to be better re-created through montage as pure communicative distance: first, we have the barber qua Hynkel's 180 degree countershot as a piece of archive footage showing an actual crowd of those times, and then the barber and Hannah look at each other from an imprecise distance.[33]

In this distance, which is the distance a stage would classically grant, lies essentially the ethical, civic, and political value of classical tragedy. It is an imitation of the world, not really in the sense that it "copies" reality, but rather because it reproduces in its very structure the equivalence of contraries at the core of imitation as such. The latter is the second-order mimesis. Such an equivalence grounds both classical tragedy as the narrative instrument by which myth is rationalized and the more broadly philosophical "speculative reason," through which something becomes itself only by means of its opposite[34]—in other words, synthesis derived from the deployment of thesis and antithesis, as a resolution of their opposition.

A brief digression around speculative reason is essential here in order to shed light on its "negative counterpart," catharsis, which is one of the key concepts of our argument. Hölderlin attempts to trace a fundamental link between classical tragedy and speculative reason, but what he finds instead as the outcome of his own research is a notion that significantly diverges from speculative reason and from what the traditional Aristotelian legacy would seem to prescribe: classical tragedy must typically leave its conflicts unsolved. So, instead of the link between classical tragedy and speculative reason he was looking for, Hölderlin, according to Lacoue-Labarthe, is compelled to deviate his research on the roots of classical tragedy toward something that articulates binary couples of contrary terms like speculative reason but that does not solve the opposition in any way—unlike speculative reason. Instead of solving the opposition, it maximizes it. The name of this particular logic is the one we have already encountered: hyperbologic. Hyperbologic (the logic of paradox: that which pushes the opposite terms to their extreme to envisage their equivalence) grounds speculative reason while remaining distinct from it; the sheer equivalence of the contraries that, unlike speculative reason, does not contemplate any resolution.[35] Only the kind of distance achieved through catharsis can achieve this equivalence, not a resolution like standard Hegelian *Aufhebung*. As Lacoue-Labarthe concludes, "The more the tragic is identified with the speculative desire for the infinite and the divine, the more tragedy presents it as a casting into separation, differentiation, finitude. Tragedy, then, is the catharsis of the speculative."[36] The equivalence of contraries can only be ascertained and distanced but not solved in a superior conceptual synthesis. The citizen is supposed to find his or her place in society on the basis of this unsolvable equivalence between self and other, absence and presence, and the like. And only a stage, only some kind of distance with regard to one's inconsistencies could help the subject find a way through his or her own inconsistencies by means of social and political practice.[37]

Speculative reason (the "dialectic") is quite recognizably at stake in *The Great Dictator*. Hynkel's symbol is not a swastika, but two crosses. On one hand, it could be read simply as a reference to "double-crossing." On the other hand, in the wake of all these hints pointing at hyperbologic, one is tempted to read it as a reference to double negation: the root itself of standard (Hegelian) dialectic, the "negation of the negation." Because *The Great Dictator* is neither classical tragedy nor classic dialectic, it is structured by the hyperbologic of paradox at the core of speculative reason while still distinct from it by the inextricable connection between mimesis and the equivalence of contraries. Early in the film narrative, during World War I, the Jewish barber and commander Schultz (Reginald Gardiner) engage in a flight. Suddenly, the plane spins a few times, after which it is turned upside down. Heads downward, the two passengers do not seem to realize that they are flying in an inverted position. The barber leans out and sees the sun below the plane; they open a flask and the water spills out upward. In other words, this gag perfectly illustrates the equivalence of contraries: there is no difference between side and reverse-side—at least according to the perceptions of the unaware characters, who for a little while believe they are still flying properly. Nevertheless, there is a difference. During this funny scene, an editing cut changes the point of view so that the viewer now watches the scene upside down the same way the characters are, whereas before the cut, the point of view was "commonly gravitational." In so doing, this editing cut both emphasizes the equivalence of contraries and posits a kind of ironic distance from it. What was once in classical tragedy a matter of stage is now a matter of editing. This axiom could easily be extended to the whole of Chaplin's aesthetic attitude; his cinema can be justifiably seen as a possible answer to the following question: how can a strictly theatrical form like his kind of comedy be at the same time purely theatrical and quintessentially cinematic?

This difference that nevertheless persists between reversed positions in this scene leads us to a crucial point that should be made absolutely clear. The coincidence between the two opposites does not imply that there is absolutely no difference between them. The point is rather that their difference *is nothing*—but that kind of hyperbological nothing that coincides with everything. It is a very affecting, influential, ponderous kind of nothing. It is a productive nothing, as Lacoue-Labarthe puts it. Chaplin and Hitler, the barber and Hynkel, are not, of course, the same thing. Their difference consists in a kind of nothing (the moustache), which is at the same time what makes them equal *and* absolutely distinct, since they wear it for entirely different purposes—the moustache as something endowed with all the powerful, influential nothingness of myths. Similarly, according to what was affirmed earlier in this essay, totalitarianism and democracy are not to be conceived as identical. The "nothing" that separates them is a purely formal *but crucial* difference, the one between the two kinds of theatrical distribution illustrated above.

The Great Dictator has been from the very beginning a film evidently about mimesis: the standard mimetic relationship between Chaplin and his Tramp is now redoubled thanks to another uncanny semblance: Hitler. As much as it is a film about mimesis, *The Great Dictator* is also a film about paradox, the logic of which can be called "hyperbologic." This convergence between second-order mimesis and paradox is inherent in the very roots of the concept of mimesis, that is, in its original articulation in ancient Greek philosophy. But this articulation also provides another insight that is pertinent to *The Great Dictator*: in classical tragedy, when the community self-represents its own myths through mimesis, we have basically the hyperbologic (paradoxical) deployment of the equivalent opposites. However, unlike "speculative reason" at the core of dialectics proper, it offers no possibility for resolution. How then are we to deal with these unsolvable opposites? The ethical answer, coming again from Aristotle, is catharsis—something that, in this film by Chaplin as well as in the other two analyzed later, takes the shape of a sort of theatrical distance re-created within the cinematic medium and outside tragedy, which used to be catharsis's original proper form.

SOCIETY ON A STAGE AND UNDER THE GUILLOTINE

Monsieur Verdoux and *Limelight* seem to be conceived as a logical continuation of what was formulated in *The Great Dictator*. The hard kernel of *Monsieur Verdoux* is unmistakably hyperbological, starting with the name of the main character: "ver doux," "sweet worm." And the second thing we see him doing after tending roses is picking up a worm from the ground and sparing its life. At the same time, Verdoux is a cruel serial killer of rich widows and a tender family man. He is the former in order to financially be the latter.

Bazin compiled a notorious structuralist analysis of this film, which generated many directly linked critical interventions: for instance, the passionate exploration of the mythological nature of Chaplin's worldwide success by José França (*Le self-made mythe*) or the detailed list, compiled by Jacques Bernard Brunius, of quotations from the previous Tramp movies contained in *Monsieur Verdoux*. According to Bazin, the film regards the myth of the Tramp as the myth of the irreducible incompatibility with society and provides a definite confirmation of that myth by turning its values completely upside down.[38] The Tramp is eternally unfit with regard to society; whereas the rich, successful courter of women, Verdoux, is hyper-fit. However, the latter sins against society anyway, because he puts into practice society's presuppositions ("business justifies anything") with excessive zeal, up to murder. By "myth," Bazin means an appearance that produces a significant "actual" response in reality. As we have seen in *The Great Dictator*, the existence of such a myth blurs the borders between nature and art: we are still fully inside second-order mimetic dynamics then. This myth has also to do precisely with the equivalence of contraries: the incompatibility between man and society is in place when the former is either too much or too little what society asks him to be. Verdoux is captured only thanks to a photograph of him, shown in the film during the very first scene and then forgotten until the narrative climax shortly before the end: it is Verdoux's image that ties him to his destiny—that is, to his contradictions. It is his appearance, or more precisely the recording of his appearance in the photograph, that exposes his duplicity. And it is his appearance as well that connects him to the Tramp, as both played by Chaplin.

Verdoux shares a number of features with the other great nemesis of the Tramp: Hynkel. Both are first and foremost excellent organizers: their time is inflexibly scheduled in order to grant the maximum efficiency to their deeds. Unlike the Tramp, who only knows the present instant, they know no im-

provisation at all: they *plan* all the time, and they organize all their movements according to a centripetal principle. In other words, there is a center
toward which all their frenetic activities are finalized: Hynkel's office, Verdoux's family mansion.

Indicatively, Verdoux's downfall derives partly from an unplanned meeting that breaks his certitudes. When he meets by chance on the street a sweet
young girl (Marilyn Nash) who is ready to sacrifice everything for her invalid husband, Verdoux initially plans to poison her, but he gives up because
he sees himself in the girl; he has carried out all of his misdeeds to care for
his invalid wife. Some years later, another casual meeting with the girl
proves to be even more traumatic: that same girl has married a gun trader. In
other words, she embodies exactly as he does the paradoxical coincidence of
the moral opposites. It is at this point that he decides to confess and to admit
to the police all that he has done. Why? "I have to accomplish my destiny,"
he says. Again, it is a matter of mimesis qua hyperbologic and of the necessity for it to be a theatrical second-order one, as already illustrated by *The
Great Dictator*. Mimesis as paradox is not simply a matter of coincidence
between opposites. A certain kind of representational distance (a stage, typically) is required in order to "stabilize" the infinite "electrical" tension between the two opposite terms. This distance is exactly what the young girl
lacks; she only embodies the coincidence between opposites. Unlike the
young girl, Verdoux chooses catharsis and the stage upon which it will be
enacted, a very theatrical public trial, where he lectures the audience with
more than one theatrical monologue. And so he finally becomes nothing;
while the guards and various other bystanders frenetically look for him in a
crowded hall, he joins the searching crowd while remaining perfectly unnoticed. He repeats the same gag during the trial: the lawyers proclaim him "a
monster here among us in this court," pointing directly at Verdoux, but he
turns his head behind, as if himself looking for the monster. He is not himself
anymore, he literally looks for himself as much as the others do: by acting on
the public stage, and especially by overtly admitting his contradictions, Verdoux manages to "be nothing" since he reveals himself as being nothing
more than a faithful illustration of the values of society. His contradictions
are not his own, but society's. The Chaplinian myth of "the incompatibility
with society" now applies to society itself instead of the misfit Tramp: it is
society that is ultimately incompatible with itself, because it ruthlessly condemns precisely the one that most zealously dared adhere to society's presuppositions. As a result, society itself proves to be nothing more than its own
myth, nothing more than an imaginary solution for a real, insurmountable
contradiction, the ultimate mimetic paradox, to put it in Levi-Straussian
terms.[39] The mask (the myth) and the face (society) blur into each other. The
young girl, unlike the "nothing" that he has become, avoids catharsis and
thus still "is" someone; she still holds to first order, so to speak, and ends up

adhering to society. In his trial, Verdoux prepares the most terrifying trap society could ever fall into: a stage. Seemingly separating the world from its representation, society from its myths, the stage Verdoux jumps onto in the final courtroom scene demonstrates with the perfect rigor of the hyperbologic that the real myth is off, and not on, the stage. Its name is society.

This point can be summarized as follows. Society self-represents through a myth it abundantly identifies with, recalling the myth of the Tramp. As Bazin demonstrates in full detail, for instance, by emphasizing the last shot showing Verdoux walking away in the exact same way the Tramp used to walk at the end of his movies.[40] Thus, Chaplin reverses the Tramp and obtains Verdoux, someone who is both the Tramp and his exact opposite—in effect, an equally mythical figure due to its inseparability from the Tramp. In doing so, Chaplin has created another symmetrical myth: the myth of the ultimate enemy of society, someone society can never identify with, unlike with the Tramp. But there is more. Chaplin complicates the mythic symmetry by using the courtroom, the stage on which society aims to celebrate the myth of its ability to contain its own ultimate enemy, as the site where Verdoux—embodied by the duplicity of his own actor, who repeatedly played the Tramp (who is both Verdoux and Verdoux's opposite)—instead demonstrates that his contradictions are society's own contradictions. Verdoux and society being alike, society now is the enemy of society itself. This way, the level of myth (Verdoux as the myth of the anti-Tramp) rejoins second order, which is hyperbologic, the coincidence between opposites. In other words, society's self-representation consists of the representation of the coincidence of opposites.

As a result, the ultimate coinciding opposites are then society and the myth it creates as the opposite of itself, since both are essentially and irretrievably contradictory. Thus, society rejoins myth at the void intersection between art and nature that has been already defined as the productiveness of nothingness, the absence of identity—or, where every identity is untenable because each is contradictory. In other words, society is nothing but its own self-representation, a kind of self-copying where the model does not precede the copy but comes along with it, which is what we have called second order and leads us back to our premise on myth and mimesis following Lacoue-Labarthe. Moreover, what makes *Monsieur Verdoux* a particularly vertiginous maximization of the paradox at the core of *The Great Dictator* is the fact that it does not properly shift from first order to second. Its very starting point relies on a second-order kind of shift: Verdoux is not at all a copy of the Tramp, as in the case of the barber, but his "hyperbologic twin," that is, someone who is the equivalent of the Tramp and yet his exact opposite. So what we have instead of a shift from first order to second is a shift that is entirely within the second order, that is, a shift from a second-order mimetic dynamic pertaining to Chaplin's character to one pertaining to the entity that, in the broader sense, produces, justifies, and sustains that character: society.

BEYOND MYTH

Limelight makes a rather anomalous third episode of the "trilogy" analyzed here. The reason is deceptively simple: whereas the other two films were built on paradox, mimesis, and myth, *Limelight*'s horizon is assuredly "post-mythical," since Calvero is basically Chaplin deprived of his own myth. To elaborate, in *The Great Dictator* and *Monsieur Verdoux* (two films that do not cast the Tramp), Chaplin's myth still took a form largely derived from the Tramp, either as someone similar (the barber) or opposite (Verdoux, who, as Bazin points out, steps toward the scaffold in Chaplin's typical Tramp-like style of walking). Although both films can be easily read as a kind of fare-well to the Tramp, *Limelight* is probably the first film in which that figure is nowhere to be seen or relied upon for meaning. This means that, after the Tramp, Chaplin comes back to the original notion of myth as relevant within his universe regardless of the Tramp character presence in all its forms and variations. *Limelight* embodies the notion of Bazin's definition of myth—a collective condensation of social impulses gaining a peculiar kind of "transcendent" existence of its own, which transcends, notably, personal biography. In other words, this film is about "social transcendence" at its purest, namely the kind that Chaplin himself has attained in the eyes of the world regardless of its character. But, more importantly, it is especially about the lack of social transcendence.

Although the Tramp is not involved this time, we have again two coinciding opposites. The two contraries are Calvero and Charles Spencer Chaplin himself. The actor, and not his character, faces and embodies his own fears (failure, senility, death), projecting them upon Calvero. Yet, it is necessary to push the analysis a little further and to recur once again to an intuition by Bazin. Is it really all about failure, aging, and death? Isn't anything else at stake? Actually, there is: the fear to be nothing in itself.[41] What Chaplin fears "through" Calvero is that his own success, the success that Calvero has lost along the way, has nothing to do with himself, but is something entirely dependent on the relationship between him and the public. Chaplin/Calvero is afraid that his life does not exist "in" itself but only "for" others. He is literally a creature of the stage: "I do not love the theater, but neither can I stand the sight of the blood that circulates in my veins." Indicatively, at night he dreams of performing once more on stage his "flea trainer" number, where he trains a flea that obviously does not exist, but whose existence is suggested to the public by the trainer's gaze following its imaginary somersaults in the air. According to an elementary oneiric logic, Calvero fears becoming that flea, something that does not exist if not activated by the gaze of the viewers. Immediately thereafter, Calvero takes a sad look at the completely empty pit in front of the stage; then he stares into the camera, while a dissolve shows an identical close-up of the now-awakened Calvero, who also stares into the camera, but without a countershot: he is on his bed and not on a stage, so there is no pit nor audience. This means that the "second" Calvero is in fact Chaplin looking for our gaze, just as Calvero, a few seconds before, was looking for the gazes of the theatrical audience who were supposed to sit in front of him. Since his own myth is alien to him, he looks for it in that "outside" where it only can be located—that is, in the eyes of those who believe in it, like Thereza later in the film. In other words, *through* the screen, he looks for a stage, a place where he can settle frontal eye contact with the audience: a stage-like representational distance beyond theater and the theatrical apparatus, like in the final scene of *The Great Dictator*, where, as many critics have noticed, Chaplin himself seems to be addressing us, and not just the barber. Another paradox: Calvero's audience (the vacant seats) is an absent presence, while Chaplin's (ourselves watching him without being seen by him) is a present absence.

The myth of Chaplin lives in place of Chaplin, and Calvero is just the negative proof that Chaplin would be nothing without his myth. Like Hitler, he is but his moustache. Calvero is precisely what remains after the departure of all that myth represents. He is Chaplin as a human, and not as a living legend. However, the point of this "mythless nothing" (Calvero) lies else-where. Once again, it has to do with mimesis. The relationship between Calvero and Thereza is assuredly of an imitative kind. They both need self-confidence, and both get it by imitating each other's confidence. This mutual imitation is what they do throughout the movie: they react against adversities by taking inspiration from each other. Sometimes, there is also a significant ambiguity with regard to the symbolic implications they're attached to: Does the scene where Columbine dies amid her friends trying to distract and con-sole her allude to Thereza (who plays her, and who used to be immobilized in a bed and unable to walk, just like Columbine) or rather to the actually dying Calvero? Who consoles whom? But this spiral of reciprocal imitation is not eternal. The first-order copy-model relationship is not the last word: accord-ing to the by now well-known paradox of mimesis, one term of the imitative relationship is actually accomplished only when the other is reduced to noth-ing—second-order mimesis. This reduction is exactly what happens in the very last scene: a tracking shot connects Calvero's dead body with Thereza's triumphant dancing onstage. They were both striving so that one or the other (or both) could be a successful stage performer (sometimes Calvero sup-ported Thereza; other times she supported him), and this is finally achieved when Calvero accepts what he has been all along but was afraid to be: nothing (i.e., dead) if not "for the others." If the ethical and political value of classical tragedy's catharsis consists in facing the fact of "being nothing," *Limelight* adds a crucial specification: "if not for the others" and the representational distance indispensable to establish all this is again the stage. It is on a stage that Calvero can transfer his own mastery to Thereza. Only a stage can "stabilize" the opposites Calvero/Chaplin by transferring to another human being his own legend. *Limelight* abundantly emphasizes stages, indulging in several long and frontal shots of the performers onstage—in other words, indulging in the properly theatrical point of view. It is again the theatrical apparatus beyond theater (that is, in cinema) that grants this abstraction, and this dynamic is probably what made Bazin write his enigmatic statement: "the greatness of *Limelight* is one with the greatness of the cinema itself; it is the most dazzling display of its very essence, abstraction *by way of incarnation*."[42] Calvero is Chaplin "incarnated," as the human being beyond myth, but only insofar as he submits to that kind of self-abstraction that only second-order theatrical catharsis makes possible. After Chaplin had ultimately mythologized himself, his character could no longer be supposed to sustain his myth, since Chaplin no longer needed it to: it had instead to reduce to zero (to "abstract") Chaplin's myth and to embody his human side *beyond* myth. It had to be more human than the man himself. Finally, the year itself when these events are set is highly paradoxical: 1914. The film enacting the ultimate dismissal of Chaplin's myth takes place at its very beginning, that is, in the exact year when Charles Spencer Chaplin debuted on the big screen.

We have come a long way since *The Great Dictator*'s "simple" deployment of paradoxes through resemblances. Calvero's paradox of mimesis is considerably different from, and more elaborated than, Hynkel's. From one film to the other, with *Monsieur Verdoux* in the middle, Chaplin refined his stance on mimesis; yet the core of all three movies is equally and recognizably mimesis as paradox and paradox as mimesis. Did Chaplin consciously envisage them as a trilogy dealing with this mimetic logic of paradox we have called "hyperbologic"? It is hard to say. However, several elements from those very same years do point to a conscious intention on his part to systematically explore mimesis and paradox at that stage of his career. Shortly before the time of *The Great Dictator*, Chaplin conceived a film project in which Napoleon escapes "from St. Helena with the help of a self-sacrificing double who takes his place."[43] Resemblance was thus clearly one of his major concerns. Yet this essay has hopefully made clear how resemblance (mimesis) is involved with pushing ideas to their extreme (the hyperbologic). No wonder that in an interview shortly before the release of *Monsieur Verdoux*, Chaplin stated: "Von Clausewitz said that war is the logical extension of diplomacy; M. Verdoux feels that murder is the logical extension of business."[44] In other words: Verdoux does nothing more than push the logic of business to its extreme. Another film that was never made but that Chaplin described in his autobiography,[45] offers another blatant example of the filmmaker himself pushing things to the extreme. Chaplin envisioned that film as reaching its climax with the crucifixion of Christ on the stage of an ordinary nightclub, with the person playing Christ dying for real. Here, similar to *Limelight*, the stage is the very special place where an uncanny coincidence between opposites occurs: the utmost presence of the actor, who through and with his role, coincides with his utmost absence, through his death.

CONCLUSION

In his late "trilogy," Chaplin seems to reconceive the basic features of mimesis and classical tragedy and emphasize the hyperbologic potential when applied to the relatively new medium of cinema. This effort includes the allusion to, and the reinvention through cinematic forms of the representational distance generally associated with theatrical stage, which is the classical site of the dramatization of catharsis. Moreover, it entailed finding cinematic means to render the original bond connecting together imitation on one side and the expression of paradoxes on the other, the bond at the core of both classical tragedy and speculative (dialectic) reason. In all three films, Chaplin plays mimetically with his own myth in order to redouble it and to install a basic paradox, an equivalence of contraries. And, each time the ethical lesson to be derived from this hyperbologic relies on the possibility of achieving a kind of catharsis, a kind of representational distance from the equivalence of contraries. This representational distance typically relies on *a stage*—that is, a broadly conceived theatrical apparatus. Each of the binary couples derived from Chaplin's mimetic play in these films are resolved by way of performance on a stage. Hence, these films also underline the ethical importance of a representational distance as the proper way to handle contradictions and the necessity to find for it a shape beyond its conventional form on the theatrical stage. To conclude, it is worth quoting a striking anecdote told by Theodor Adorno:

> Together with many others we were invited to a villa in Malibu, on the coast outside of Los Angeles. While Chaplin stood next to me, one of the guests was taking his leave early. Unlike Chaplin, I extended my hand to him a bit absent-mindedly, and, almost instantly, started violently back. The man was one of the lead actors from *The Best Years of Our Lives*, a film famous shortly after the war; he lost a hand during the war and in its place bore practicable claws made of iron. When I shook his right hand and felt it return the pressure, I was extremely startled, but sensed immediately that I could not reveal my shock to the injured man at any price. In a split second I transformed my frightened expression into an obliging grimace that must have been far ghastlier. The actor had hardly moved away when Chaplin was already playing the scene back.[46]

The ways of dialectic are hard to follow. Even most prodigious attempts like Adorno's "negative dialectic" can fall into various impasses: it is not easy to come to terms with the structural imbalance between the subject and the object—they cannot really "shake hands," even when this imbalance is aptly pinned down by theory. The impasses encountered by Adorno in his attempt to come to terms with dialectic are seemingly allegorized in this anecdote by his failed attempt to shake hands, that is, to make subject and object meet. Yet, by simply performing an *imitation* (Adorno's) and thus by shifting the focus from the attempted conciliation between subject and object (the hand-shake) to mimesis as such, Chaplin shows that perhaps something can overcome these impasses and reasonably claim to be placed right at the core of speculative reason. It is hyperbologic: the paradoxical logic that informs imitation.

NOTES

1. André Bazin, "Charlie Chaplin," in *What Is Cinema?* vol. 1, ed. and trans. Hugh Gray (Berkeley: University of California Press, 1967), 144.
2. Philippe Lacoue-Labarthe, "Diderot: Paradox and Mimesis," in *Typography: Mimesis, Philosophy, Politics*, ed. Christopher Fynsk and Philippe Lacoue-Labarthe, trans. Christopher Fynsk (Cambridge, MA: Harvard University Press, 1989), 260.
3. "Charlie is a mythical figure who rises above every adventure in which he becomes involved. For the general public, Charlie exists as a person before and after Easy Street and The Pilgrim. For hundreds of millions of people on this planet he is a hero like Ulysses or Roland in other civilizations" (Bazin, "Charlie Chaplin," 144). Similarly, the first pages of Bazin's "The Myth of Monsieur Verdoux" are dedicated to a depiction of Chaplin's myth focusing on the fact that his characters seem to have an existence that is independent from (i.e., that "transcends") the films they are in. See Bazin, "The Myth of Monsieur Verdoux," 102–6.
4. André Bazin, "Pastiche or Postiche: or, Nothingness over a Moustache," in *Essays on Chaplin*, ed. And trans. Jean Bodon (New Haven: University of New Haven Press, 1985), 18.
5. , Lacoue-Labarthe, "Diderot: Paradox and Mimesis," 252.
6. These three films are also the first truly spoken films Chaplin ever made. See Aner Preminger's chapter in this volume for an account of Chaplin's sound cinema. Chaplin is of course never directly mentioned in *Limelight*, and yet he is an inescapable reference behind Calvero; the main character of *The Great Dictator*, who is not the Tramp strictly speaking, shares nonetheless many features with him; Mr. Verdoux, as I will explain in greater detail, is so precise a reversal of any possible trait belonging to the Tramp that he is the Tramp himself in reverse.
7. This presupposition is suggested primarily within the rereading of Plato contained in "Typography," the initial chapter of the book of the same name. Philippe Lacoue-Labarthe, "Typography," in *Typography: Mimesis, Philosophy, Politics*, ed. Christopher Fynsk and Philippe Lacoue-Labarthe, trans. Christopher Fynsk (Cambridge, MA: Harvard University Press, 1989), 43–138.
8. Simon Louvish, *Chaplin: The Tramp's Odyssey* (London: Faber and Faber, 2009), 87.
9. Bazin, "Pastiche or Postiche," 20–21.
10. Bazin, "Pastiche or Postiche," 16.
11. Lacoue-Labarthe, "Diderot: Paradox and Mimesis," 255.
12. Lacoue-Labarthe, "Diderot: Paradox and Mimesis," 255–56.
13. Lacoue-Labarthe, "Diderot: Paradox and Mimesis," 257–59.
14. Lacoue-Labarthe, "Diderot: Paradox and Mimesis," 258.
15. Lacoue-Labarthe, "Diderot: Paradox and Mimesis," 259.

16. Charles Chaplin, *My Autobiography* (New York: Simon and Schuster, 1964), 316.

17. Bazin, "Pastiche or Postiche," 19.

18. Bazin, "Pastiche or Postiche," 16.

19. Bazin, "Pastiche or Postiche," 17.

20. Lacoue-Labarthe, "Diderot: Paradox and Mimesis," 260.

21. Jacques Derrida, "Introduction: Desistance," in *Typography*, 41.

22. Lacoue-Labarthe, "Diderot: Paradox and Mimesis," 253.

23. Philippe Lacoue-Labarthe, "The Caesura of the Speculative," in *Typography*, 231.

24. Lacoue-Labarthe, "Diderot: Paradox and Mimesis," 259.

25. Lacoue-Labarthe, "Diderot: Paradox and Mimesis," 260.

26. Derrida, "Introduction: Desistance," 41.

27. William F. Fry Jr., "Charles Chaplin: An Embodiment of Paradox (le comique et la terreur)," in *Charlie Chaplin: His Reflection in Modern Times*, ed. Adolphe Nysenholc (Berlin: Mouton de Gruyter, 1991), 62.

28. Mladen Dolar, *A Voice and Nothing More* (Cambridge and London: The MIT Press, 2006), 115–16.

29. This juxtaposition may certainly be read as simply supporting the film's theme of the meek against the strong, who are completely disconnected from the oppressed and their humanity. But it would be an unusual kind of editing choice for Chaplin, to say the least—he rarely used montage to convey that kind of conceptual suggestion.

30. Lacoue-Labarthe, "Diderot: Paradox and Mimesis," 261–64.

31. Lacoue-Labarthe, "Diderot: Paradox and Mimesis," 264.

32. Lacoue-Labarthe, "Diderot: Paradox and Mimesis," 265; "The Caesura of the Speculative," 208–9.

33. This choice emphasizes, rather effectively, the lack of realism in the speech's ability to carry across great distances without technological support.

34. As Lacoue-Labarthe observes in "The Caesura of the Speculative," "Indeed, the possibility offered by the tragic fable or scenario is that of the preservation (though to the benefit and in the sense of freedom) of the contradiction of the subjective and the objective, since the tragic hero, 'at once guilty and innocent' (as Hegel will also say) in struggling against the invincible, that is, in struggling against the destiny that bears responsibility for his fault, provokes an inevitable and necessary defeat and voluntarily chooses to expiate a crime of which he knows he is innocent and for which, in any case, he will have had to pay. Culpable innocence and the 'gratuitous' provocation of punishment are therefore the solution to the conflict: the subject manifests its liberty 'by the very loss of its liberty.' The negative, here, is converted into the positive" (216). Oedipus is of course the main inspiration for such idealist attempts to establish a fundamental relationship between classical tragedy and the "march through oppositions" by speculative reason.

35. Lacoue-Labarthe, "The Caesura of the Speculative," 227–32.

36. Lacoue-Labarthe, "The Caesura of the Speculative," 232.

37. Lacoue-Labarthe, "The Caesura of the Speculative," 218–19.

38. Bazin, "The Myth of Monsieur Verdoux," 103–5.

39. This points connects to Levi-Strauss's observation, "The purpose of myth is to provide a logical model capable of overcoming a contradiction (an impossible achievement if, as it happens, the contradiction is real)." (*Structural Anthropology*, trans. Claire Jakobson and Brooke Schoepf [New York: Basic, 1963], 229).

40. Bazin, "The Myth of Monsieur Verdoux," 103.

41. André Bazin, "The Grandeur of Limelight," in *What Is Cinema?*, 133–34.

42. Bazin, "The Grandeur of Limelight," 138.

43. David Robinson, *Chaplin: His Life and Art* (London: Penguin, 2001), 511.

44. Theodore Huff, *Charlie Chaplin* (New York: Arno Press, 1972), 293.

45. Chaplin, *My Autobiography*, 390–91.

46. Theodor Adorno, "Chaplin Times Two," in *The Essential Chaplin: Perspectives on the Art and the Life of the Great Comedian*, ed. Richard Schickel (Chicago: Ivan R. Dee, 2006), 271–72.

Chapter Nine

Charles Chaplin Sings a Silent Requiem

Chaplin's Films, 1928–1952, as Cinematic Statement on the Transition from Silent Cinema to the Talkies

Aner Preminger

FROM REVOLUTION TO EVOLUTION

Cinematic history accords Chaplin high prominence as a creator of silent films but almost completely ignores him as a significant filmmaker in the era of the talkies. While many historians and critics extol Chaplin's uniqueness in some of his sound films, they approach them in much the same way as they approached his previous silent films. They virtually disregard his contribution to the language of cinema as a medium of both picture and soundtrack. David Robinson concisely and authoritatively expresses the prevailing attitude on this issue in his book *The History of World Cinema*: "Chaplin approached the new medium with great caution; and did not risk a full talking film till 1940. *City Lights* (1931) and *Modern Times* (1936) are really silent films with a greater or lesser degree of synchronized sound effects and music."[1]

Although I do not dispute the facts adduced by Robinson, I do interpret them rather differently. As Michel Chion puts it, with the advent of synchronized sound, cinema was now (1928) a "phenomenon of *audiovisual illusion*" (Chion's italics).[2] I submit that Chion's notion precisely characterizes Chaplin's cinema as of 1928. Deploying Chion's terminology, I argue that Chaplin invented original ways of utilizing sound in *The Circus* (1928), *City Lights*, *Modern Times*, and *The Great Dictator* (1940). The fact that even Chion himself, in the numerous examples he cites from later prominent filmmakers in support of his case, ignores Chaplin's singular use of sound, bears out the urgent need for an analysis of Chaplin's audiovisual devices. Chaplin was not only an important innovator in the cinematic language of talkies, using sound in audio gags similarly to his use of props and body in his visual comedy. In all of the above-mentioned films, and later in *Limelight* (1952), he also subtly dealt with the *meaning* of sound, the differences between silent and talking cinema, and the implications of using sound technology in order to artistically represent truth and reality. I contend that in all his films during this period, Chaplin, in his own distinctive way, most deliberately and consistently wielded sound and the absence of sound with great precision and ingenuity.

In order to refine our concepts, we need to add three categories to the dichotomy between silent film and talking picture.

Audio-silent film is a motion picture in which the cinematic language and style are those of a silent film. There is use of sync sound effects and music, whether diegetic or extradiegetic. The characters never speak in sync sound, and any dialogue, if it occurs, is represented by intertitles. Chaplin's *City Lights* and René Clair's *A Nous la Liberté* (1931) are examples of audio-silent films, which are considered silent films in the literature of cinema.

Talking-silent film is an audio-silent film that sometimes includes sync sound dialogue. In these films, there may be a combination of real sync dialogue and intertitles between two close-ups in other dialogue scenes. Actors might perform the type of nonverbal communication associated with the style of the silent era, in conjunction with sync sound effects and partial dialogue.[3] Examples of talking-silent films would be *The Jazz Singer* (1927), which is regarded as the first talkie in the literature, and *Modern Times*, which is considered a silent picture in the literature. Chion uses the term "sonorized films"[4] when referring to such films, but he does not include them in his analysis of the contribution of sound to the audiovisual illusion. Actually, Chion refers to Chaplin only twice in *The Voice in Cinema*, and in both cases as the ultimate icon of silent cinema: "Chaplin defended the silent cinema as an *art of pantomime*."[5] The second time he mentions Chaplin is when talking about the burlesque: he refers to his characteristic "playing on the very situation of the human being as a dislocated body, a puppet, a burlesque assemblage of body and voice."[6]

Filmed-theater is a talking picture that uses a soundtrack to record voice, music, and sound effects, yet its cinematic language is not distinctive and may even be regressive in comparison to the aesthetic achievements of the silent film. I would even venture to suggest that in the four years during the revolutionary transition from silent films to talking films, following *The Jazz Singer* and prior to *The Blue Angel* (*Der Blaue Engel*, 1930), the films that were produced were essentially either audio-silent films, talking-silent films, or filmed-theater, all of which were far from exploiting the potential of the new medium.

It is well known that many great silent filmmakers did not survive the invention of the talkies. A small number managed to adapt to the new medium after the sound innovations of *The Blue Angel*, and some of these filmmakers were even creative and original. Chaplin, however, never made filmed-theater, and in his search for his own way into the talkies, he continued to make silent, audio-silent, and talking-silent films. Even *The Great Dictator*, as I demonstrate later, is a talking-silent film, though it is considered to be his first talking picture. Kay Dickinson seems aware of his reluctance to use concrete speech when she writes that even in "*Modern Times* he preferred more abstract, textural sounds to those of the human voice."[7] Although Dickinson recognizes that Chaplin may have done some interesting things with sound, she seems to support the prevalent view that Chaplin shunned the talking picture challenge and was stuck far behind the filmmakers who were leading the talking revolution. Adrian Daub sums up the critical consensus, stating that Chaplin first compromised in *Modern Times*, and later he "altogether abandoned his rejection of talkies for *The Great Dictator*."[8] In an illuminating analysis of Chaplin's uses of voice, words, language, and translation in *The Great Dictator*, Daub's perception is that Chaplin's use of synchronized speech is the culmination of a process of giving up his previous "rejection of talkies." Furthermore, Daub's argument is that "it is this question of voice versus image in film and the role of voice and vision in theorizations of fascism that underpin Chaplin's attempt to challenge Nazism in and through film and comedy."[9] My view is that for all the extraneous historical influences affecting Chaplin, the use of image and voice in *The Great Dictator* is the continuation of an imminent process that began much earlier in his filmmaking, not in the form of a mere "compromise," but as an inevitable consequence of Chaplin's fundamental attitude toward sound.

The following chronological examination of the films in question traces the auteur's evolution from master of silent film technique to creative innovator of cinematic language within talking pictures.

THE CIRCUS

The Circus is about essential aspects of silent cinema, mute comedy, pantomime, and the clown figure that Chaplin perfected. Moreover, the film confronts the audience with the relation between reality and artistic representation. In one of Chaplin's iconic gags, the Tramp is lost in a maze of mirrors, and we witness a total blurring of his many reflections that appear in them, a moment in which one cannot distinguish between the figure and its reflection.

The camera functions as an observing eye represented by the dominant circle as a graphical motif throughout the film, duplicating the traditional circus ring. The film opens with an iris shot of a circle of light centered on a star—a circus emblem. A woman on horseback leaps through the paper star in the raised hoop—a circle—tearing it away. At the film's end, the Tramp stands at the edge of the huge circle that marks the area of the dismantled circus tent. The Tramp sits down outside this circle, picks up the paper torn at the beginning, and crumples it into a ball. He gets up, moves away from the camera toward the horizon as the iris of the camera closes around him, and he vanishes in the ring of light, which becomes smaller and smaller, fading into a black screen. The film's ending accentuates the recurring circular geometry of the film's décor: the round tent, the loop with its star, the light circles, and the iris. Thus, the circular form is a dominant motif in the film. It is especially prominent in the circus performances, where the shapes of the ring and small stage, the spotlight on the performers, and the peephole through which the Tramp looks into the circus world from outside the tent are all round. Clearly, the domain inside the circle—circus—represents the world of art. Outside is "reality." But "art" refers here specifically to Chaplin's art of silent comedy, that is, pantomime, the Tramp.

The Circus is a veritable requiem for the silent cinema. Unlike his colleagues in Hollywood who immediately sought to emulate the type of sound picture introduced by *The Jazz Singer*, Chaplin did not hurry into the technological race. Rather, he seemed now to take his time and mourn silent cinema's death through artistic effort.

The audition sequence in which the Tramp attempts to join the circus can be understood as alluding to the Hollywood film industry. In the course of the audition, the various gags define the essence of comedy and the relation between Chaplin's sophisticated art and the tradition of circus slapstick. The clowns in the circus are the ones fighting for their dying art, namely, silent comedy as seen now by modern viewers. The Tramp, representing Chaplin's art, however, manages to breathe new life into these tired routines due to his "artless" gestures (that are actually his reaction to his concrete situation in the film's "reality") and also due to his spontaneity and improvisations, all transcending the mechanical clichés of circus slapstick.

Two unique scenes in the film demonstrate Chaplin's keen awareness of the power of sound. Most of the gags in both scenes are based on the potential of sound. The possibility of sound is underlined by sound's conspicuous absence when it is visually dramatized. The scenes present sound, as well as its production, as the Tramp's enemy and thus, by iconic association, as the enemy of Chaplin the artist. The Tramp inadvertently finds himself in the lion's cage, at risk of death, as a result of an accident related to the sound-producing organ—his mouth. The overseer instructs him to blow a pill into a sick horse's mouth through a plastic tube, the Tramp's mouth at one edge of the tube and the horse's mouth at the other. The horse's blowing power—its sound-producing force—exceeds that of the Tramp's.[10] The Tramp, shocked by the pill stuck in his mouth, rushes in panic straight into the lion's cage. Once trapped in the cage, the Tramp's aim is to ensure silence so as not to awaken the lion. Sound, here, is the source of horror, of mortal danger, and the expression of its destructive power is latent in the lion's roar, which is not heard. The Tramp walks about on tiptoe so as not to make any noise. When he opens the door of the neighboring cage and is terrified by the leopard there, he is alarmed again by the slamming of the gate between the two cages—again a sound that the spectator *sees* but does not hear. After this, the lion's water trough falls from the shelf and the Tramp catches it at the last moment, preventing it from hitting the floor and making noise. The scene's climax occurs when a dog arrives and, instead of helping him, begins to bark fiercely at the Tramp, who is terrified that the lion will stir. The Tramp covers his ears to avoid hearing the dog's bark, a bark that we only *see*, as if he could thereby prevent it from reaching the lion. This gesture represents Chaplin's self-irony: despite the Tramp's attempts to shut his ears and si-lence the cinema's soundtrack, as it were, Chaplin is smart enough, *we* know, to understand that it is impossible to cover the audience's ears and quite impossible to hold back the entrepreneurial producers of talkies and techno-logical advance.

In this scene, two things happen that distinguish it from the rest of the film, both relevant to our subject. Each of the obstacles and dangers in the sequence hinges on sounds that the audience does not hear. For the first time Chaplin is working with pseudo-audio gags in a manner similar to the way in which he used visual jokes in the past. The second thing we notice is his choice not to use synchronous sound effects, even though by 1928, a year after *The Jazz Singer* was released, there was no technical reason not to do so. Conspicuously absent are the sounds of the Tramp's footsteps, the noise of the clanking door, the roars of the leopard and the lion, and of course the barking of the dog. The absence of these sounds is a consistent artistic choice that is dramatized by the Tramp's covering of his ears.

Here Chaplin is proposing a new way of using sound, namely, sound as a concept rather than as a diegetic audio component of the soundtrack. He draws the audience's attention to the absence of the sound by silencing it. At this early stage of talking movies, Chaplin chooses not to apply the new technology, yet he is not ignoring it. Rather, his conscious refusal to diegeti-cally deploy sound becomes the subject of (and the comic force behind) these gags. He magically performs the feat of "turning off" the sound, which in the films of other creators is already "on." This fits well with Rachel Joseph's general observation in her essay "Chaplin's Presence," earlier in this volume, about Chaplin's obsession with the "ways that presence and absence emerge, miss one another, and disappear."[11] This example is probably one of the first in cinematic history where sound is used in its punctuating function, in Chion's terminology, but in a privative, soundless, sense. Chion states that "synchronous sound brought to the cinema not the principle of punctuation but increasingly subtle means of punctuating scenes without putting a strain on the acting or the editing."[12]

Later he mentions the use of a "barking of a dog off-screen"[13] as an example of a possible sound punctuation. Ironically, he gives this as a general example, ignoring *The Circus*'s dog-barking scene in which Chaplin applies the same idea, but in the *negative* sense. We can say that the nonexisting barking sound effect of the onscreen barking dog suggests the notion of an *off sound-space* or maybe a *negative sound-space*. In other words, what is seen onscreen has a distinctive sound: it is *seen* that the sound is there and heard by the characters, but *not heard* by the audience. It is the concrete availability of sound that enables Chaplin to extend the semiotics of pantomimic indirect expression to the acoustic dimension.

Interestingly, from the present viewpoint that sees *The Circus* as a response to the advent of sound, it is remarkable that Chaplin began production of this movie in 1925, the year that AT&T had already started experimenting with sync sound.[14] It is not surprising that Chaplin, as a sensitive barometer of his times, should use his art to reflect innovations that were being explored in his own industry, even though he was in no hurry to immediately incorporate them. In this context, how can one fail to note that the source of the Tramp's mortal danger represented by the roaring lion recalls the famous MGM icon?

CITY LIGHTS

By the time of Chaplin's next film, *City Lights*—made three years after *The Circus*—the sound revolution was technologically complete and some talkies, like *The Blue Angel*, were successfully exploring the artistic potential of the new medium. Despite this potential, Chaplin was still pursuing his experimentation with sound in the formal framework of the silent movie. Released during the initial stages of the talkie, *The Circus* makes no direct statement about its being a silent film; *City Lights*, however, asserts in the intertitle: "A Romantic Comedy in Pantomime," signaling to Chaplin's audience that he was still in the (audio-) silent movie business.

In the extensive commentary on *City Lights*, there is no mention of the allusion inherent in its plot to the dilemma of incorporating synchronized sound, which then engaged Chaplin. The film focuses on the Tramp's infatuation with a blind flower girl (Virginia Cherrill) whose sight would be restored if she could undergo a newly discovered and expensive operation. The Tramp, who loves the poor girl, obtains the money needed for the operation.

The price they both have to pay for fulfilling this wish is his disappearance from her life, for the relationship between them is based on an illusion: the Tramp has falsely allowed her to believe that he is wealthy. The girl, rejoicing in her restored sight, cannot understand why her benefactor has vanished, and she waits in vain for him to reappear.

By the end of the picture the Tramp, who has just been released from jail, materializes beside her new flower shop. He is excited to see her but does not reveal himself to her. She treats him like a strange bum pursuing her. His appearance amuses her, and she even mocks him. In the end, pitying him, she offers him a coin. Now, by the touch of his hand, she realizes that he is the man for whom she has been waiting. The film ends with alternating close-ups of the two of them, interspersed with the following intertitles of dialogue:

The girl: You?

The Tramp: You can see now?

The girl: Yes, I can see now.

The blind girl's situation represents—though inversely—the situation of the cinema audience embracing the coming of the talkies after having been deprived of synchronized sound in silent pictures. When she is blind, she perceives reality by means of either hearing or touch, depending on the context. Through the eye operation, the latest development in surgical technology, she acquires an additional sense, which radically transforms her perception of reality. The dear price, however, is the loss of love or simply the disappearance of the Tramp from her life. The final scene actually casts doubt on the blessing inherent in this new ability. Sight only hinders the girl from correctly identifying the "real" person. She catalogs the Tramp according to external visual signs and classifies him according to social clichés. Only when she returns to the sense of touch, the original sense through which she has experienced life, does she discover that he is her benefactor.

In 1931, both the audience and the makers of talking films were in a situation similar to the experience of the formerly blind girl, if we swap "audio" for "visual." Both cases deal with people switching from experiencing reality in a limited fashion through the loss of one sense, to accessing it both aurally and visually. Sound technology gave the film audience an additional means of experiencing a sense of realism when watching motion pictures. The addition of sight created a similar situation for the blind girl. However, as Chaplin sees it, cinema has only hindered its own authentic expression of inner experience by providing this added realism. According to his use of it, sound can be powerful only if it does not enhance realism but rather provokes the imagination. Much later, in 1964, Chaplin articulated this idea in his autobiography, relating his being depressed at the time by a young critic's remark that *City Lights* lacked realism: "Had I known what I do now, I could have told him that so-called realism is often artificial, phony, prosaic and dull; and that it is not reality that matters in a film but what the imagination can make of it."[15] When Chaplin says just before these words: "I found myself agreeing with him,"[16] he also expresses his sober realization and fear that sound might lead to the death of the love affair between himself and his audience. This fear was certainly understandable regarding the Tramp figure, but perhaps no less so regarding Chaplin the filmmaker. In his essay "The Paradox of the 'Dictator': Mimesis, Logic of Paradox, and the Reinstatement of Catharsis in *The Great Dictator*, *Monsieur Verdoux*, and *Limelight*," Marco Grosoli argues that "*The Great Dictator* and *Monsieur Verdoux* can be easily read as a kind of farewell to the Tramp,"[17] but we actually see here that this insight of Chaplin's was already expressed in *City Lights*.

The Tramp's final sentence—"You can see now?"—is fraught with meaning. Its plain sense is "was the operation a success?" The subtext is "now you can see that it's me," "now you can see that I lied to you and that I'm not rich," and perhaps, "now you can understand that you were mistaken when you mocked me." On the symbolic and philosophical levels, however, its meaning is, "now you can see that this achievement came at a great price." In Rachel Joseph's discourse this would mean "now you can see that I'm both present and absent," or more specifically in my discourse, "my presence is valid only in silent cinema."

In *City Lights* Chaplin makes use of the soundtrack in gags that are linked to the film's theme. The blind girl first encounters the Tramp when he nonchalantly passes through the "obstacle" of a parked limousine. The girl hears the car doors opening and shutting and judging by sound alone, she believes that he is a rich man who has just stepped out of the limousine. In contrast to other sound effects actually used by Chaplin in the film, this particular sound is conspicuous in its absence—just like the one with the Tramp in the lion's cage. Their first encounter, a reverse analogy to their encounter at the end of the film, stems from an error on the realistic level, which arises from a perception of reality through hearing, but leads to a deeper inner truth, as we see later in the film.

In contrast to his strategy in *The Circus*, where real sound is salient through its absence in the soundtrack, Chaplin uses a form of stylized sound effect to draw attention to itself in *City Lights*. A distinct example occurs when the Tramp swallows a whistle, and its sound bursts out of his stomach during the party at the millionaire's house. Prominent in this scene is the prolonged contest between the synchronized music of the band, a conventional controlled synchronous sound, and the uncontrolled eruptions of whistling from the depths of the Tramp's belly—Chaplin's new approach to the use of sound. Though sound is now associated with both the Tramp and the band, he is the odd man who will soon be out.

The film's opening scene already establishes some of the terms in which stylized sound is conjoined to the visual representation of sound, in the visual narrative. The mayor (Henry Bergman) is giving a solemn speech at a fancy inauguration of a new sculpture. His speech sounds to us like gibberish, but the listeners' reaction indicates that to them it is quite intelligible. Technically, the mayor's speech, and later the speech of the actress standing beside him, was produced by Chaplin, speaking gibberish sprinkled with real words, very quickly, through a kazoo.[18] This technique is what Chion defines as "verbal chiaroscuro."[19] The strange speech is an audio gag that makes the characters look ridiculous and creates a cinematic equivalent of what in ordinary speech is called "nonsense." We are presented with a trenchant satire of politicians blabbering on at assemblies and ceremonies without saying anything. From a self-reflexive point of view, Chaplin is once again stating artistically that the aesthetic richness of the sound lies solely in the music, the acting, the tone, and not in the content of the speech, which he ridicules. It is interesting to mention that the mayor's gibberish and the actress's gibberish are distinctively different, though both are performed by Chaplin himself, who thus proves to be a vocal art virtuoso. Each one has its own music, color, and intonation. The actress's speech is high-pitched and feminine, whereas the mayor's is deep and masculine. This scene demonstrates that Chion's statement about "Chaplin's protest against the voice, under the name of the speech"[20] is not quite accurate. Actually, here Chaplin uses voice as material for his gags. In fact, he protests only against words as verbal information and the realistic quality that it lends to cinema. Nevertheless, Chion's terminology helps to bring out the importance of this scene, though he never once refers to it. The speech used by Chaplin in this scene is what Chion defines as emanation speech: "A speech which is not necessarily heard and understood fully and in any case is not intimately tied to the heart of what might be called the narrative action. . . . Emanation speech, while the most cinematic, is thus the rarest of the three types of speech, and, for complex reasons, the sound film has made very little use of it."[21] Later, Chion mentions that Jacques Tati, Tarkovsky, Fellini, and Ophuls use emanation speech[22] and surprisingly ignores Chaplin who, as we have just seen, actually invented this form of speech in *City Lights*.

In the same way that Dziga Vertov experimented with slow motion and fast motion in the silent cinema era to produce images of distorted reality, Chaplin experimented with the soundtrack to produce distorted sounds that make no attempt at realism, and they often satirize mimetic sound-film practices. Whereas Vertov's visual effects became part of the language of cinema, other filmmakers rarely adopted Chaplin's techniques in *City Lights* for parodying speech. But, as we've just learned from Chion, his techniques were important in the development of the cinematic utterance.

Unlike in *The Circus*, Chaplin experiments with diegetic sound in *City Lights*. Now the music is not external to the narrative or the plot—not a mere musical accompaniment for emotional manipulation; rather, the characters themselves hear it together with the movie audience. At the solemn moment of the inauguration, as the drape is removed from the monument, the Tramp is exposed sleeping peacefully on the huge stone figure. The Tramp, embarrassed, attempts to climb off, but his clothes are caught on the statue. The orchestra, having continued to play routinely, is now playing the national anthem. The Tramp is unable to release himself and stand properly at attention. This need to stand at attention for the anthem is utilized by Chaplin in further gags, emphasizing the contrast between the pomposity of the dignified crowd and the authentic spontaneity of the Tramp. The characters thus respond to sound in a way that is similar to the reaction of his characters to props and sets in his silent movies.

To better appreciate Chaplin's strategy of minimizing his use of sound together with his use of its absence, it is well worth noting Chion's illuminating remarks on the avoidance of sound: "Godard unmasks conventional sound editing all the more in the way he avoids the usual practice of mixing many tracks at once, such that our attention is not grabbed by breaks and cuts in the sonic flow—in some of his films he limits the tracks to two."[23] Later, talking about the importance of silence, he adds, "it was necessary to have sounds and voices so that the *interruption* of them could probe more deeply into this thing called silence."[24] In this passage, Chion also mentions Bresson and Godard as exponents of the use of silence. In the light of Chion's perceptions, it seems that Chaplin was actually the first to set the concept of silence as a powerful sound element in cinema and to explore practically the detailed grammatical rules of applying it, starting with *City Lights* and further developing it in his next "audio-talking films," as we see later.

After 1931, the talkies completely captured the imagination of both audiences and filmmakers. The filmmakers, for their part, either embraced the new medium or dropped out (of whom Buster Keaton, David Griffith, and Erich von Stroheim are outstanding examples). Chaplin produced no films for five years after *City Lights* until 1936, when he released *Modern Times*. This was his first talking-silent film, for in addition to sound effects and music, it also contained synchronized speech.

MODERN TIMES

Modern Times is about the wearing out of the "little man" in modern technological society, the clash between the individual and his or her needs, and the alienated mass in industrial society, with its economic goals and its demand of efficiency. The simple man is the victim of this conflict. Personal and emotional relationships among people have become a luxury one must strive for. Happiness and liberty are attainable only in insanity or in prison; maybe art alone can enable grasping them. The shot in which we see the Tramp caught between the cogwheels of the monstrous machine gives a poetic, graphic expression of the film's essence. We have here a visual metaphor of man caught and squashed by the wheels of the machine. On one obvious level Chaplin, who was very poor as a youth, is now the successful, wealthy artist who identifies with the small man devoured by capitalist industry. However, there is also a clear sense in which Chaplin, the silent filmmaker, is contending here with sound technology. Metaphorically the machine that sucks up the Tramp and threatens his existence is the technology of the talkies that threatens Chaplin. The factory's mad production line represents Hollywood's production line, and the machine's wheels could represent the wheels of filming and projection apparatus.

The scene that strongly confirms this reading is the one in which the Tramp treats himself to a cigarette in the seclusion of the factory bathroom. Suddenly the tyrannical factory boss (Allan Garcia), the epitome of capitalist industry, appears on the screen in the form of a talking picture, "Big Brother"–style. [25] From the imperious huge screen we see (and also hear!) a close-up of a man speaking and browbeating the small figure standing helplessly below—surely, Charles Chaplin, the silent actor, director of silent films, who works with props, decor, and acting without words. Integral to Chaplin's unique strategy for using sound throughout this film is the interplay between the in-sync speech coming from above, dramatizing a virtual reality, and the speechlessness in the "actual" reality in the factory.

The director Chaplin intersperses speech conveyed by synchronized sound with speech communicated through intertitles and bodily gestures in the style of the silent film. When characters communicate interpersonally, Chaplin shoots scenes in silent cinema mode. He employs synchronized speech only to provide *impersonal* verbal information and conveys it through modern mechanical equipment: radio in the prison, a phonograph in the scene where the feeding machine is demonstrated, and the "visual intercom" screen in the scenes where the manager gives orders to his workers through the screen. Implicit here is Chaplin's view of the speaking voice in sound cinema. The voice is mechanical and alienating, suggesting a lack of communication. In these scenes human contact is possible only in the absence of the voice. Furthermore, within this film, vocal speech represents power: it is not *speaking with* but rather *speaking at* the public, a theme fully developed in Chaplin's next film, *The Great Dictator*.

Chaplin explicitly verbalizes this idea later where the marvels of the automatic feeding machine are being demonstrated to the manager. The recorded instructions conclude with the words "Let us demonstrate with one of your workers, for actions speak louder than words." "Actions speak louder than words" is said verbally by a talking machine (a talkie), where action is *acting*, as performed by Chaplin. Acting is not just more effective or efficient; it is louder, better heard.

Chaplin's exploration of the expressive possibilities of stylized sound led to further innovations, as seen in two of the prison scenes. In the first, the Tramp sits in his prison cell reading a newspaper about protests and riots performed by the hungry and unemployed located far beyond the prison walls, while in the background we hear the sound of birds chirping. Apart from the fact that the sound is not synchronous because we do not see the source of the sound, it is also mimetically paradoxical, because in prison no birds can be heard, not even offscreen. Chaplin uses sound that is nonsynchronous and incongruous with the site of the action in order to express cinematically and without words that although the Tramp is in prison, he is freer (and more fortunate) than the people outside. The disparity between the newspaper headlines and his own situation, as expressed in his actions and by means of the soundtrack, creates a poetic gag that asks a philosophical question, one that recurs throughout the entire movie: what is the meaning of freedom and what is the connection between internal freedom and external freedom? This use of sound nicely illustrates what Chion calls audiovisual dissonance or counterpoint: "Audiovisual counterpoint will be noticed only if it sets up an opposition between sound and image on a precise point of meaning."[26]

In the scene that follows, between the Tramp and the minister's wife (Mira McKinney), Chaplin creates a series of gags around obtrusive sound. The scene is built upon an intimate situation in which the characters suffer from stomach rumblings; this time it uses sound with no visible origin, though of course we know its source. Although the sound actually emitted by their stomachs is not loud, they are embarrassed, convinced that the others can hear it. Chaplin has chosen a sound as the source of the problem that distresses the characters, and, as usual, he amplifies and exaggerates it to unrealistic proportions. As a form of cinematic utterance, we may call what he does in this scene an audio close-up (or close-up in sound-space). If in the visual close-up, the camera allows us to see details that realistically we would not be able to see with the naked eye, the close-up in sound-space allows us to hear things that realistically we would not be able to hear without cinematic sound equipment. Hence, just as Griffith created the close-up in space by means of the camera, and as Eisenstein created the close-up in time by means of the montage, so Chaplin created the close-up in sound-space. Here Chaplin also employs a variety of sound elements, all related to the gas theme, thus maintaining a unity of style throughout the soundtrack. The Tramp turns on the radio so that the sounds emitted by it may override the rumbles coming from his stomach. Much to his embarrassment, what comes on is a commercial for gastritis medication, which only further emphasizes, through words rather than mere sound, what he was hoping to conceal, and he turns the radio off at once. Similarly, when the minister's wife wants to take a pill to calm her rumbling stomach, she pours herself some soda water from a siphon, which makes a loud noise as the gas escapes from the bottle. This noise frightens the Tramp, who reacts disproportionately. Yet the intensity of his reaction is consistent with the previous reactions to his stomach's weak grumblings. The synchronized sound of the barking of the minister's wife's dog plays an important role in this scene, compounding the characters' embarrassment and their inability to conceal their intimate secret. Sound, then, is both what needs to be concealed and what draws attention to itself. Unlike the scene in *The Circus*, in which a barking dog—seen but not heard by the audience of silent cinema—calls the lion's attention to the vulnerable Tramp, this embarrassing scene includes a dog whose audible barking in response to the Tramp's and the parson's wife's gurgling stomachs calls further attention to their social embarrassment.

Toward the film's end, we get an exciting surprise—actually one that Chaplin's public had been awaiting for eight years since *The Circus*. For Chaplin was approaching a critical turning point in the evolution of the Tramp, as well as in his audiovisual articulation. Thus, upon his release from jail one last time, the Tramp finds the girl he saved (Paulette Goddard) waiting for him. She tells him that she has found work as a dancer in a restaurant. The girl introduces him to the owner, who offers him a job as a waiter but asks him a critical question: "Can you sing?" (It is all in intertitles, of course.) The Tramp's answer is hesitant. The boss offers him a trial. The Tramp gestures to his girlfriend that he cannot sing at all. In order to understand the magnitude of this moment, we have to consider the attitude of cinema viewers in 1936, nine years after *The Jazz Singer*. They have already seen two (audio-) silent films by Chaplin and are now almost at the end of his third, but this virtuoso actor has not yet opened his mouth to produce synchronized sound. The restaurant owner who asks him if he can sing is asking this question on behalf of millions of viewers of Chaplin's films, as well as his colleagues in Hollywood. Chaplin talks about this moment in his autobiography where he tells of the theater manager's response to the disastrous preview of *City Lights*: "Now I want to see you make a talkie, Charlie—that's what the whole world is waiting for."[27] In his essay in this volume, Benjamin Click argues that the opening scene in *The Great Dictator* is a response to "the aesthetic question Chaplin audiences have tacitly been asking: how will silent film's greatest star be heard in synchronized sound?" And Click adds that Chaplin realized that "To talk he [the Tramp] would have to step off his pedestal, the pedestal of silent film."[28] Once again, my point is that this insight of Chaplin's was already dramatized in *Modern Times*.

The Tramp's anxiety centers on remembering the *words* to the song, and when he forgets them, he must improvise. He starts his show, which is a mixture of dance, pantomime, and gibberish singing. Here Chaplin does open his mouth and does not disappoint his contemporary audience's expectations. He produces a voice, but ironically, his nonsense syllables are hardly what they were expecting. He shows that he can delight his audience with his unusual song in gibberish—his emanation song, to extend Chion's terminology. Again, he has proven to his audience that acting, dance, pantomime, and music can tell a story better than voiced words. Once again, Chaplin, faithful to his artistic vision, succeeds in expressing his deep doubt about the artistic quality of the new talking medium, given the effectiveness of his old style upgraded by the new technology of the talking medium.

At the end of this film, after the Tramp has opened his mouth for the first time, there is no way back. Chaplin goes on grappling with the role of speech in cinema through experiments that explore sound as a means of cinematic utterance. The result that hits the screens four years later is *The Great Dictator*.

THE GREAT DICTATOR

Although *The Great Dictator* is considered a "talkie"—Chaplin's first full-dialogue picture—I perceive it as a talking-silent film that is transformed, during its final scene, into a real talking picture. True, the characters speak without the use of intertitles throughout the movie, but this film more often than not employs the cinematic language of Chaplin's silent ones. Moreover, Chaplin constructs the two characters that he plays—the Jewish barber and the dictator Hynkel—in a sense as two opposing variations of the figure of his Tramp—what Grosoli calls "second-order mimesis."[29] In the final sequence, the two characters merge into one. The latter composite character, in turn, separates himself from the Tramp and transforms into Chaplin, the man. He talks the way Chaplin spoke and much like the way other people sometimes spoke in the talking pictures of the era. Whereas both Hynkel and the barber suffer from speech impediments, the new superimposed personality is verbally articulate. The Jewish barber is timid and barely speaks during much of the film. Hynkel himself emits various strange sounds, yet they are mostly shouts, shrieks, beastly roars, childish wails, and gibberish spiced with a few intelligible English or German words. Furthermore, when he has to speak one-on-one or on the telephone with Napaloni (Jack Oakie), Hynkel becomes tongue-tied and desperately needs the assistance of his verbally articulate propaganda minister, Garbitsch (Henry Daniell), who is always at his side.

Beyond being a penetrating and brilliant satire on Hitler and Nazism, one could also regard *The Great Dictator* as a film about identity. As Truffaut has suggested, this film, too, fits into the general scheme that characterizes Chaplin's work and is thus divided into two parts, the vagabond and the most famous man in the world.[30] In *The Great Dictator* Chaplin deals with the "identity problem" in part by choosing to play the two diametrically opposing roles in the film: the victim and the victimizer. He also uses the soundtrack, especially the speech evasion of the characters he plays, as a cinematic means of exploring the nature of their identity. The psychological split, a dominant motif in the film, has thematic parallels in the dualities of talkies versus silent films: speech and silence, speech and gibberish, and a synchronous soundtrack in combination with, or in contrast to, visual narrative.

In many scenes, Chaplin's soundtrack continues his experimentation with audio gags and his quest for the right cinematic grammar. At the beginning of the film, in the scene where the cannon fires, before the shell bursts forth, we hear a human sound much like someone clearing his throat. After that the cannon fires a dud shell. Here Chaplin personifies the cannon, by means of the soundtrack, as "diseased" or ineffective. The sound is diegetic though not realistic. Just as in his silent films, where Chaplin created montages with visual elements that do not connect with one another realistically, here he fashions an "inappropriate" soundtrack by juxtaposing the sound of the throat clearing with the picture of the cannon misfiring. Chaplin is thus expanding the audio-aesthetics he developed in his earlier work.

The firing of the cannon by the Jewish barber marks Chaplin's first appearance in this film. With his left hand, he prepares to pull the string that will fire the cannon, and with his right, he covers his ear to protect himself from the noise—as futile a gesture as it was for the Tramp in the lion's cage in *The Circus*. In other words, Chaplin is still trying to shut his ears to the threat of sound, even though he has reconciled himself to the need to open his mouth. Unlike the situation in *The Circus*, this time he is not the victim of external factors producing the dangerous sound. Here, he fully collaborates, being the one producing the menacing sound. He "carried talking pictures with one hand and protected himself from them with the other."[31]

Immediately after firing the shell, the Jewish barber falls flat on the ground, shocked by the power of the sound. When he rises, he picks up his binoculars to watch the flight of the shell. The common practice in films during this period was to juxtapose the image of the person using the binoculars pointing offscreen with a shot of the character's point of view framed through the contours of a binocular-shaped mask. Chaplin changes this pattern for a nonrealistic "audio point of view." The camera shows the distant landscape in a long shot without the binocular mask effect and with no framing of the flying shell. On the soundtrack, however, we hear the whistling of the shell as it cuts through the air. Actually, it is only by means of the soundtrack that the audience understands that the shell is indeed in flight toward its destination. The shrieking of the shell is heard only while the binoculars are pressed to the gunner's eyes and ceases the moment he lowers them from his face. This technique allows the soundtrack to establish an audio point of view in a nonrealistic way. Chaplin here develops the code he created in *City Lights,* where he uses sounds that come from an unseen source (e.g., the sound of the swallowed whistle)—in this case the sound of a flying shell that cannot be seen. By contrast, when the source of the sound *is seen* through the camera lens, the fact that the sound is not heard is even more effective. According to Chaplin's audio-cinematics, synchronous sound, which imitates reality, weakens cinema's power, whereas merely suggested "unheard sound" or heard sound from unseen sources, enhances it.

When Hynkel dictates a letter to his secretary (Nita Pike), he utters many sentences in gibberish, but she types only a single character. Hynkel is amazed but continues dictating; this time just one word, but now she begins a long run of typing on her typewriter. Again, this is a gag built on the sound-track—a cinematic representation of the fact that translation from one language to another is never direct and one-to-one but entails a transformation. Structurally, this scene is intimately related to the Hynkel macaronic speech discussed later.

In the scene of the military parade Chaplin does not show us the weapons of war, but only Hynkel and Napaloni (Mussolini) looking at the parade. The audience knows what the two are looking at through the changing soundtrack and the two onlookers' matching responses. Again, we witness the use of a nonsynchronous soundtrack and a reaction of the viewer—two elements essential to the pattern of the cinematic utterance in creating meaning while avoiding showing the object viewed. In this case, Chaplin uses the sound's function of unification, in Chion's terminology, by substituting the "heard space"[32] of the military parade for the visual spectacle of it.

Chaplin further develops the use of close-up in sound space in the scene when the Jews hide a coin in a single muffin as a way of drawing lots to determine who will go on the suicide mission to assassinate Hynkel. Hannah (Paulette Goddard) believes the plot is ridiculous and decides to thwart the scheme by hiding coins in all the muffins without their knowledge. In this amusing scene, each of the characters secretly passes his coin to someone else, with the eventual result that the Jewish barber receives all of them. Each time the barber finds another coin in his muffin, he swallows it. Chaplin treats us to a laugh at the barber's discomfort through the soundtrack when we hear the coins clinking against one another as they meet in his stomach. As in *Modern Times*, Chaplin uses a nonrealistic sound close-up here to create a funny gag that also advances the film's plot through the nonverbal information that it conveys.

Chaplin also uses music differently from the usual practice in cinema. The national anthem at the opening of *City Lights* is such an example. In *The Great Dictator*, however, there is a special use of music in the scene where the barber gives someone a shave. The radio plays Brahms' *Fifth Hungarian Rhapsody*—a rare occasion, along with his use of the Prelude to Act I of Wagner's *Lohengrin* to accompany Hynkel's globe ballet, in which Chaplin uses music other than his own—and the barber matches his shaving motions to the music. The usual practice in cinema is to fit the music to the given scene in order to add an emotional dimension to what is seen. In this case, however, Chaplin switches the order and fits the barber's functional movements to given music, thus producing a kind of modern ballet choreography. Once again, Chaplin is proposing alternative codes for connecting picture and music—codes that are particularly suited to Chaplin's cinematic language, because his cinema is often closer to dance and music than to theatrical drama.

One of the most notable examples of Chaplin's distinctive use of a soundtrack in this film occurs in the first scene, where Hynkel makes a speech in front of an aroused and cheering crowd. Hynkel's gibberish, especially in its hysterical, menacing intonation, chillingly reflects the threat of violence inherent in the distorted charisma of the dictator. Like the mayor in *City Lights*, much of his gabble is meaningless. This time, the effect is not only ludicrous but also horrifying, since Hynkel is using his rhetorical skills, conveyed to us through "tone, cadence, and accent,"[33] as well as gesticulation, to spread hate. This device artistically exposes the mechanism of totalitarian demagogy at its most effective. When we compare this scene, which seems to us absurd and ridiculous, with contemporary newsreels of Hitler's speeches, we can see astonishing parallels between the actual and parodied dictator's performance styles. And as Marco Grosoli puts it: "Hitler is himself an imitation because he 'stole' from the Tramp his unmistakable moustache."[34]

In this scene, Chaplin also expresses his attitude to cinematic sound as a means of conveying information. A radio announcer relates the content of Hynkel's speech to listeners throughout the world. His text is not a straightforward translation of the gibberish but a false description, prepared in advance, of what we see and hear, rendering the content more genial. The conspicuous comical contrast in tone between the actual speech and parallel "running commentary" for public relations and propaganda purposes vividly dramatizes the vicious deceitfulness of Hynkel's message. Thus, Hynkel's supposedly translated text turns into Chaplin's metatext, which gives a richer interpretation to the performance that we see and hear. This effect is akin to the dictation scene with the typist discussed earlier. It is also illuminating as to what happens in the transposition from one medium (audiovisual) to another (verbal), and vice versa, a point that Chaplin never fails to drive home.

In the dictator's speech, the humanized microphones bend back in reaction to the mounting aggressiveness of his delivery and then snap back at him. It appears that not only language rejects his "speech," but the public address system cannot "contain" it. Here the *machine* is humanized, as opposed to the feeding robot in *Modern Times*, which is ultimately a dumb machine. This audiovisual gag is also a unique plastic expression of the rivalry and hostility between the dictator and the media, when they fail to yield to his every whim. It furthermore reflects Chaplin's thirteen-year struggle with the soundtrack.

Also in this scene, Chaplin breaks accepted codes of soundtrack editing in order to enrich the cinematic articulation. When Hynkel raises his hand as a sign to his audience to applaud, the sound of clapping immediately reaches top volume, without the customary gradual amplification of a fade-in. In the same way, the sound ceases immediately when Hynkel gestures that it should stop, without any gradual fade-out. This nonrealistic control of the volume of the sound, which also works as an audio gag, uses the soundtrack to emphasize the dictator's absolute control over his audience. It also inverts the humanization of the microphones, this time rendering the human crowd a veritable machine. We have here another example of the unconventional way in which Chaplin plays with the rules of soundtrack editing, extends the boundaries of the language of vocal utterance, and creates a language of his own that suits the theme of his film and his artistic style.

This speech is no mere conventional gibberish, but a sophisticated variation on the emanation speech. Chaplin's sophisticated use of words, both in English and in German, illustrates what Chion classifies as loss of intelligibility[35] speech. The characters' names are used as a means of enriching the statement. The führer Adolf Hitler is transmuted by the radio voice-over into "the phooey, Adenoid Hynkel." Chaplin plays with the sound similarities and with the connotations of phooey and adenoid (polyp). Herman Göring is called Herring—a montage of "Her" from Herman and "ring" from Göring; it sounds similar and it suggests a bad smell. Joseph Goebbels is called Garbitsch, that is, trash. These last meanings are consolidated in a verbal fragment of Hynkel's gibberish speech, when he says: "Oh, Herring shouldn't smelten fine from garbitsch und Garbitsch shouldn't smelten fine from herring." This part of the speech, like other parts that are not pure gibberish, is highly effective as satire. Chaplin contrives new ways of producing meaning from words, unrelated to their informational import. He speaks macaronically, acting out language in general, as it were. Thus, Benito Mussolini is rechristened Benzino Napaloni, a montage of Benito, Napoleon, Mussolini, and polony (sausage); Italy is Bacteria, a montage of Bactria of Alexander's empire and the microorganism. Austria becomes Osterlich, which alludes to the bird ostrich and echoes Austerlitz, the famous Austrian defeat to Napoleon.[36] Finally, the "double cross," substituting for the swastika, obviously connotes betrayal (double-crossing). The satirical distortion of names in itself is more literary than cinematic; nevertheless, here these names punctuate the gibberish, as do the few real words sprinkled here and there. Thus, we can see that although the scene is more similar in character to silent cinema than to the talkies, its soundtrack is rich and innovative in its use of sound, vocabulary, and cinematic grammar.

The second time that Hynkel makes a speech, again in gibberish, occurs mostly off-camera. That is, we hear the dictator's roars of gibberish, but we *see* a close-up of the loudspeaker—the mechanical mediator—through which the speech is being transmitted and the hysterical responses of the Jews in the ghetto. Conspicuous is the response of the Jewish barber, who jumps in horror headfirst into a barrel. Besides being a developed variation on the barber blocking his ear in the cannon scene earlier in the film, this ostrich-like image recalls Chaplin's self-irony projected in the lion cage scene in *The Circus*. In this specific context, it is also suggestive of the world's reaction to Hitler's speeches—figuratively burying its head in the ground.

At a critical moment toward the film's conclusion, Chaplin sheds his disguises—the disguises of Hynkel, of the Jewish barber, of the Tramp, and of an actor. Simultaneously, he finally discards the last barrier to sound from himself as artist. Chaplin gives his own monologue. He is shown in close-up, without his traditional Tramp makeup, his gray hair and his wrinkles giving away his true age (fifty-one). He sends the world an unequivocal message, the absolute opposite of gibberish, the complete and crystalline, universal and humanistic worldview of Chaplin the man. This speech is well articulated. He speaks in favor of resistance to tyranny and of refusal to obey arbitrary orders opposed to basic human laws, orders that serve unjust people and allow humans to rule and trample one another. This speech affirms freedom, human solidarity, love, and tolerance. If at the end of *Modern Times* Chaplin had surrendered to the need to use his voice to show us that he could also sing, at the end of *The Great Dictator* he surrenders to the need to use meaningful words.

Having thoroughly mastered the cinematic meaning of sound and having explored the creative possibilities of a "nonverbal" soundtrack for thirteen years in four films, Chaplin now articulately uses words with great ease and permits himself an especially long monologue, which is not customary in cinema. This extraordinary monologue, transcending the fictional confines of the film, serves to convey the extreme urgency of the message. It emphasizes the importance of the issues and the feeling that in order to stop Hitler it is necessary to make use of every means available, including words, which until now have not been among his artistic means of expression.

ASSIMILATION

Indeed, Chaplin's next film arrives seven years later, and this time it is talking cinema in every sense: *Monsieur Verdoux* (1948). Here, it seems that Chaplin has fully mastered the new medium of audiovisual illusion. He has fully assimilated the new medium, no longer struggling with verbal communication. He has finally adopted the conventional language of talking cinema. His new products constitute a synthesis between his unique artistic language and the prevailing codes of talkies. In this sense, his first "conventional" realistic talking film lends appropriate perspective to his long experimentation with and development of sound in cinema. I illustrate this claim by pointing out three scenes in which sound is used along the lines we have traced so far.

The first murder we see, by the serial killer Henri Verdoux (Charlie Chaplin), is conveyed by cinematic means that Chaplin had previously developed in *City Lights*.[37] Verdoux takes Lydia Floray (Margaret Hoffman), his first victim, to the bedroom while reciting his regular seduction speech. As she enters the room, he lurks outside by the window. Lydia goes on with the realistic dialogue while Verdoux's monologue suddenly waxes poetic—stylistically out of character. Here Chaplin uses two contrasting modes of speech to heighten tension in view of the impending murder, an audiovisual counterpoint. As Verdoux enters the room, the camera remains outside in the corridor for a while. The romantic music now switches to horror music and is cut abruptly. The soundtrack is completely silenced. The corridor night shot dissolves into the same corridor in an early morning shot, and the chirping of birds is heard on the soundtrack. This maneuver employs another audiovisual counterpoint, more mimetic than that in *Modern Times*, because in this case birds could possibly be outside the window. Here the sound effect whose origin is offscreen (sound punctuation) serves as a counterpoint to the extradiegetic music that precedes it. The combination of the empty corridor with total silence is a very powerful "audio-image" that obliquely points to the murder that is taking place behind the door.

When Annabella Bonheur (Martha Raye) appears at Verdoux's wedding,[38] jeopardizing his conspiracy by exposing his imposture and fraud, she first appears in the form of a threatening sound.[39] Both the audience and Verdoux hear her distinctively vulgar laughter before she is actually seen in the crowd. Again, Chaplin uses the sound synecdochically, as a foreboding of horror; he emphasizes and exaggerates it to a nonrealistic degree; the sound of what cannot be seen is intended to enrich the scene, to raise the tension, and it certainly creates an audiovisual macabre gag.

Finally, the last unexpected encounter between the totally defeated Verdoux and the girl (Marilyn Nash), the only purported victim for whom he has a soft spot, resonates with the final scene of *City Lights*. Beside the common narrative motifs, this scene in *Monsieur Verdoux* is styled as a silent film piece within a conventional talking film.[40] The woman who became rich is behind the window of a fancy car, watching Verdoux, who at this point seems completely devastated. He moves his lips, talking inaudibly, while she is heard talking from the car very realistically. This semi-silent nonverbal scene powerfully expresses the characters' love for each other, which they are unable to realize, since they are unable to overcome Verdoux's tragic flaw. Also, the woman's ability to talk contrasted with Verdoux's corresponding disability not only brings him back to the "Tramp" position, but also audibly expresses their new reversed positions—a twisted variation, in both sound and mise-en-scène, on the factory bathroom scene in *Modern Times*, where the factory manager speaks from the screen to the mute tramp. As usual, the active-passive talking relationship mirrors the power hierarchy.

Thus, *Monsieur Verdoux* well attests to the applicability of Chaplin's innovative use of sound to any talking picture (e.g., Chion's list above, Hitchcock's *Frenzy*, Bergman's *Hour of the Wolves*) beyond the four films discussed here.

CONCLUSION

Four years later, in *Limelight*, Chaplin reverts to the subject that had never ceased to engage him since 1928. If *The Circus* is a requiem for the clown—a film that sums up silent cinema—then *Limelight* sums up the totality of Chaplin's cinematic oeuvre. It is a requiem for the artist who is still making films but feels that the end is already imminent and it is time for a farewell. In Rachel Joseph's words, "Calvero rehearses his eventual disappearance."[41]

In the final scene of *Limelight*, Calvero (Charles Chaplin) and his partner (Buster Keaton) put on a skit, playing the parts of two musicians trying unsuccessfully to perform a violin and piano duet. Tuning their instruments, they get into trouble that leads to absurd states of loss of control, trampling on the violin and pulling out the piano strings. After their instruments are completely destroyed, the piano is miraculously well tuned without the wrenched-out strings, Calvero, like a magician, pulls out a new violin from behind him and plays it masterfully and most expressively. Keaton accompanies him with matching grace and technique. The wonderful duet ends with Calvero's premeditated falling off the stage into the band's big drum. In this scene, the gags are all built around the struggle with the sound-emitting musical instruments. Keaton and Calvero are overwhelmed by the preparatory tasks of setting up the music notes and tuning their instruments. In spite of anticipating the tuning problem—they even have a tuning wrench and a wire cutter—the powerful piano and the delicate violin seem at first to be too much for them to cope with. They lose control. The humanized instruments "behave" like a monstrous enemy. With unrelenting thoroughness and persistence they stretch their instruments beyond their limits, until the violin and piano strings all snap. They seem to be taking the piano apart to get at its secrets and not out of sheer rage. Only after the instruments are destroyed and the men have suffered blows and humiliations through them do they gain control over them, seduce them like lovers, bend them to their will and needs, and finally perform brilliantly. They do not ignore sound and are not helpless before it. They investigate it like true artists, struggle with it until they master it, and then use it in the best way—just as Chaplin himself did in all his earlier films, as we saw earlier. But at this climactic moment, the triumphant performance having been achieved (self-reflectively, it is this very film), that is also the moment to bow out. One has to step off the stage. This powerful moment is a turning point inspired by the insight that their original art form has passed away, and cinema has actually become a new art that is alien to them. They belong to a generation that no longer exists. However painful, Chaplin resigns to this reality of being passé and kills Calvero as Calvero killed his stage persona in the premeditated gag. Once more, like in *The Great Dictator*'s final scene, the character and its mirrored reflection become one and they both reflect the filmmaker Charles Chaplin. Highly significant is the way Calvero dies, to wit, amid performing—surely, an actor's dream. Yet his actual deathbed in the gag devised by Calvero, which turns out to be Calvero's *real* death, is none other than the big drum. The most delicate instrument, his violin, in his hand, he dies in the drum that represents the roughest and most aggressive sound in the orchestra. Of course, Calvero in the film looks as Chaplin did in 1952, but in his dreams, Calvero appears as the Tramp in his typical costume. In this final scene, however, Calvero is dressed in semi-Tramp garb, and side-by-side with his partner Buster Keaton, the spectacle is that of the two great old masters of slapstick and silent cinema.

NOTES

1. David Robinson, *The History of World Cinema* (New York: Stein and Day, 1981), 168–70.

2. Michel Chion, *Audio-Vision: Sound on Screen*, trans. Claudia Gorbman (New York: Columbia University Press, 1994), 5.

3. The use of the term talking-silent film requires a careful examination of the difference between a stylized talking-silent film and poor acting in a talking picture. Consistency and unit of style are key elements here, but this issue is beyond the scope of this chapter.

4. Michel Chion, *The Voice in Cinema*, trans. Claudia Gorbman (New York: Columbia University Press, 1999), 12.

5. Chion, *The Voice in Cinema*, 102.

6. Chion, *The Voice in Cinema*, 131.

7. Kay Dickinson, ed., *Movie Music, The Film Reader* (London: Routledge, 2003), 2.

8. Adrian Daub, "Hannah, Can You Hear Me?—Chaplin's *Great Dictator*, 'Schtonk,' and the Vicissitudes of Voice," *Criticism* 51, no. 3 (summer 2009): 452.

9. Daub, "Hannah, Can You Hear Me?" 452.

10. This gag is transformed into the Tramp's swallowing the whistle in *City Lights*, the Tramp's stomach rumblings in *Modern Times*, and the Jewish barber swallowing the coins in *The Great Dictator*.

11. Rachel Joseph, "Chaplin's Presence," 121.

12. Chion, *Audio-Vision*, 49.

13. Chion, *Audio-Vision*, 49.

14. Robert. C. Allen and Douglas Gomery, *Film History: Theory and Practice* (New York: McGraw-Hill, 1985), 91–104.

15. Charles Chaplin, *My Autobiography* (New York: Simon and Schuster, 1964), 382–83.

16. Chaplin, *My Autobiography*, 382–83.

17. Marco Grosoli, "The Paradox of the 'Dictator': Mimesis, Logic of Paradox, and the Reinstatement of Catharsis in *The Great Dictator*, *Monsieur Verdoux*, and *Limelight*," 154.

18. Chaplin writes that he created the soundtrack of this scene using his own voice and an instrument in his mouth. Charles Chaplin, *My Life in Pictures* (New York: Grosset & Dunlap, 1974), 34.

19. Chion, *Audio-Vision*, 176.

20. Chion, *Audio-Vision*, 12.

21. Chion, *Audio-Vision*, 177.

22. Chion, *Audio-Vision*, 177.

23. Chion, *Audio-Vision*, 42–43.

24. Chion, *Audio-Vision*, 56–57.

25. Orwell's *1984* was published in 1948 but the origin of this image is probably in Fritz Lang's *Metropolis* (1926).

26. Chion, *Audio-Vision*, 38.

27. Chaplin, *My Autobiography*, 329.

28. Benjamin Click, "Chaplin's Sound Statement on Silence: *The Great Dictator* as Rhetorical Encomium," 192.

29. Grosoli, "The Paradox of the 'Dictator,'" 141.

30. François Truffaut, *The Films in My Life*, trans. Leonard Mayhew (New York: Simon and Schuster, 1978), 62.

31. Paraphrasing Nehemiah, 4:11.

32. Chion, *Audio-Vision*, 47.

33. Daub, "Hannah, Can You Hear Me?" 451–52.

34. Grosoli, "The Paradox of the 'Dictator,'" 141.

35. Chion, *Audio-Vision*, 177.

36. This observation I owe to Odeya Kohen-Raz, "The Ethics of 'Contra-Lying' in Narrative Holocaust Films," in *Just Images: Ethics and the Cinematic*, ed. Boaz Hagin, Sandra Meiri, Raz Yosef, and Anat Zanger (Newcastle: Cambridge Scholars Publishing, 2011), 167.

37. Charles Chaplin, *Monsieur Verdoux*, France, 1948, 0:22:47–0:28:38.

38. Chaplin, *Monsieur Verdoux*, 1:31:50.

39. Chaplin, *Monsieur Verdoux*, 1:32:20.

40. Chaplin, *Monsieur Verdoux*, 1:41:50.

41. Joseph, "Chaplin's Presence," 131.

Chapter Ten

Chaplin's Sound Statement on Silence

The Great Dictator *as Rhetorical Encomium*

Benjamin Click

"The world awaits your word." "You must speak." "You must. It's our only hope." These are the last three lines spoken to a Jewish barber reluctantly impersonating a ruthless dictator about to address a conquered nation. These lines also applied to Charlie Chaplin, the actor who played the roles of the unnamed Jewish barber and the dictator Adenoid Hynkel in his first full talkie, *The Great Dictator* (1940). Begun in 1937 and released in 1940, the film marked Chaplin's last great critical as well as commercial success. With its release, the world literally did await Chaplin's first spoken word. Presented with this situation, Chaplin enjoyed what rhetoricians would call a kairotic[1] or timely moment to make an argument about the strengths and limitations of the spoken word, and *The Great Dictator* needs to be read rhetorically as such.

Although it has been praised as an antiwar satire, examined as a forerunner of propaganda films that would proliferate in the American cinema during World War II, and generally recognized as Chaplin's belated acceptance of the talking picture—and it *is* all of these things—*The Great Dictator* should also be read as a specific form of rhetoric, epideictic rhetoric.[2]

The classical concept of epideictic rhetoric, as summarized by rhetorical theorists Chaïm Perelman and Lucie Olbrechts-Tyteca, was speech concerned with praise or blame on topics "apparently not controversial and without practical consequences." Such speeches were often "the central attraction at festivals" and their efficaciousness was "assessed as a work of artistic virtuosity."[3] Unlike forensic oratory that sought audience adherence in matters of guilt or innocence regarding a past act, or deliberative oratory that sought adherence on the course of action for a future policy, epideictic oratory was concerned with praise or blame with regard to a present state of affairs. The speaker's interest lay in what was beautiful or ugly.

Perelman and Olbrechts-Tyteca, however, claim a greater argumentative significance for the epideictic genre than it had previously been afforded, asserting that it "forms a central part of the art of persuasion" designed to "secure a proper degree of adherence from the audience" regarding "particular values recognized by that audience." Originally the ancients "readily confused the concept of the beautiful, as the object of the speech . . . with the aesthetic value of the speech itself." Perelman and Olbrechts-Tyteca convincingly argue that the effectiveness of the speech is not based solely on aesthetic beauty of the speech (artistic virtuosity), but on the argumentative "aims the speaker has set himself" and how well he or she established a sense of communion centered on those particular recognized values. Therefore, epideictic rhetoric has "significance and importance for argumentation, because it strengthens the disposition toward action by increasing adherence to the values it lauds."[4] Granted, epideictic rhetoric was and is often denigrated as a less consequential and merely belletristic form of rhetoric, but Perelman and Olbrechts-Tyteca disagree. They claim this form to be more central to a twentieth-century New Rhetoric because the "recognized values" are more in dispute and in need of definition (or of being made up) in a larger and more diverse society.

Thus, on one level, I argue that Chaplin delivers *The Great Dictator* as a form of epideictic rhetoric, implicitly and deftly praising silence, censuring sound, and promoting the values engendered by silent film—beauty and unity without totalizing effect. I employ Kenneth Burke's concepts of rhetorical identification and perspective by incongruity to illustrate how Chaplin cautions against an unpleasing aesthetic embodied by vocalized language in film and the potential dangers of speech. His rhetoric seems to imbue silence with an annealing authority to repair the "state of Babel after the Fall," to use Burke's terms as analogous to the state of silent film since the advent of the talkie.[5] However, Chaplin encounters a dilemma. The moments of beauty and unity that he creates through silence seem unsustainable by silence alone as the film progresses.

Thus, on another level, I show how Chaplin works to resolve the dilemma created by his affinity for pantomime and the audience expectation that he embrace the talking mode of the changing industry. My analysis reveals that, in struggling with this dilemma, Chaplin provides a complex representation of the possible corruption of speech and the underappreciated virtues of speech and ultimately recognizes the potential dangers of imposed and voluntary silence as well. By the film's conclusion, punctuated by Chaplin's stunning speech for humanity and followed by the coda of "Look Up, Hannah,"[6] Chaplin resolves the seemingly inescapable and agonistic binary that exists between his aesthetic sensibilities and those of the talkie, thus reconciling his own ambivalence about the potential for both to coexist.

My argument proceeds in three stages. First, applying classical and contemporary rhetorical thought, I contextualize the film's release as a kairotic moment for Chaplin—explaining how the film can simultaneously function as deliberative as well as epideictic rhetoric. Next, employing the film's narrative as the rhetorical structure of an argument, I analyze how Chaplin juxtaposes scenes of silence and sound to make his statement on the value of silence and the dangers of language. Last, applying recent scholarship on the rhetoric of silence and rhetorical listening, I examine the film's last scene, focusing on the concluding speech as a final unifying moment. This application reveals Chaplin's last appeal to the value of silence, the potential uses of speech, and the possibilities of unifying the two mediums without diminishing the *beauty* of silent film and the *vitality* of the talkie, terms that Chaplin ascribed to each medium respectively.

FROM DELIBERATIVE TO EPIDEICTIC RHETORIC: RHETORICAL CONTEXT AND KAIROS OF *THE GREAT DICTATOR*

The film's opening announces its kairotic moment—what classical rhetoric defines as situational time, an opportunity or moment to address a specific and timely issue: "This is the story of a period between the two World Wars—an interim in which Insanity cut loose. Liberty took a nose dive, and Humanity was kicked around somewhat." The syntax of the line and its casual diction personifying abstract concepts imply the film's comic intent and its rhetorical goal of restoring the usurped values of sanity, liberty, and humanity. The line also transparently glosses the rise of fascism and its stronghold in Europe, evinced by Hitler's Nazi Party at the time of the film's release, October 1940. Understandably, film and cultural historians as well as biographers focus on the deliberative motive of *The Great Dictator*. They reconstruct the film's historical moment of emergence and reception, illuminating America's resistance to the war and tracing the film's censorship problems from the Hays Office as a result of its overt political message. Thus, they see the film as a form of political rhetoric effecting some influence and future action by those in public office.[7]

In terms of audience, then, *The Great Dictator* functions as what Burke calls a "kind of timely topic, such as that of the satirical cartoon, which exploits commonplaces of a transitory nature."[8] Like the satirical cartoon, the film derives its deliberative persuasiveness because its audience lives "under one particular set of circumstances," therefore making "certain images more persuasive in one situation than another."[9] For example, as anti-war satire, the film parodies the "certain images" of real-life events and characters that rely on the commonplace ideology of war's ridiculousness: misunderstandings between nations, obstinate world leaders, blind adherence of the masses, misguided subordinates of an evil dictator, obscene war machines (Big Bertha), and absurd combat gear (a faulty bulletproof suit, a parachute hat that doesn't open). Character parodies were obvious to the viewers at the time. Hynkel is Hitler, Benzino Napaloni (Jack Oakie) is Mussolini, Marshall Herring (Billy Gilbert) is Hermann Goering, Propaganda Minister Garbitsch (Henry Daniell) is Joseph Goebbels; Tomania is Germany; Bacteria is Italy; Osterlich is Austria; Tomania's ghetto residents were Jews of Nazi Germany.

Through his comic artistry, in particular ridicule, Chaplin tempers the harsh reality of the subject matter as in his two silent films in the age of talkies (i.e., the dehumanization of the factory worker in *Modern Times* [1936] and poverty in *City Lights* [1931]). By the release of *The Great Dictator*, filmgoers had witnessed "certain images" of the harsh reality of Nazism through newsreels: Hitler exhorting crowds at the Nuremburg rallies, German Panzer tanks rolling into Poland, victory parades in Warsaw, and German soldiers marching past the Arc de Triomphe. For some critics, ridicule hardly seemed a fitting response. Of course, only later did Chaplin realize the film's nearly inappropriate kairotic (and political) moment of release: "Had I known the actual horrors of the German concentration camps, I could not have made *The Great Dictator*."[10]

Political rhetoric has long employed ridicule as a rhetorical device. The epideictic genre uses it as well because it can condemn "eccentric behavior which is not deemed sufficiently important or dangerous to be repressed by more violent means."[11] Thus, Chaplin's ignorance of the Nazi's "bestial murders and tortures" and his urging of Roosevelt, after the film's release, to immediately open a second front in Europe, lessens the claim that he used ridicule solely to effect some future policy action. Rather, its use suggests a broader and subtler rhetorical project—an encomium to silent film: one that ridicules the insidious uses of speech and reveals the impotence of such uses to bring about unity without a totalizing effect.

While some regard *The Great Dictator* as antiwar satire, others see it as a precursor to World War II propaganda films. For example, historian Robert Cole views Chaplin as a "natural propagandist" and "political idealist determined to make the world see its problems and their solutions from his point of view."[12] However, a rhetorical understanding of the uses of propaganda clarifies the epideictic aspects of the film. Rhetorically speaking, *The Great Dictator* is not this extreme form of deliberative rhetoric because by its conclusion the audience faces no real controversy about either the values that Chaplin promotes or what action it should take. Moreover, the temporal distinction between deliberative and epideictic rhetoric further supports Chaplin's epideictic motives. Deliberative rhetoric is concerned with future action, epideictic with the present. The former seeks action to be taken; the latter seeks to "increase the intensity of adherence to the values held in common by the audience and the speaker."[13] Promoting values of broad appeal in his films, at most, Chaplin believed that "laughter [could] help check the— the— the bad behavior in the world."[14] Politically speaking, *The Great Dictator* may have increased its audience's adherence to the values of democracy, but it did little to move them toward action. It would take Pearl Harbor for that. Not surprisingly, Chaplin, the entertainer, downplayed any propaganda aspect of the film in a 1940 interview: "But don't think for a moment that I am trying to sell propaganda. I am far too experienced a showman to believe that anyone will pay his way into a theatre to be preached at."[15]

The distinction that Perelman and Olbrechts-Tyteca make between the propagandist and the educator also illuminates Chaplin's epideictic motives. Unlike the propagandist who must initially "gain the good will of his audience," the educator is "commissioned by the community to be the spokesperson for the values it recognizes, and, as such, enjoys the prestige attaching to his office."[16] Chaplin had already gained the good will of his audience, and he enjoyed the prestige of being silent film's greatest star. Possessing such status, he successfully resisted making a film in which *he* talked. In discussing *City Lights*, Chaplin states, "I was determined to continue making silent films, . . . and that as a pantomime, and in that medium I was unique and without false modesty, a master."[17] His "master" status, combined with the fact that no other American filmmaker produced a successful critical and creative feature-length silent film during the 1930s, ensured his prestige. In a sense, then, with *The Great Dictator*, Chaplin assumes the role of educator who "promotes the values he is upholding," values forged in twenty-five years of making silent film.

As a "master" pantomime and entertainer/educator, Chaplin seems at least as interested in the values engendered in that art as in persuading political bodies to dispense with appeasement and isolationism, especially given that Hollywood "discreetly avoided making overt anti-Nazi films," and a Gallup poll showed "96 per cent opposition to America's entry into a war."[18] The epideictic rhetor predominantly promotes "the values that are shared in the community [because] no immediate practical interest is ever involved."[19] However, the absence of a practical interest only partially diverts us from the ostensible political motive of the film. The question of shared values still remains, with the difficulty of assuming that the movie-going public aligned with Chaplin regarding the values of silent cinema.

At the start of 1931, Chaplin realized that the talkie had "come to stay," that it "had more vitality than silent film, though less beauty."[20] His early recognition of the staying power of the talkie created an exigence for Chaplin to find a way to achieve the beauty of silent film while maintaining the vitality of the talkie. *The Great Dictator* would be that unifying device.[21]

Movie audiences wanted the "vitality"[22] that sound cinema offered. Even if the question of whether "the 'little fella,' voiced or unvoiced, was becoming archaic in the rapidly changing social climate of the 1930s,"[23] Chaplin was still a major star at the end of the decade. Thus, the issue of shared values slightly complicates the understanding of rhetorical motive—but only slightly. The concept of a "universal audience," what Perelman calls "all of humanity, or at least all those who are competent and reasonable," assists us here.[24] He distinguishes between particular and universal audiences, asserting that the speaker addressing a particular audience "might rely on arguments that are foreign or even directly opposed to what is acceptable to persons other than those he is presently addressing."[25] He recognizes the apparent danger of a "composite audience" (universal audience) because the speaker "has to resolve into its constituent parts for the purposes of argumentation."[26] In a sense, for twenty years, Chaplin needed only to be the prestigious spokesperson of his medium for him to gain adherence with the universal audience—he was an iconic, international star. But with synchronized sound in film, the universal audience had shifted. Chaplin would have to accommodate them by speaking in movies, and he would rely on his status to promote the values previously shared when the medium was essentially silent.

What then are the values that the community has entrusted its prestigious spokesperson to promote? Those engendered and best conveyed by what Chaplin found most valuable in silent film: beauty and unity. More specifically, Chaplin's particular audience anticipates the typical emotional binaries of the beautiful and the ugly at the forefront of his films—good/evil, gentleness/harshness, community/division, democracy/authoritarianism. For Chaplin and his audience, pantomime most effectively and emotively expressed those values. There exists a universal, unifying quality in pantomime; its beauty transcends vocalized language. It circumvents language barriers, allowing all to witness and appreciate its beauty. Chaplin understood this. In a 1925 interview, Chaplin said, "Where words leave off, gesture begins . . . the final motions of the soul are speechless . . . of an incomparable beauty."[27] But by 1931, Chaplin realized that the talkie had "more vitality" than silent film, even if it had "less beauty."[28] Moreover, he knew that the Tramp was becoming "less purely comic than he used to be" and was "growing more and more human."[29] Although the claim refers to the Tramp in *City Lights*, it pertains to my argument because it suggests the limitations Chaplin faced in employing pantomime to express the full range of human emotion. He resolves those limitations in *The Great Dictator*'s conclusion by transitioning from the actor playing the all-but-silent barber in order to deliver a speech for humanity.

To undertake the analysis of how Chaplin promotes these values, we can view the narrative structure of the film as following the rhetorical structure of argument: exordium (introduction), narration (statement of the issue), proof, and conclusion. Chaplin uses the opening intertitles and first scene on the battlefield as his introduction; the headline montage that follows showing passage of time and the newsreel narrator as his statement of the issue; scenes juxtaposing synchronized voices with silent film staples as his proof; and the film's final two scenes, the humanity speech followed by the "Look Up, Hannah" coda, as his conclusion.

EXORDIUM (AN INTRODUCTION) AND STATING THE CASE: THE TRAMP REMAINS SILENT

The first two intertitles and the opening scene with the Jewish barber introduce the epideictic discourse that will follow. Like Quintillian's "good man speaking well," Chaplin, an icon—reputable and trustworthy—relies on audience recognition of his film ethos to tacitly understand the irony of the first intertitle: "Note: Any resemblance between Hynkel and the Jewish barber is purely coincidental." Nothing about the resemblance is coincidental—it is purposeful mimesis. However, the Chaplin/Hitler resemblance belies the complexity of playing the dual role, as explored in Marco Grosoli's essay in this book, "The Paradox of the 'Dictator': Mimesis, the Logic of Paradox, and the Reinstatement of Catharsis in *The Great Dictator*, *Monsieur Verdoux*, and *Limelight*." Grosoli shows how Aristotelian second-order mimesis extends beyond, yet relies on, resemblance to show the paradox of Chaplin the myth (persona) and Chaplin the person (141–145). As in his previous films, the emotional binaries of the beautiful and the ugly play out in this one as well with one difference: Chaplin represents and performs both the beautiful (the barber) and the ugly (Hynkel). The audience will be drawn to the gentle, endearing, and innocent barber and repelled by the ridiculous, ferocious, and pernicious Hynkel.

The next intertitle identifies what has been censured and implies what needs to be praised. Censuring the virtues is vice; restoring them is virtue. Insanity has "cut loose." Liberty has taken a "nose dive." And humanity has been "kicked around somewhat." The fate of liberty and humanity, staple values of Chaplin films, is at stake. Thus, these intertitles imply the question: what has threatened these broad and abstract values and brought about such insanity? Restoring them brings unity, and sanity returns. This second intertitle suggests the complexity of the value of unity. It calls attention to our common humanity, which Chaplin later pleads for in his speech to the citizens of Osterlich. Moreover, to deliver that plea Chaplin must step out of character, thus achieving a unity of persona wherein silent film's greatest actor finds his place in the talkie.

The film then moves to its opening scene and responds to the aesthetic question Chaplin's audience have tacitly been asking: "how will silent film's greatest star be heard in synchronized sound?" Chaplin realized, "To talk he [the Tramp] would have to step off his pedestal, the pedestal of silent film."[30] But Chaplin wouldn't allow it; thus, the voice of the mythic Tramp figure, manifested in part by the barber, is stifled throughout *The Great Dictator*. The mistaken identity element of the film allowed Chaplin to incorporate the art of silent film through both the barber and Hynkel. But it is his rhetorical choice of *how* to keep the Tramp figure silent that gives celebratory power to silent film. Throughout the film, the barber is commanded to speak and has no audience to hear; he is silenced by others as a way to highlight the beauty of silent film; he is questioned but kept from answering; and he is asked to remain silent (until the final scene). In terms of speech, the barber is passive to others' voices. His scant utterances are either truncated or reduced to mere monosyllabic words—sometimes directly placed there by outside agents.

Throughout the opening war scene, reminiscent of *Shoulder Arms*, the barber speaks sparingly, in short, sometimes barely audible responses ("Yes sir," "What's that?" "Sorry sir," "Capitan? Whowho?"). Moreover, he performs several silent film bits: dancing with an undetonated bomb, riding an antiaircraft gun as if on a mechanical bull, fumbling with a live grenade, inadequately shouldering arms, and hanging upside down from a plane's open cockpit.

The barber's lengthier, yet still short, vocal responses highlight the comic incongruity of inappropriate vocal responses amid the backdrop of war. For example, when Colonel Schultz (Reginald Gardiner) asks, "Comrade, help," when he is injured after being shot down, the barber politely replies, "Only too glad to oblige, sir." This scene gives way to one of the film's great iconic moments, one that effectively combines silent pantomiming with synchronized sound—the upside-down plane scene. It contains vaudevillian wordplay ("General Smelloffel") and several language gags—Colonel Schultz: "How's the gas?" (concerned whether his plane has enough fuel to make it to friendly territory.) The Barber: "Kept me up all night." The verbal humor enhances the pantomiming that it accompanies through humorous incongruity. The audience sees the plane rolling, but it appears to right itself. However, when they witness the barber's pocket watch floating skyward and water from a canteen flowing upward, they realize the plane is flying upside down. This is followed by another incongruity in which verbal humor complements pantomime. The barber hangs upside down from a plane about to crash while making quizzical faces as Colonel Schultz waxes eloquent about Tomania in the spring with "Hilda tending the daffodils." This opening scene ends with the barber in the army hospital suffering from amnesia, literally out of the picture and silent.

The introduction of the film offers a concession to the talkies because Chaplin uses synchronized sound to speak. Rhetorically, it accommodates the expectations of both universal and particular audiences by presenting the ethos of its speaker—Chaplin the beloved silent film star. It's a standard ethical appeal to establish, or, in this case, maintain the reputation/character of the rhetor (good will, good character, and good sense). For the remainder of the film, the barber often refrains from speaking, even though he has the opportunity to speak freely when he returns to his home in the Jewish ghetto, and eventually becomes silent by film's end.

As the dramatic action of the first scene ends, the statement of the issue emerges; Chaplin introduces the case for the dangers of speech, implicitly calling for its censure. The narrator states stentoriously, "Hynkel, the dictator, ruled the nation with an iron fist. Under the new emblem of the double cross, liberty was banished, free speech was suppressed, and only the voice of Hynkel was heard." Thus, the narrative structure of the film sets up the need to restore liberty, free speech, and polyphonic voices of all people.

PROOFS: BURKE'S "PERSPECTIVE BY INCONGRUITY" AND PANTOMIMIC ATOM CRACKING

From this point on, the film juxtaposes silence and sound within and between both Hynkel's and the barber's scenes (the two never meet). Chaplin's juxtaposition exemplifies Burke's concept of "perspective by incongruity," a term he employed "for understanding human motive in forming and reforming congregations."[31] It "designates one way of transcending a given order," "refers to the methodic merger of particles that had been considered mutually exclusive," "merg[es] categories once felt to be mutually exclusive," "see[s] two angles at once."[32] As an analytical tool specifically applied to language, it is "a method for gauging situations by verbal 'atom cracking' wherein you wrench a word loose from one category and apply it to a different category."[33] As a conscious and systematic tool of persuasion of or identification with an audience, it is a "planned incongruity." Burke values its use in combating Thorstein Veblen's concept of "trained incapacity," that "state of affairs whereby one's very abilities can function as blindnesses."[34] Specifically, in order to analyze how the juxtapositions work, we should apply how Burke connects Veblen's trained incapacity to Dewey's notion of occupational psychosis. Basically, occupational psychosis refers to the ways in which individuals or groups orient themselves by obeying the "thought patterns" of their occupational interests, thereby becoming incapable of recognizing other possible thought patterns. But perspective by incongruity can

suddenly introduce other patterns, breaking up their entrenched mental habits. In other words, social environment reflects a society's method of production and can go unchecked without perspective by incongruity.

This same relationship influences the production of cultural works. A.
Bowdoin Van Riper's "In the Shadow of Machines: *Modern Times* and the
Iconography of Technology" examines the complexity (and reflexivity) of
that relationship in his analysis of *Modern Times*, referencing the photography of Lewis Hines and WPA murals as examples. Chaplin, however, resisted the impulse to follow rapid technological advancement in American
society that became synonymous with methods of production in film (incorporating synchronized sound). In a sense, then, Chaplin applies aspects of
silence to the scenes of talk to expose the occupational psychosis of the
thoroughgoing genre of the talkie. Such application reorients audience perspective through the incongruity. For Chaplin, the talkies represented Veblen's concept of "trained incapacity" in that the very ability to use synchronized sound distracted its audience from the unifying beauty of silent
film. Thus, Chaplin's planned incongruity of juxtaposing silence (pantomime) and sound (speech) moves audiences *out of* their customary habits of
perception now engrained by twelve years of talkies and *into* remembering
the art of the silent film. But realizing the inevitable permanency of the
talkie, Chaplin offers a solution to the occupational psychosis created by both
the talking film and Hitler's rhetoric—a solution employing both sound and
silence.

Chaplin relies on perspective by incongruity throughout *The Great Dictator*, structuring it to alternate between moments of silence and moments of
sound. He wrenches loose both pantomimic image and vocal utterance from
their typical categories—pantomime belongs in silent film, vocal utterance to
talking film. In doing so, he reveals the difference between "breaking up"
mental categories and totalizing. Thus, perspective by incongruity bridges
different orientations while also (and by) breaking up the already totalized
worldviews entailed by those orientations. Burke recognized that "the practiced rhetorician relies greatly upon images to affect men's ideation."[35] Chaplin, as the practiced pantomime, realizes the same. At times, he fuses pantomime and speech into one scene in order to "see two angles at once." At
others, he employs them separately. In doing either, he theoretically helps his
audience gauge situations involving speech's aesthetic and real-world use.

After the accommodations that satisfy audience expectation and curiosity
in the opening war scene, the second scene, Hynkel's initial speech, disturbs
both the beauty of the silent routines as well as the gentle and humorous
vocal performance of the barber. It begins with a five-minute tour de force of
Chaplin burlesquing the macaronic vocal ranting and strident physical gestures of Hitler. The scene simultaneously incorporates speech and pantomime. Both the war scene and Hynkel's speech induce laughter, but it is the

audience's gauging of the situation that affords Chaplin's planned incongruity its epideictic power. Chaplin as the barber reinforces the aesthetic and communal values the audience expects from him, and his pantomimic virtuosity produces intimacy and a vast range of emotions. Juxtaposing sound with silence amplifies those values by giving the audience what it had *not* ever heard—Chaplin talking. Although we hear the barber talk, we are not disturbed by the sound. We feel quite differently when we hear Hynkel's voice.

As Richard Schickel notes, the vocal parodying of Hitler was not technically difficult for Chaplin: "Almost every comedian of his era could talk 'Dutch'—long, nonsense speeches featuring a few recognizable German words . . . and a lot of gutturals."[36] The silent pantomiming that supplements Hynkel's speech works much like the rhetorical figure of accumulation wherein scattered points are brought together and listed. Chaplin brings together a list of pantomimic standards to accompany the verbal utterance of Hynkel's speech: Hynkel pouring water down his pants, tightening his belt, wiping mock tears from his eyes with his tie, cradling an imaginary Aryan baby, fluttering eyes and fondling imaginary locks in mock imitation of the Aryan maiden, being manipulated by the microphone (reminiscent of the physical manipulation of the feeding machine from *Modern Times*), pouring water in the ear and spitting it out the mouth, and ending the speech with the standard pratfall down a flight of stairs. The abundance of silent, comic moments work incongruously with Hynkel's condemnatory shouts of "die Juden," and the harrowing grunting and groaning.

Another layer of the pantomime/speech juxtaposition is at play throughout the scene—one that further exposes the potential dangers of speech. The voice-over translation of Hynkel's rant euphemizes Hynkel's inflammatory rhetoric, which calls for domination of Europe and the world, parsing the statement into: "In conclusion, the Phooey remarks that for the rest of the world, he has nothing but peace in his heart." The verbal incongruity points out the ability of language to deceive—what is actually said is not what is actually relayed. The voice-over is followed by Chaplin's pantomimic ridicule of Hynkel, providing Chaplin's audience with Hitler/Hynkel from two angles at once—the demented and dangerous dictator and his ridiculous doppelganger.

The rhetorical figures in Chaplin's verbal lampooning of Hynkel are numerous as well. But more pertinent to our discussion of the dangers of speech, they eerily illustrate what Burke warned of in his discussion of the classical use of such figures. Contrary to viewing them as merely "obtrusive, sheer decadent decoration," he recognizes that "even the most ostentatious of them arose out of great functional urgency," stating that both pagan and Christian rhetoric has been historically emboldened by such verbal affectation.[37] For example, although comedically delivered, Chaplin's speech mimics precisely the kinds of rhetorical devices that Hitler deployed to gain the frenzied support of his followers—disparagement (*extenuatio*): "Democracy est strunk," "Liberty est strunck," "Freesprechen est strunck"; digression (*digressio*): recalling Herring and Garbitsch, as the voice-over says, "His Excellency recalls the struggles of his early day, shared by his two comrades"; antithesis (*contentio*): "Die Aryan" vs. "Die Juden"; taking the audience into partnership (*communicatio*); and the obvious raising of the voice to the point of frenzy for purposes of amplification (*augendi causa*).[38] The combining of pantomime, vocal performance, and the disjunctive voice-over highlights both the real danger of speech and the ridiculousness of Hynkel. Thus, Chaplin himself realized the possibilities of working his art into the medium of talkies: in pantomime the ridiculous (ugly) and beautiful can be coincident, both unifying and deconstructive.

In addition, the scene imitates the artistic proofs[39] that also led to tragic acts perpetrated against the Jews. In "The Rhetoric of Hitler's 'Battle'," Burke identifies Hitler's major rhetorical tropes that established his rhetorical effectiveness. In Hynkel's opening speech and throughout the film, Chaplin burlesques each one, thus reducing them to the ridiculous, a form of the ugly: inborn dignity ("The Aryan, Ah, the Aryan maiden"); projection device (the scapegoating of the Jews—"die Juden, die Juden!"); symbolic rebirth (the conflation of poison and mania is obvious in the call for a new "Tomania"); commercial use (attacking Jewish finance, leaving Aryan finance in control—this idea is illustrated in the next scene in the ghetto and later when Hynkel seeks Jewish finance to fund his war).[40]

The fused verbal and silent images embodied in the Hynkel speech represent a twofold ideation: the ridiculousness of Hitler and the beauty and effectiveness of pantomime. However, Chaplin complicates his stance on the beauty of silence and the dangers of speech as the scene ends. Following his incendiary oration against the Jews, Hynkel heeds Garbitsch's advice about "rousing the people's anger" toward them and enacting "violence against the Jews." Hynkel responds: "Perhaps you're right. Things have been quiet in the ghetto lately." Both men recognize and fear the subversive power of silence. As Kennan Ferguson in "Silence: A Politics" asserts: "Those who wish to build and reinforce community mention silence as a threat to community, as failure and malfunction. Silence is that which is imposed upon marginalized groups, for example, so it is easily assumed that silence must be overcome."[41]

The next scene cuts to the ghetto as the barber returns home after his release from the hospital. Unlike the battlefield scene where he moves between the Tomanian army and the enemy, in the ghetto the barber rejoins his community. His presence is appreciated there. Yet, even with a sympathetic audience to listen, the barber still doesn't speak; instead, Chaplin gains adherence from his film audience for the value of silence as we witness the film's second silent dance scene, this time between a storm trooper and the barber. The dance begins after the barber is caught washing off the linguistic signifiers of his marginality—the double cross and "Jew" painted on his window. A storm trooper approaches and reprimands the barber. Refusing to be pushed around, the barber slaps him in the face with a paintbrush, making the storm trooper appear to be in whiteface. As he tries to escape the clutches of his nemeses (another storm trooper has joined in on the harassment), Hannah (Paulette Goddard) clobbers both storm troopers and (accidentally) the barber over the head with a frying pan. With one storm trooper knocked unconscious, the dazed barber begins a seemingly clumsy silent dance with the dazed, white-faced storm trooper. The performance, however, is anything but clumsy—it illustrates the "bodily intelligence" of Chaplin the skilled pantomime—a concept that James Caron explains in his essay, "Chaplin's 'Charlie' as Merleau-Ponty's Phenomenological Everyman or How Bodily Intelligence Manifests the Personae, Styles, and Fable of Slapstick." After the "dance" ends and the barber has regained his wits, Hannah says, "thanks, Mister! You were wonderful. I enjoyed that" and "that did me good." Here she not only speaks of fighting back against her oppressors, but also acknowledges the artistic virtuosity of the silent dance that Chaplin has just performed.

When other storm troopers return and attempt to hang the barber, Colonel Schultz, upon recognizing the barber, says, "Don't you remember? You saved my life." On one hand, the line explicitly advances the plot; the barber now has an ally who can save his life and peace can be restored in the ghetto. On the other hand, the line recalls for the audience the first scene between the barber and Schultz—a scene in which limited dialogue from the barber accompanies the pantomimic gags of shooting a gun, flying a plane, and drinking water. Both the immediate and recalled scenes represent a space wherein Chaplin creates cohesion between dialogue and silence—a place of coexistence between the two.[42] Whereas Hannah's acknowledgment of the barber's courage validates Chaplin's artistic virtuosity and the beauty of the pantomime, Schultz's comment reminds the audience of the possibilities of silence and sound coexisting. As we soon see, Schultz will request silence of the barber only later to request that he speak. Thus, as the barber, Chaplin functions as that agent of "epideictic rhetoric [who] tries to establish a sense of communion centered around particular values recognized by the audience."[43] For the particular audience of Chaplin fans, those values would be in pantomime, a medium in which he knew he was "without false modesty, a master."[44] They would recognize the beauty of the pantomime and the unifying qualities engendered by silent film—a democratic medium of sorts in which the spoken word cannot disrupt meaning because of language barriers or linguistic limitations. For the universal audience, Chaplin mediates the modes of silent film and the talkie, revealing how the two can aesthetically coexist. His argument for the values of silent film presents (if not convinces) the universal audience with reasons that "are of a compelling character, that they are self-evident, and possess an absolute and timeless validity, independent of local or historical contingencies."[45]

The barber finally does "remember" and is reminded of his role. From this point in the film, he remains relatively silent, the virtue of Chaplin's mythic Tramp figure restored. Moreover, Chaplin ingeniously makes comic use of how his silence is preserved. For example, when the barber tries to speak, Hannah silences him with a hand over the mouth or vocally interrupts the man she has just praised ("shh," "quiet," etc.). Examples such as this proliferate throughout the film, serving as reminders to the barber (and Chaplin's audience) to maintain (and thus value) silence.

THE FAILINGS OF SPEECH AND OF INSTRUMENTS OF WRITING

Until the last scene, the barber projects a variation of the iconic persona that Chaplin had established in the Tramp in order to simultaneously remind the audience of the beauty of pantomime and to promote the values engendered in that art: beauty, gentleness, unity, the "whole range of emotions." In stark contrast, through Hynkel, he demonstrates not only the failings of speech and its implements, but also their potential to create dangerous congregations. Even by demonstrating the failings of Hynkel's speech as an instrument of rationality, Chaplin is demonstrating its effectiveness as an instrument of power and also its effectiveness in his own hands as an instrument of subversion, since he himself uses speech to parody Hitler and, if not to make him ridiculous, to reveal his ridiculousness.

The audience has already witnessed the amplified parody of Hynkel's nonsensical, macaronic vocal utterances and his exaggerated, pantomimic gesturing in his opening speech. Chaplin now juxtaposes silence and sound in a series of short bits in which Hynkel discards the implements of writing (a writing pad, a typed page, pens and pencils) against the contrapuntal clash of macaronic speech. His vocal utterances increase the audience's reaction to the visual depiction of his struggle. In these sequences, Chaplin censures the dangers of speech, writing, and language in general while simultaneously revealing the potential inadequacy of language to effective communication, whatever the medium.

In ludicrous fashion (a bugle call), Hynkel summons his secretary to take a letter. As she prepares to write, Hynkel transforms into a grotesque figure, snorting as he moves slowly toward his stenographer, planning to seduce her. He grabs the pad, throws it aside; she faints, dropping the pencil. Next, he dictates a letter while his secretary types. His lengthy sentences, spoken in "Dutch," receive one click of the keys; conversely, his short sentences yield a rapid, nonstop clacking of keystrokes and ringing of several returned carriages. Chaplin's facial expressions humorously punctuate Hynkel's vocal utterances that have failed to translate to what the secretary is typing. When he takes the letter to his desk and begins to sign his name, the pen set fails him. In frustration, he condemns his secretaries, not the implements of language: "I'm surrounded by nothing but incompetent, stupid, sterile stenographers." In perfect alliterative diction Hynkel demeans the very people he dictates to and is dictator of. Of course they *are* sterile—because of him; nothing fertile grows from one espousing ideas and another prevented from responding to them. Any rhetoric of assent becomes impossible in such a model. Moreover, in leveling criticism, his speech does not fail him—it is hurtful, effective. However, in trying to communicate with another in writing, Hynkel's language is imprecise, misunderstood. Chaplin's histrionic gesturing and vocal performance offer a comic perspective on the potential dangers of language, suggesting that such abuses ultimately fail to unify speaker and listener.

The next scene, Hynkel's famous silent dance with the globe set to the Prelude to *Lohengrin*, is considered one of Chaplin's great virtuoso performances in pantomime. The full rhetoric of the performance, however, relies on the silent routine that follows in the barbershop. Moreover, the juxtaposition of the two begins to reveal the tenuousness of Chaplin's encomium that values one mode of expression, silence (pantomime) over another (speech). Both scenes are pantomimes but unequal in terms of their moral value, as the following analysis illustrates.

Despite the overt, elegant grace, Hynkel's dance is obscene, absurd, and disturbing, exemplifying his megalomania and narcissism and representing division, conquest, and dominance. The macabre use of this opera's prelude containing the famous bridal chorus implies Hynkel as groom and world as bride. In analyzing *Mein Kampf*, Burke explains the "sexual symbolism that runs through Hitler's book" and how Hitler considered the masses as "feminine." "As such, they desire to be led by a dominating male," who "woos them—and when he has won them he commands them."[46] Chaplin's silent dance with the globe reveals Hynkel's sickening qualities (division, conquest, domination) in ways that his vocal/pantomime performance of Hynkel's first speech does not. That speech oscillates between vocalized fawning over the Aryan race and overt impassioned disdain for the Jews—the delivery matches the intent. The dance, in contrast, belies those appalling qualities because it is graceful, alluring, and arresting; yet the incongruity of performance and intent create the scene's sinister disturbance. Again, the silence of pantomime (set to music) best captures those qualities. The bursting of the globe functions in two ways: as the apocalyptic end that must come from the obsessions of a dictator seeking world dominance as well as the bursting of that dictator's delusions of that possibility. Either way, the scene ends in destructive disunion. It ushers in the barber performing a Tramp-like bit in the next scene and functions as a counterstatement to what has just transpired.[47]

Back in the ghetto, over the barbershop's radio, the announcer immediately signals the change of perspective that will ensue: "This is 'The Happy Hour Program.' Make your work a pleasure. Move with the rhythm of music. Our next selection Brahms' Hungarian Dance #5." Reminiscent of a similar barbershop scene cut from the Chaplin short "Sunnyside" (1918), the barber shaves a customer to the rhythm of the music. Every aspect of the scene counters Hynkel's chilling globe ballet. Rather than diminishing humanity through dictatorial dominance, the scene restores it through community. The once empty and cobwebbed barbershop now draws customers from the neighborhood; it has once again become a common gathering place where the radio reaches the community. Despair is replaced with happiness. Work as servitude is replaced by work as pleasure. Melancholic rhythm is replaced by lively rhythm. The anti-Semite Wagner is replaced by the humanist Brahms. And the repugnance of the globe ballet is replaced by the light laughter of slapstick. The restoration is only temporary, as Hynkel's harrowing address to the "children of Israel" follows "The Happy Hour Program." The two broadcasts parallel the incongruity between the globe ballet and the barbershop chair routine—the former involves one person, takes place in a sterile solitary space, and is pervaded with a sinister portent. The latter involves two people, takes place in a communal space and is enlivened with good-naturedness. But the social cohesion briefly attained in the ghetto can last only so long because the voice of Hynkel disrupts the unity and hope Hannah had earlier expressed: "Wouldn't it be wonderful if they let us live and be happy again?" Such happiness will not survive as Hynkel plans another pogrom in the ghetto.

The scene that follows further supports the turn in Chaplin's encomium to silence that reveals his ambivalence to the unifying possibilities of speech. When Colonel Schultz suggests that such a course of action is ill advised and speaks in the "cause of humanity," Hynkel imposes silence and sends him to the "marginalized group" in the concentration camp. In this case, imposed silence functions as repression of speech on behalf of humanity and punishment for the speaker; the scene forecasts the necessity of Chaplin's impassioned speech for humanity toward the film's end. Moreover, the scene illustrates the strategic uses of silence in political conflict, specifically, as Ferguson asserts, how silence "must be rethought as not only a site of repression but also a nexus of resistance or even as a potentiality for creation."[48] Throughout the film, Chaplin deploys pantomime as that "nexus of resistance": with the barber trying to avoid battle, fighting the storm troopers, and escaping capture. In this scene, however, he applies it to Hynkel. The pantomime signals resistance to Hynkel's foreboding speech and simultaneously mocks the tyrant. Feeling ridiculously remorseful over what he perceives as Schultz's betrayal, Hynkel breaks down and weeps. The short pantomime of resistance begins when Hynkel enshrouds himself in a cape. With his wrath toward the Jews intensified as a result of Schultz's speaking for the "cause of humanity," Hynkel reaches for the text of the radio address from Garbitsch. As he does, he entangles himself in the cape, which temporarily prevents him from accessing language designed to inspire and unite "the sons and daughters of the double cross." As a result of his increased wrath, he further divides the citizens of Tomania when he redirects his address to the "children of Israel." Just as the barber's silent dance of resistance with the storm troopers temporarily staves off their return, Hynkel's short pantomime only delays the inevitable authority that his speech wields.

The harrowing address that follows dislocates the citizens of the ghetto, forcing them to flee to Osterlich, once again demonstrating the failure of speech to unify without causing further division. Up to this point in the film, Chaplin has established the ghetto as a locus of unity, community, gentleness, kindness, and beauty—all values of Chaplin's silent films. The scenes between the barber and Hannah, his customers, the Jaeckel family, and the ghetto community represent those values. Metaphorically, the ghetto signifies a liminal space where the potential for silence (silent film) and sound (the talkie) to coexist may be explored. For example, the barber's silence to Hannah's excited talk begins their romance, while he is "mak[ing] her beautiful." The barbershop chair routines produce the laughter of mirth, not the laughter of derision. In the ghetto, when one speaks, another listens. The pogrom ends all that, and the last scene in the ghetto with Hannah and the barber on the roof reiterates Chaplin's claim for unity and beauty, only now we sense Chaplin's ambivalence that silence alone can promote such values.

Once more, he orients our perspective through the juxtaposition of silence and sound. As the strains of Wagner's prelude begin, the barber announces the end of one symbol of unity and beauty: "There goes the barbershop." As he silently watches it burn, his back turned toward the camera, Hannah, as if trying to reclaim that unity and beauty, tells him: "Nevermind. We can start again. We can go to Osterlich; it's still a free country. Mr. Jaeckel says it's beautiful there. . . . Now we can go together." Chaplin purposely breaks the solemnity of the scene with a brief cutaway to Hynkel playing the piano in order to invoke the symbol of speech's evil embodiment. He then cuts back to the rooftop for the scene's final sequence that will forecast the film's closing speech. Hannah looks up at the stars and vocalizes the hope of restoring the values of beauty and unity while rejecting those exemplified by Hynkel: "Look at that star; isn't it beautiful? One thing Hynkel, with all his power, can never touch is that." Two points about the scene should be made here. The barber announces the destruction of the film's silent signifier for unity (the barbershop), which gives way to Hannah's vocal assertion of hope.

Interestingly, the scene also suggests Chaplin's attitudes about his relationship with studio bosses and the ethos of United Artists, which he formed in 1919 with other "stars"—Mary Pickford, Douglas Fairbanks, D. W. Griffith, and David O. Selznick—as a way to claim artistic autonomy. The rhetorical identification here is with the notion that they were stars and deserved protection from the movie moguls.

The scenes in the ghetto come to an end, and the barber's role as an active character diminishes as he and Colonel Schultz are captured. Schultz signals that diminished role when he tells the barber, who has just been apprehended, "Remember your silence will be appreciated." The multiple meanings of the line confer its rhetorical power. Politically, silence protects likeminded resistors to the war. Epideictically, silence acknowledges the artistic merit of Chaplin's customary mode of performance in the present (in this film) and the future (by generations to come). Furthermore, Schultz will need the barber to remain silent so that he can do the talking for the barber, as we witness later in the film.

Chaplin now reorients the film's perspective to a different kind of unity, a deceitful alliance between Benzino Napaloni and Hynkel. The scene represents a bad kind of unification (totalization), not be confused with the good kind. He frames the perspective with a short silent montage of Hannah crossing over into Osterlich, enjoying the bounty of the good earth with the Jaeckel family, and writing to the barber about the "beautiful country" and being "together again." In this place, unlike in Hynkel's mansion, the implements of writing do not fail when they are used for good. All features of this scene support the idea of beauty existing without vocalized sound. Pastoral images portray men, women, and children in harmony with one another. People talk, yet no sound is necessary to witness their communication.

Chaplin invokes a perspective of incongruity as these silent images of beauty and unity are threatened by the voice of Hynkel. Dining with his inner circle, he toasts: "To the invasion of Osterlich." The film's penultimate scene involves Hynkel and Napaloni trying to talk each other out of invading Osterlich. Napaloni must remove his troops from the border, and Hynkel must agree not to invade. The scene serves as Chaplin's final rhetorical proof in his argument for the inadequacy of speech as evinced in the stalemated negotiation. The two dictators are what Wayne Booth calls "fanatical nonlisteners," incapable of producing any honest discourse because neither will compromise. The scene ends in "rhetrickery," Booth's term for "dishonest communicative arts producing misunderstanding."[49] We witness only one side of this rhetrickery—Hynkel's. He follows Garbitsch's instructions to agree to Napaloni's demands with the intent to invade Osterlich once Napaloni's troops are removed from the border.

In some of the movie's funniest moments, Chaplin highlights the deceitfulness of their rhetoric through the perfect mixture of physical slapstick amplified by limited dialogue. Hynkel decides to declare war on Bacteria when he hears that Napaloni's troops are on the Osterlich border. However, once again, Chaplin reveals Hynkel's inability to employ the implement of writing—the pen. In trying to sign the declaration, he reprises his earlier burlesquing of the same action. Ultimately, the two dictators meet and attempt to find common ground on which to establish a treaty. Chaplin illustrates their inability to access speech to convey common goals when each dictator swallows hot mustard. It silences them—leaving them only wild gestures punctuated with truncated vocal outbursts. When Hynkel finally does agree to the treaty, he signs it in deceit, allowing Napaloni to think that he will not attack Osterlich, despite having given his spoken word. In the previous scene Chaplin exposed the indeterminacy and inadequacy of speech; in this one, he now imposes silence via slapstick comedy to censure tyranny and its agents.

Structurally, the Hynkel/Napaloni scene ends the laying out of proofs against the dangers of speech. Chaplin has sufficiently made the case that words can be dangerous, that the occupational psychosis promoted by the use of synchronized sound has unceremoniously diverted its audiences from the values of silent film, a problem that may be reconciled only by the effective uses of silence in synchronized sound films. Yet, in describing his process of writing a silent picture and how *The Great Dictator* differed from that process, Chaplin hints at the dilemma that he faced, suggesting that he was working out the merits of the talkie while still maintaining the values of silent film: "I think in terms of action, pantomime, and as I dictate I act. I construct every part in terms of pantomime and go through each part, building it, extracting all the value that is in it. For this picture, I needed dialogue—not too much . . . but some. And what I have used is, I think, effective, because it is sparing."[50] The word "dictate" is especially telling in that much like Hynkel/Hitler, Chaplin, too, was notoriously egocentric and dictatorial as an authority figure. Given the mounting pressure to finally make a talkie, Chaplin had to develop a means of working in the new mode without fully embracing it or forsaking his preferred mode of expression.

Contemporary rhetorical theorist Cheryl Glenn, resurrecting silence as a powerful rhetorical tool, argues against the longstanding notion that silence is subordinate to speech and that speech points out silence. She argues against Picard's assertion that "it is language and silence that makes man human. The word has supremacy over silence." Countering Picard, she asserts, "it is silence that reveals speech at the same time that it enacts its own sometimes complementary rhetoric."[51] Revealing and enacting are precisely Chaplin's own intuitive rhetorical means for recognizing the equal footing that silence maintains in regard to speech: "For this picture I needed dialogue—not too much, because it is essentially a picture of action."[52] The creation of the barber/Hynkel characters allowed for that complementary rhetoric, and *The Great Dictator* is a vehicle for enacting it.

Unfortunately, critics praise only Chaplin's parodic portrayal of Hitler in the form of Hynkel while diminishing his invention of the barber. Schickel states that Chaplin's interest was "much more with Hynkel" and that the character "stirred him to some of his best work."[53] Even more effusive in his praise, Kyp Harness hyperbolizes: "Chaplin's portrayal [of Hynkel] throughout the film is a tour de force, one of his greatest performances of all and certainly his greatest performance in a sound film."[54] Additionally, both disparage Chaplin's performance of the barber. Schickel contends that in "playing a variant on his Tramp character, the comic routines are less extended, less lyrical than they had previously been."[55] And Harness almost laments that Chaplin's performance as the barber emphasizes his sedentary, passive nature" as compared to the "heroic, dynamic Tramp," claiming to be "no more than a symbol, an amiable, nostalgic ghost of the departed Tramp, merely powerless under Hynkel."[56]

Such critiques, based on the simple aesthetic binary of the characters, miss the more complex and compelling argument of the film's epideictic purposes. They also fail to recognize Chaplin's rhetorical awareness of the kairotic moment. Scholars such as Roger Manvell identify what Chaplin already knew: that in the "rapidly changing climate of the 1930s," the Tramp was becoming "archaic," "unable to embody or universalize the common feelings of the time."[57] Thus, Chaplin's comic routines as a variation of the Tramp are "less extended" and "less lyrical,"[58] which makes perfect rhetorical sense because, juxtaposed with talk, they heighten the beauty of the silent routine while revealing the potential "ugliness" of the spoken word as well as its potential power. Moreover, they give presence to the possibility for the values of each to coalesce. Chaplin must be praised for his use of the barber, not censured, because this variation and performance of the figure provided the best means for the encomium on silence and sound that the film ultimately delivers.

CONCLUSION: TWO ORATIONS, RECONCILING BINARIES, AND CHAPLIN'S SOUND STATEMENT ON SILENCE

Epideictic rhetoric "praises or attacks a man," showing him and all he represents as worthy of honor or the reverse. In satirizing Hitler, Chaplin attacks; yet in doing so, he also praises himself through satire, as an expert in the art of pantomime and the medium synonymous with his name, silent film. He adheres to the epideictic dictum to treat "all other considerations with reference to this one." However, like the orator, he also understands that he must do what is honorable. In differentiating the deliberative and epideictic orator,

Aristotle states that the latter does not "consider whether his acts have been expedient or not, but often makes it a ground of actual praise that he has neglected his own interest to do what is honourable."[59] Applying Aristotle's distinction to Chaplin, we now may reinterpret his last great work and, in particular, the final two orations as not neglecting, but rather realizing that silent film will no longer be the sole medium (Chaplin's own interest) in which he performs. In delivering the humanity speech in his own voice, Chaplin does the honorable thing; he uses the discourse that is not in his own interest. What is more, the speech functions to remind and implore film audiences to remember the beauty of silence.

Perelman states that "the speaker's reputation is not the exclusive end of epideictic discourse, but at most a consequence" of it, an idea particularly relevant to Chaplin's final speech.[60] Granted, the speech received varied critical appraisal and, to some critics, may have seemed like "spectacle."[61] However, Chaplin's choice about *how* to end the film warrants a different analysis. Originally, he had filmed an ending that included a scene of dancing storm troopers, a scene that would seem consistent with the parodic elements of the film. Given that he discarded it and chose the speech for humanity and the "Look Up, Hannah" coda instead, we might conclude that his reputation could not have been the exclusive end of his epideictic endeavor.[62] He had built his career on silent pantomime using one timeless character—the Tramp. For the end of this film, he dispenses with any variation of that figure, offering instead an emotional encomium that exhorts both the particular audience (fans of Chaplin's silent films) and the universal audience (all filmgoers, all of humanity) to recognize the film as a model wherein values of beauty and unity are delivered through sight and sound. The film represents unification without totalizing. Furthermore, Chaplin delivers that praise in the film's most beautiful use of sound.

More than anything, Chaplin understood what the public wanted from him and his films: "an evening's entertainment."[63] This attitude is one of the two functions of epideictic discourse, artistic virtuosity. However, being "mawkish," "fatuous," "feeble," or "preachy" (all adjectives used to describe the speech) makes entertainment difficult. The general feeling at the time was that Chaplin, the comedian, ceases to entertain at this point in the film. As Dilsy Powell states, the speech is "so blatantly out of harmony with what has gone before as to nullify much of the effectiveness of the preceding two hours."[64] But as the final emotional appeal in his encomium, the speech structurally creates the *only* coherent and harmonious ending the film could have had. More than just a plea for humanity, it is a powerful exhortation that works in seamless harmony with the rest of the film's rhetoric.

Recalling Chaplin's claim, "where words leave off, gesture begins," expands our understanding of his use of planned incongruity in the film, particularly in the final speech. Throughout the film, Chaplin highlighted such expressiveness of motion—of gesture—either featuring silent film routines such as the dances or calling attention to gesture in vocalized performances such as Hynkel's speech. However, Chaplin delivers this speech virtually without motion or gesture, yet imbued with expression that is verbal, vocal, visual, and up close. It follows the announcement by Propaganda Minister Garbitsch that "liberty, democracy, and equality are words to fool the people." His words threaten true community; he demands "absolute obedience" to Tomania (i.e., imposed silence) and warns: "let him who refuses beware." His command is met with silence.

The words that follow provide an incongruous perspective. As the barber rises to speak, he slowly transforms into Chaplin. The barber's last gesture is a gentle bow to Garbitsch's gesture of dangerous rhetoric, the "Hail Hynkel" salute. The barber's bow may be read as recognition of this danger, but not capitulation to it. Instead, the speaker, now Charlie Chaplin, will refute it using speech, not gesture. Chaplin's only gesture in the speech, the raising of his hand, occurs simultaneously with the word, "unite." His oration relies on numerous rhetorical tropes and schemes to return the values of liberty, democracy, and equality to the citizens of Osterlich, and it also reconciles the use of sound and silence for his film audience. Its soaring rhetoric not only praises the values of beauty and unity but also offers aesthetic guidance on how silence and sound can enact such values. Chaplin's plea is met with the sound of thunderous cheering.

The opening line, "I don't want to be an emperor—that's not my business," implicitly refers to Chaplin himself. It's a line fraught with meaning. No longer the "emperor" of the silent era, Chaplin willingly accedes the role in favor of finding beauty through unifying the medium in which he performed and the one that has replaced it. Chaplin understands his "business" is not that of the talkie, but that of silent film; not political figure, but entertainer. After the closing call to "unite," Chaplin's disembodied voice exhorts Hannah to "look up," recalling several instances of looking up in the film, countering some and reinforcing others. For example, Hynkel's fear-inducing moans over the loudspeaker cause Hannah, the barber, and the ghetto residents to look up and scatter in fear into darkness (i.e., the basement, the trunk). In contrast, the rooftop scene directs Hannah, the barber, and the audience to look up to the stars overhead, to escape through the visual.

Accordingly, Chaplin's exhortation for Hannah to look up enhances the humanity speech's plea for unity by merging the verbal images of beauty that follow. The speech claimed, "We all want to help one another"; "In this world there is room for everyone." "The airplane and radio have brought us closer together. The very nature of these things . . . cries out for universal brotherhood—for unity of us all." Now in the coda Chaplin's word images convey beauty (the clouds lifting, the sun breaking through, the winged soul of man flying into the rainbow) and require visual imagination—verbalizing them alone is inadequate. This is why Hannah must "look." When Mr. Jaeckel (Maurice Moscovitch) asks, "Hannah, did you hear that?" She gestures for him to remain silent. Her physical ability to hear represents what synchronized sound has only physically delivered. Looking up, she says, "listen." Chaplin's plea to "look" joins the film's last word, "listen," compelling his audience to make sense of what it hears. Thus, Chaplin's speech responds to the opening lines of the last scene: "the world awaits your word," and "you must speak." With Hannah's last spoken word, "listen," what is heard are the final strains of the coda, celestial strings. What is seen is Hannah's uplifted face bathed in light. What is remembered is *The Great Dictator* as Chaplin's sound statement on silence.

NOTES

1. We have no exact equivalent to the Greek notion of *kairos*, but we come close when we use the term to mean occasion, right time, opportunity, or season.

2. Classical rhetoric divided rhetoric (the art of public speaking) into three forms: deliberative (political), forensic (legal/judicial), and epideictic (demonstrative). Deliberative rhetoric dealt with expedient issues affecting future action, its intent to sway the audience on public policy. Forensic rhetoric dealt with past acts to determine guilt or innocence of the accused. Epideictic rhetoric dealt with present issues and was celebratory or censorial in nature, often called a rhetoric of display. Classical rhetoric, as reconceived by twentieth-century rhetorical theorists such as I. A. Richards, Kenneth Burke, and Chaïm Perelman, is called the "New Rhetoric," and it expands the classical notion of rhetoric beyond the medium of public speaking to encompass rhetorical effect in all forms of discourse—ad campaigns, billboards, iconic images, fashion, film, and so on. For these rhetorical thinkers, rhetoric embodies the broad study of communication and understanding; recognizes discourse of all kinds as seeking to motivate people and that meaning is found in intention and effect; and offers an alternative to formal argumentation and instead identifies knowledge emerging within communities that share assumptions and beliefs (Bizzell and Hertzberg 14–15). However, the classical designations of the three forms of rhetoric—deliberative (political), forensic (legal), and epideictic (celebratory)—still serve as useful designations for rhetorical analyses in terms of codifying rhetorical forms and inherent motive of the form.

3. Chaïm Perelman and Lucie Olbrechts-Tyteca, *The New Rhetoric: A Treatise on Argumentation* (Notre Dame, IN: University of Notre Dame Press, 1969), 48.

4. Perelman and Olbrechts-Tyteca, *The New Rhetoric*, 47–51.

5. Re-envisioning Aristotle's notion that rhetoric is the "faculty for observing the available means of persuasion," Burke replaces the term "persuasion" with "identification." For Burke, identification is a means of one individual or group becoming "consubstantial" with another individual or group—that is, sharing the same "substance" or occupying common ground. Therefore, recognizing identifications often reveals rhetorical motive where it is not usually recognized. In Kenneth Burke, *A Rhetoric of Motives* (Berkeley: University of California Press), xiii, 20–23.

6. Here I differentiate between the two, although often both are conflated and referred to as the "Look Up, Hannah" speech. In his autobiography, Chaplin himself referred to both under one heading, "The Concluding Speech of The Dictator," a rather ironic reference, since the speech is actually delivered by Chaplin the man, not the barber or Hynkel. In Charles Chaplin, *My Autobiography* (New York: Simon and Schuster, 1964), 399–400.

7. See David Robinson, *Chaplin: His Life and Art* (New York: McGraw-Hill, 1985), 510, 516. Robinson offers further reactions of Roosevelt to the film and Chaplin's overt political

speeches after its release, in which he calls out "official Washington" and "official London" to open a second front to win the war.

   8. Burke, *A Rhetoric of Motives*, 63.
   9. Burke, *A Rhetoric of Motives*, 63.
   10. Chaplin, *My Autobiography*, 392. Interestingly, many antiwar satires owe a debt to Chaplin's film, if not directly influenced and inspired by it: *Dr. Strangelove*, *Wag the Dog*, *Catch-22*, to name a few.
   11. Perelman and Olbrechts-Tyteca, *The New Rhetoric*, 206.
   12. Robert Cole, "Anglo-American Anti-Fascist Film Propaganda in a Time of Neutrality: The Great Dictator, 1940, " *Historical Journal of Film, Radio and Television* 21, no. 2 (2001).
   13. Perelman and Olbrechts-Tyteca, *The New Rhetoric*, 52.
   14. Charles Chaplin and Kevin J. Hayes, *Charlie Chaplin: Interviews*, Conversations with Filmmakers Series (Jackson: University Press of Mississippi, 2005), 92.
   15. As early as 1931, Chaplin denied any propagandist agenda: "I am always suspicious of a picture with a message. Don't say that I'm a propagandist." Robinson, *Chaplin*, 458.
   16. Perelman and Olbrechts-Tyteca, *The New Rhetoric*, 52.
   17. Chaplin, *My Autobiography*, 325.
   18. Robinson, *Chaplin*, 506.
   19. Perelman and Olbrechts-Tyteca, *The New Rhetoric*, 52.
   20. Chaplin and Hayes, *Charlie Chaplin*, 90.
   21. We may also argue that his attempt to make *Modern Times* his initial talkie supports the thesis that he saw silent film as a unifying mechanism that could create this union between the two mediums.
   22. Interestingly, the naming of film technologies signals the escalation from mere movement of silent films to the vitality of talkies. For example, kinetoscope (meaning "movement vision") is followed by "biograph" or "vitagraph" (meaning "life writing").
   23. Roger Manvell, *Chaplin*, The Library of World Biography (Boston: Little Brown, 1974), 29.
   24. Chaïm Perelman, *The Realm of Rhetoric* (Notre Dame, IN: University of Notre Dame Press, 1982), 14.
   25. Perelman and Olbrechts-Tyteca, *The New Rhetoric*, 31.
   26. Perelman and Olbrechts-Tyteca, *The New Rhetoric*, 31.
   27. Chaplin and Hayes, *Charlie Chaplin*, 81.
   28. Chaplin and Hayes, *Charlie Chaplin*, 90.
   29. Chaplin and Hayes, *Charlie Chaplin*, 90.
   30. Richard Schickel, *The Essential Chaplin: Perspectives on the Life and Art of the Great Comedian* (Chicago: Ivan R. Dee, 2006), 56. Indeed, Chaplin had the idea of talking in *Modern Times*; he wrote a script for it and even filmed part of it before returning to the silent medium.
   31. Kenneth Burke, "Introduction," *Attitudes toward History*, 3rd ed. (Berkeley: University of California Press, 1984).
   32. Kenneth Burke, *Permanence and Change: An Anatomy of Purpose*, 3rd ed. (Berkeley: University of California Press, 1984), liv, lv, 69; Burke, *Attitudes toward History*, 269.
   33. Burke, *Attitudes toward History*, 308.
   34. Burke, *Permanence and Change*, 7.
   35. Burke, *Attitudes toward History*, 308–14.
   36. Schickel, *The Essential Chaplin*, 29.
   37. Burke, *A Rhetoric of Motives*, 67.
   38. Burke, *A Rhetoric of Motives*, 67.
   39. I use the phrase here in the classical sense. Inartistic proofs in rhetoric include eyewitnesses, testimony, and demonstration; artistic proofs are those created by the rhetoric, means of persuasion that rely on the appeals, enthymemes, and example.
   40. Kenneth Burke, *The Philosophy of Literary Form: Studies in Symbolic Action*, 2nd ed. (Baton Rouge: Louisiana State University Press, 1967), 202–3
   41. Kennan Ferguson, "Silence: A Politics," in *Silence and Listening as Rhetorical Arts*, ed. Cheryl Glenn and Krista Ratcliffe (Carbondale: Southern Illinois University Press, 2011).

42. Although he would never achieve the sustained artistic statement of combining panto-mime with dialogue as in *The Great Dictator*, Chaplin would continue to include pantomime in all of the remaining films in which he acted.

43. Perelman and Olbrechts-Tyteca, *The New Rhetoric*, 51.

44. Chaplin, *My Autobiography*, 325.

45. Perelman and Olbrechts-Tyteca, *The New Rhetoric*.

46. Burke, *The Philosophy of Literary Form*, 195.

47. I borrow this term from Kenneth Burke's book *Counter-Statement*, in which he offers literary artists a "counterstatement" to the current "view of the day" in terms of narrative elements, universal themes, and the role of the artist. Kenneth Burke, *Counter-Statement*, 2nd ed. (Berkeley: University of California Press, 1968).

48. Ferguson, "Silence: A Politics," in Glenn and Ratcliffe, *Silence and Listening as Rhetor-ical Arts* (Carbondale: Southern Illinois University Press, 2011). In his investigation of rhetori-cal effects of silence in politics, Ferguson also extends the groundbreaking work of Cheryl Glenn, *Unspoken: A Rhetoric of Silence* (Carbondale: Southern Illinois University Press, 2004), which examines "how silence takes many forms and serves many functions, particularly as those functions vary from culture to culture" (15).

49. Wayne C. Booth, *The Rhetoric of Rhetoric: The Quest for Effective Communication*, Blackwell Manifestos (Malden, MA: Blackwell, 2004).

50. Chaplin and Hayes, *Charlie Chaplin*, 94.

51. Glenn, *Unspoken*, 3.

52. Chaplin and Hayes, *Charlie Chaplin*, 94.

53. Schickel, *The Essential Chaplin*, 29.

54. Kyp Harness, *The Art of Charlie Chaplin: A Film-by-Film Analysis* (Jefferson, N.C.: McFarland, 2008), 165.

55. Schickel, *The Essential Chaplin*, 29.

56. Harness, *The Art of Charlie Chaplin*, 164, 169.

57. Manvell, *Chaplin*, 29–30.

58. Schickel, *The Essential Chaplin*.

59. Aristotle, W. Rhys Roberts, Ingram Bywater, and Friedrich Solmsen, *Rhetoric* (New York: Modern Library, 1954), 32, 33, 56, 57.

60. Perelman and Olbrechts-Tyteca, *The New Rhetoric*, 50.

61. Perelman and Olbrechts-Tyteca, *The New Rhetoric*, 50.

62. Chaplin did enjoy delivering the full text of the "Look Up, Hannah" speech and re-printed it in his autobiography. Additionally, we see similar speeches in his talkies following *The Great Dictator*; however, none is delivered by Chaplin the person, only by characters Chaplin plays.

63. Chaplin and Hayes, *Charlie Chaplin*, 81.

64. Schickel, *The Essential Chaplin*, 234.

Bibliography

Adams, James Truslow. *The Epic of America.* Boston: Little, Brown, and Company, 1931.

Adas, Michael. *Machines as Measures of Men: Science, Technology, and Ideologies of Western Dominance.* Ithaca, NY: Cornell University Press, 1992.

Adorno, Theodor. "Chaplin Times Two." In *The Essential Chaplin: Perspectives on the Art and the Life of the Great Comedian,* edited by Richard Schickel, 267–72. Chicago: Ivan R. Dee, 2006.

Allen, Robert C. *Horrible Prettiness: Burlesque and American Culture.* Chapel Hill: University of North Carolina Press, 1991.

Allen, Robert C., and Douglas Gomery. *Film History: Theory and Practice.* New York: McGraw-Hill, 1985.

Anderson, Sherwood. *Perhaps Women.* New York: Boni and Liveright, 1931.

Aristotle. "Poetics." In *The Complete Works of Aristotle,* 2316–40. The Revised Oxford Translation. Edited by Jonathan Barnes. Volume 2. Princeton, NJ: Princeton University Press, 1984.

Aristotle, W. Rhys Roberts, Ingram Bywater, and Friedrich Solmsen. *Rhetoric.* New York: Modern Library, 1954.

Arnheim, Rudolf. *Film as Art.* Berkeley: University of California Press, 1957.

Auerbach, Jonathan. *Body Shots: Early Cinema's Incarnations.* Berkeley: University of California Press, 2007.

Auslander, Philip. *Liveness: Performance in a Mediatized Culture.* London: Routledge, 1999.

Bakhtin, Mikhail. *Rabelais and His World.* Translated by Helene Iswolsky. Bloomington: Indiana University Press, 1984.

Barthes, Roland. *Image-Music-Text.* Edited and translated by Stephen Heath. New York: Hill and Wang, 1977.

Barton, Robert, and Annie McGregor. *Theater in Your Life.* Belmont, CA: Wadsworth Publishing, 2008.

Bataille, Georges. "Un-Knowing: Laughter and Tears." Translated by Annette Michelson. *October* 36 (spring 1986): 89–102.

Bazin, André. "Charlie Chaplin." In *What Is Cinema?,* 144–53. Edited and translated by Hugh Gray. Volume 1. 1948. Reprint, Berkeley: University of California Press, 1967.

———. "The Grandeur of Limelight." In *What Is Cinema?,* 124–39. Edited and translated by Hugh Gray. Volume 2. 1952. Reprint, Berkeley: University of California Press, 1971.

———. "The Myth of Monsieur Verdoux." In *What Is Cinema?,* 102–23. Edited and translated by Hugh Gray. Volume 2. 1952. Reprint, Berkeley: University of California Press, 1971.

———. "The Myth of Stalin in Soviet Cinema." In *Bazin at Work: Major Essays and Reviews from the Forties and Fifties*, 23–40. Edited by Bert Cardullo and translated by Alain Piette and Bert Cardullo. 1950. Reprint, New York: Routledge, 1997.

———. "Pastiche or Postiche: Or, Nothingness over a Moustache." In *Essays on Chaplin*, 15–21. Edited and translated by Jean Bodon. 1945. Reprint, New Haven, CT: University of New Haven Press, 1985.

Behind the Screen. Directed by Charles Chaplin. Mutual Films, 1916. http://archive.org/details/ CC_1916_11_13_BehindtheScreen.

Benjamin, Walter. "The Work of Art in the Age of Its Mechanical Reproducibility." In *The Work of Art in the Age of Its Technological Reproducibility and Other Writings on Media*, 19–55. Edited by Michael W. Jennings, Brigid Doherty, and Thomas Y. Levin. Translated by Edmund Jephcott, Rodney Livingstone, Howard Eiland, and others. Cambridge, MA: Harvard University Press, 2008.

Bergson, Henri. *Le Rire: Essai Sur La Signification du Comique.* 7th ed. Paris: Félix Alcan et Guillaumin Réunies, 1911.

———. "Laughter." In *Comedy*, edited by Wylie Sypher, 61–192. Baltimore: Johns Hopkins University Press, 1980.

———. *Laughter: An Essay on the Meaning of the Comic.* Translated by Cloudesley Brereton and Fred Rothwell. New York: Macmillan, 1911.

Billington, David P. *Power, Speed, and Form: Engineers and the Making of the Twentieth Century.* Princeton, NJ: Princeton University Press, 2006.

Billington, David P., and Donald C. Jackson. *Big Dams of the New Deal Era: A Confluence of Engineering and Politics.* Norman: University of Oklahoma Press, 2006.

Bizzell, Patricia, and Bruce Hertzberg. *The Rhetorical Tradition: Readings from Classical Times to the Present.* New York: Bedford/St. Martin's, 2000.

Black, Donald D. "Pathological Laughter: A Review of the Literature." *The Journal of Nervous and Mental Disease* 170, no. 2 (1982): 67–71.

Booth, Wayne C. *The Rhetoric of Rhetoric: The Quest for Effective Communication.* Blackwell Manifestos. Malden, MA: Blackwell, 2004.

Brinkley, Alan. *The Unfinished Nation: A Concise History of the American People.* Volume 2, *From 1865.* 4th ed. Boston: McGraw Hill, 2004.

Brod, Harry, and Michael Kaufman, eds. *Theorizing Masculinities.* Thousand Oaks, CA: Sage Publications, 1994.

Brodersen, Momme. *Walter Benjamin: A Biography.* Translated by Malcolm R. Green and Ingrida Ligers. New York: Verso, 1996.

Brook, Peter. *The Empty Space: A Book about the Theatre: Deadly, Holy, Rough, Immediate.* London: Touchstone, 1995.

Brunius, Jacques Bernard. "Monsieur Verdoux encore et toujours aux ordres de l'amour." *La revue du cinéma* 2, no. 11 (1948): 29–42.

Burke, Kenneth. *Attitudes toward History.* 3rd ed. Berkeley: University of California Press, 1984.

———. *Counter-Statement.* 2nd ed. Berkeley: University of California Press, 1968.

———. *Permanence and Change: An Anatomy of Purpose.* 3rd ed. Berkeley: University of California Press, 1984.

———. *The Philosophy of Literary Form: Studies in Symbolic Action.* 2nd ed. Baton Rouge: Louisiana State University Press, 1967.

———. *A Rhetoric of Motives.* Berkeley: University of California Press, 1969.

A Burlesque on Carmen. Directed by Charles Chaplin. Essanay, 1915. http://archive.org/ details/CC_1915_12_18_ABurlesqueOnCarmen.

Butler, Judith. *Gender Trouble: Feminism and the Subversion of Identity.* New York: Routledge, 1990.

———. *The Judith Butler Reader.* Edited by Sara Salih with Judith Butler. Malden, MA: Blackwell, 2004.

Callahan, Sean. *Margaret Bourke-White: Photographer.* New York: Bulfinch, 1998.

Caron, James E. "From Ethology to Aesthetics: Evolution as a Theoretical Paradigm for Research on Laughter, Humor, and other Comic Phenomena." *Humor: International Journal of Humor Research* 15, no. 3 (2002): 245–81.

———. "Grotesque Naturalism: The Significance of the Comic in *McTeague*." *Texas Studies in Literature and Language* 31, no. 2 (summer 1989): 288–317.

———. "Silent Slapstick Film as Ritualized Clowning: The Example of Charlie Chaplin." *Studies in American Humor* 3, no. 14 (2006): 5–22.

Carrigan, Tim, Bob Connell, and John Lee. "Toward a New Sociology of Masculinity." In *The Making of Masculinities: The New Men's Studies*, edited by Harry Brod, 63–97. Boston: Allen & Unwin, 1987.

Carroll, Noel. *Comedy Incarnate: Buster Keaton, Physical Humor, and Bodily Coping.* Malden, MA: Blackwell, 2007.

Chaplin, Charles. "A Comedian Sees the World." *Woman's Home Companion* (September 1933): 7–10, 80, 86–89; (October 1933): 15–17, 102, 104, 106, 108; (November 1933): 15–17, 100, 102, 104, 113, 115, 116, 119; (December 1933): 21–23, 36, 38, 42, 44; (January 1934): 21–23, 86.

———. *My Autobiography.* 1964. New York: Simon and Schuster, 1978.

———. *My Life in Pictures.* New York: Grosset & Dunlap, 1974.

———. *My Trip Abroad.* New York: Harper's, 1922.

Chaplin, Charles, and Kevin J. Hayes. *Charlie Chaplin: Interviews.* Conversations with Filmmakers Series. Jackson: University Press of Mississippi, 2005.

Chauncey, George. *Gay New York: Gender, Urban Culture, and the Making of the Gay Male World, 1890–1940.* New York: Basic Books, 1994.

Chion, Michel. *Audio-Vision: Sound on Screen.* Translated by Claudia Gorbman. New York: Columbia University Press, 1994.

———. *The Voice in Cinema.* Translated by Claudia Gorbman. New York: Columbia University Press, 1999.

The Circus. Directed by Charles Chaplin. United Artists, 1928. Burbank, CA: Warner Home Video, 2004. Two-Disc Special Edition DVD.

City Lights. Directed by Charles Chaplin. United Artists, 1931. Chatsworth, CA: Image Entertainment, 1994.

Clayton, Adam. *The Body in Hollywood Slapstick.* Jefferson, NC: McFarland, 2007.

Cole, Robert. "Anglo-American Anti-Fascist Film Propaganda in a Time of Neutrality: The Great Dictator, 1940." *Historical Journal of Film, Radio and Television* 21, no. 2 (2001): 137–52.

Connell, R. W. *Gender.* Cambridge, UK: Polity, 2002.

———. *Masculinities.* Berkeley: University of California Press, 1995.

A Countess from Hong Kong. Directed by Charles Chaplin. Universal, 1967.

Cressey, Paul Goalby. *The Taxi-Dance Hall: A Sociological Study in Commercialized Recreation and City Life.* Chicago: University of Chicago Press, 2008.

Daub, Adrian. "Hannah, Can You Hear Me?—Chaplin's *Great Dictator*, 'Schtonk,' and the Vicissitudes of Voice." *Criticism* 51, no. 3 (summer 2009): 451–82.

Dauer, Francis W. "The Nature of Fictional Characters and the Referential Fallacy." *The Journal of Aesthetics and Art Criticism* 53, no. 1 (1995): 31–38.

Derrida, Jacques. "Différance." In *Deconstruction in Context: Literature and Philosophy*, 396–420. Edited by Mark C. Taylor. Chicago: University of Chicago Press, 1986.

———. "Introduction: Desistance." In *Typography: Mimesis, Philosophy, Politics*, 1–42. Edited by Christopher Fynsk and Philippe Lacoue-Labarthe. Translated by Christopher Fynsk. Cambridge, MA: Harvard University Press, 1989.

———. *Of Grammatology.* Translated by Gayatri Chakravorty Spivak. Baltimore: Johns Hopkins University Press, 1976.

———. *Positions.* Translated by Alan Bass. Chicago: University of Chicago Press, 1981.

———. *Specters of Marx: The State of the Debt, the Work of Mourning, and the New International.* Translated by Peggy Kamuf. New York: Routledge, 1994.

Dickinson, Kay, ed. *Movie Music, the Film Reader.* London: Routledge, 2003.

A Dog's Life. Directed by Charles Chaplin. First National Pictures, 1918.

Dolar, Mladen. *A Voice and Nothing More*. Cambridge and London: The MIT Press, 2006.

Doss, Erika. "Toward an Iconography of American Labor: Work, Workers, and the Work Ethic in American Art, 1930–1945." *Design Issues* 13, no. 1 (spring 1997): 53–65.

Douglas, Mary. *Purity and Danger: An Analysis of the Concepts of Pollution and Taboo*. London: Routledge, 1991.

Eco, Umberto. "The Comic and the Rule." In *Travels in Hyperreality*, 269–78. Translated by William Weaver. San Diego: Harcourt & Brace, 1986.

Ellis, Jack C., and Betsy A. McLane. *A New History of the Documentary Film*. New York: Continuum, 2005.

Evelinoff, Boris. Letter to Arthur Kelly. 12 December 1935. Charlie Chaplin Archive, Cineteca di Bologna, Bologna, Italy.

———. Letter to Charles Chaplin. 12 December 1935. Charlie Chaplin Archive, Cineteca di Bologna, Bologna, Italy.

Ferguson, Kennan. "Silence: A Politics." In *Silence and Listening as Rhetorical Arts*, edited by Cheryl Glenn and Krista Ratcliffe. Carbondale: Southern Illinois University Press, 2011.

Fielding, Raymond. *The American Newsreel: A Complete History*. 2nd ed. Jefferson, NC: McFarland, 2004.

Filene, Peter G. *Him/Her/Self: Gender Identities in Modern America*. Baltimore: Johns Hopkins University Press, 1998.

"The Floorwalker." Directed by Charles Chaplin. Mutual Films, 1916. http://archive.org/details/CC_1916_05_15_TheFloorwalker.

França, José-Augusto. *Le self-made myth*. Lisbon: Inquirito, 1954.

Freedman, Russell. *Kids at Work: Lewis Hine and the Crusade against Child Labor*. London: Sandpiper, 1998.

Fry, William F., Jr. "Charlie Chaplin: An Embodiment of Paradox (le comique et la terreur)." In *Charlie Chaplin: His Reflection in Modern Times*, edited by Adolphe Nysenholc, 61–66. Berlin: Mouton de Gruyter, 1991.

Gittelman, Sol. "Fritz Lang's *Metropolis* and Georg Kaiser's *Gas I*: Film, Literature, and the Crisis of Technology." *Teaching German* 12, no. 2 (autumn 1979): 27–30.

Glenn, Cheryl. *Unspoken: A Rhetoric of Silence*. Carbondale: Southern Illinois University Press, 2004.

Glenn, Cheryl, and Krista Ratcliffe. *Silence and Listening as Rhetorical Arts*. Carbondale: Southern Illinois University Press, 2011.

The Gold Rush. Directed by Charles Chaplin. United Artists, 1925. Chatsworth, CA: Image Entertainment, 1994. DVD.

Gordon, Mel. *Lazzi: The Comic Routines of the Commedia dell'arte*. New York: Performing Arts Journal Publications, 1983.

The Great Dictator. Directed by Charles Chaplin. United Artists, 1940. Chatsworth, CA: Image Entertainment, 1994. DVD.

Gunning, Tom. "The Cinema of Attraction: Early Film, Its Spectator and the Avant-Garde." *Wide Angle* 8, no. 3/4 (1986): 229–35.

———. "Mechanisms of Laughter: The Devices of Slapstick." In *Slapstick Comedy*, edited by Tom Paulus and Rob King, 137–51. New York: Routledge, 2010.

Hamper, Ben. *Rivethead: Tales from the Assembly Line*. New York: Warner Books, 1992.

Harness, Kyp. *The Art of Charlie Chaplin: A Film-by-Film Analysis*. Jefferson, NC: McFarland, 2008.

Hearn, Jeff. *The Gender of Oppression: Men, Masculinity, and the Critique of Marxism*. New York: St. Martin's Press, 1987.

Hine, Lewis. *Empire State Building*. Munich: Prestel-Verlag, 1998.

———. *Men at Work*. 1932. Reprint, New York: Dover, 1977.

Howe, Lawrence. "Charlie Chaplin in the Age of Mechanical Reproduction: Reflexive Ambiguity in *Modern Times*." *College Literature* 40, no. 1 (January 2013): 45–65.

Huff, Theodore. *Charlie Chaplin*. New York: Arno Press, 1972.

———. *The Early World of Charles Chaplin*. New York: Gordon Press, 1978.

Jacobs, Lewis. *The Rise of the American Film*. New York: Harcourt-Brace, 1939.

Bibliography 217

Jaffe, Ira S. "Chaplin's Labor of Performance: *The Circus* and *Limelight*." *Literature Film Quarterly* 12, no. 3 (1984): 202–10.
Jameson, Frederic. *Postmodernism, or the Cultural Logic of Late Capitalism*. Durham, NC: Duke University Press, 1991.
The Jazz Singer. Directed by Alan Crosland. Warner Bros., 1927.
Joyce, Lucia. "Charlie et Les Gosses." *Le Disque Vert* 3, nos. 4–5 (1924): 76–78.
Kamin, Dan. *The Comedy of Charlie Chaplin: Artistry in Motion.* Lanham, MD: Scarecrow, 2008.
Kasson, John. *Civilizing the Machine: Technology and Republican Values in America, 1776–1900*. New York: Grossman, 1976.
Kerr, Walter. *The Silent Clowns*. New York: Alfred A. Knopf, 1975.
Kibler, M. Alison. *Rank Ladies: Gender and Cultural Hierarchy in American Vaudeville*. Chapel Hill: University of North Carolina Press, 1999.
Kimmel, Michael S. *Manhood in America: A Cultural History.* 2nd ed. New York: Oxford University Press, 2006.
Kline, Ronald R. "Ideology and the New Deal 'Fact Film' *Power and the Land*." *Public Understanding of Science* 6, no. 1 (January 1997): 19–30.
Kohen-Raz, Odeya. "The Ethics of 'Contra-Lying' in Narrative Holocaust Films." In *Just Images: Ethics and the Cinematic*, edited by Boaz Hagin, Sandra Meiri, Raz Yosef, and Anat Zanger, 158–83. Newcastle: Cambridge Scholars Publishing, 2011.
Komarovsky, Mirra. *The Unemployed Man and His Family.* 1940. Reprint, New York: Arno Press, 1971.
Lacan, Jacques. *The Four Fundamental Concepts of Psychoanalysis*. Edited by Jacques-Alain Miller. Translated by Alan Sheridan. New York: W. W. Norton, 1978.
Lacoue-Labarthe, Philippe. "The Caesura of the Speculative." In *Typography: Mimesis, Philosophy, Politics*, 208–47. Edited by Christopher Fynsk and Philippe Lacoue-Labarthe. Translated by Christopher Fynsk. Cambridge, MA: Harvard University Press, 1989.
———. "Diderot: Paradox and Mimesis." In *Typography: Mimesis, Philosophy, Politics*, 248–66. Edited by Christopher Fynsk and Philippe Lacoue-Labarthe. Translated by Christopher Fynsk. Cambridge, MA: Harvard University Press, 1989.
———. "Typography." In *Typography: Mimesis, Philosophy, Politics*, 43–138. Edited by Christopher Fynsk and Philippe Lacoue-Labarthe. Translated by Christopher Fynsk. Cambridge, MA: Harvard University Press, 1989.
Langer, Susanne. "The Great Dramatic Forms: The Comic Rhythm." In *Feeling and Form*, 326–50. London: Routledge & Kegan Paul, 1953.
Levi-Strauss, Claude. *Structural Anthropology*. Translated by Claire Jakobson and Brooke Schoepf. New York: Basic Books, 1963.
Levy, Stephen. *The Perfect Thing: How the iPod Shuffles Commerce, Culture, and Coolness*. New York: Simon and Schuster, 2006.
Lienhard, John. *Inventing Modern: Growing Up with X-Rays, Skyscrapers, and Tail Fins*. Oxford: Oxford University Press, 2006.
Limelight. Directed by Charles Chaplin. United Artists, 1952. Burbank, CA: Warner Home Video, 2004. DVD.
Louvish, Simon. *Chaplin: The Tramp's Odyssey*. London: Faber and Faber, 2009.
Lynn, Kenneth S. *Charlie Chaplin and His Times*. New York: Simon and Schuster, 1997.
Mac an Ghaill, Máirtín, and Chris Haywood. *Gender, Culture and Society: Contemporary Femininities and Masculinities*. New York: Palgrave/Macmillan, 2007.
Madden, David. *Harlequin's Stick, Charlie's Cane*. Bowling Green, OH: Popular Press, 1975.
Maland, Charles J. *Chaplin and American Culture: The Evolution of a Star Image*. Princeton, NJ: Princeton University Press, 1989.
———. *City Lights.* Film Classics Series. London: BFI, 2007.
———. "The Depression, Technology, and the Tramp." In *Film Analysis: A Norton Reader*, edited by Jeffrey Geiger and R. L. Rutsky. New York: Norton, 2005.
Manvell, Roger. *Chaplin*. The Library of World Biography. Boston: Little Brown, 1974.
Marx, Karl. "The German Ideology: Part I." In *The Marx-Engels Reader*, 146–99. Edited by Robert C. Tucker. 2nd ed. New York: Norton, 1978.

———. "Wage Labour and Capital." In *The Marx-Engels Reader*, 203–17. Edited by Robert C. Tucker. 2nd ed. New York: Norton, 1978.

Mauss, Marcel. *A General Theory of Magic*. London: Routledge, 2001.

McCabe, John. *Charlie Chaplin*. New York: Doubleday, 1978.

McGuirk, Charles J. "Chaplinitis." *Motion Picture Magazine* 9, no. 6 (July 1915): 85–89.

McLuhan, Marshall. "Canada: The Borderline Case." In *The Canadian Imagination: Dimensions of a Literary Culture*, edited by David Staines. Cambridge, MA: Harvard University Press, 1977.

Mellen, Joan. *Modern Times*. Film Classics Series. London: BFI, 2006.

Merleau-Ponty, Maurice. *The Phenomenology of Perception*. Translated by Colin Smith. London: Routledge & Kegan Paul, 1962.

Milton, Joyce. *Tramp: The Life of Charlie Chaplin*. New York: HarperCollins, 1996.

Modern Times. Directed by Charles Chaplin. United Artists, 1936. Chatsworth, CA: Image Entertainment, 1994. DVD.

Monsieur Verdoux. Directed by Charles Chaplin. United Artists, 1947. New York: Criterion Collection, 2013. DVD.

Mordden, Ethan. *Ziegfeld: The Man Who Invented Show Business*. New York: St. Martin's Press, 2008.

Morgan, Lael. *Good Time Girls of the Alaska-Yukon Gold Rush: Secret History of the Far North*. Kenmore, WA: Epicenter Press, 1999.

Morris, David. "Body." In *Merleau-Ponty: Key Concepts*, edited by Rosalyn Diprose and Jack Reynolds, 111–20. Stocksfield, UK: Acumen Publishing, 2008.

Mulvey, Laura. *Death 24x a Second: Stillness and the Moving Image*. London: Reaktion Books, 2006.

———. "Visual Pleasure and Narrative Cinema." In *Issues in Feminist Film Criticism*, edited by Patricia Erens, 28–40. Bloomington: Indiana University Press, 1990.

Murphy, Mary. *Mining Cultures: Men, Women, and Leisure in Butte, 1914–1941*. Champaign: University of Illinois Press, 1997.

The Music Box. Directed by James Parrott. Metro-Goldwyn-Mayer, 1932. Santa Monica, CA: Lions Gate, 2003. DVD.

Musser, Charles. "Work, Ideology, and Chaplin's Tramp." In *Resisting Images: Essays on Cinema and History*, edited by Robert Sklar and Charles Musser, 36–67. Philadelphia: Temple University Press, 1990.

My Trip Abroad Contract. Harper and Brothers Publishers to Charles Chaplin, 20 January 1922. Charlie Chaplin Archive, Cineteca di Bologna, Bologna, Italy.

The Neighbors. Directed by Edward F. Cline and Buster Keaton. Metro Pictures, 1920. http://archive.org/details/Neighbors.

Norman, Donald A. *Emotional Design: Why We Love (or Hate) Everyday Things*. New York: Basic Books, 2003.

Norwood, Stephen H. *Strikebreaking and Intimidation: Mercenaries and Masculinity in Twentieth Century America*. Chapel Hill: University of North Carolina Press, 2001.

Nye, David E. *American Technological Sublime*. Cambridge, MA: MIT Press, 1994.

Oberdeck, Kathryn J. "Contested Cultures of American Refinement: Theatrical Manager Sylvester Poli, His Audiences, and the Vaudeville Industry, 1890–1920." *Radical History Review* 66 (1996): 40–91.

"One A.M." Directed by Charles Chaplin. Mutual Film, 1916. http://archive.org/details/CC_1916_08_07_One_A_M.

Paglia, Camille. *Sexual Personae: Art and Decadence from Nefertiti to Emily Dickinson*. New York: Vintage Books, 1991.

Park, Roberta J. "Biological Thought, Athletics and the Formation of a 'Man of Character': 1830–1900." In *Manliness and Morality: Middle-Class Masculinity in Britain and America, 1800–1940*, edited by J. A. Mangan and James Walvin, 7–34. New York: St. Martin's, 1987.

Parvizi, Josef, Steven W. Anderson, Coleman O. Martin, Hanna Damasio, and Antonio R. Damasio. "Pathological Laughter and Crying: A Link to the Cerebellum." *Brain* 124, no. 9 (2001): 1708–19.

"The Pawnshop." Directed by Charles Chaplin. Mutual Film, 1916. http://archive.org/details/ CC_1916_10_02_ThePawnshop.

Peiss, Kathy. *Cheap Amusements: Working Women and Leisure in Turn-of-the-Century New York*. Philadelphia: Temple University Press, 1986.

Perelman, Chaïm. *The Realm of Rhetoric*. Notre Dame, IN: University of Notre Dame Press, 1982.

Perelman, Chaïm, and Lucie Olbrechts-Tyteca. *The New Rhetoric: A Treatise on Argumentation*. Notre Dame, IN: University of Notre Dame Press, 1969.

Perrow, Charles. *Normal Accidents.* New York: Simon and Schuster, 1984.

The Pervert's Guide to Cinema: Parts 1, 2, 3. Directed by Sophia Fiennes. Presented by Slavoj Žižek. A Lone Star, Mischief Films Amoeba Film Production, 2006. P Guide, 2006. DVD.

Phelan, Peggy. *Mourning Sex: Performing Public Memories*. London: Routledge, 1997.

———. *Unmarked: The Politics of Performance*. London: Routledge, 1993.

Pohl, Frederik, and Frederik Pohl IV. *Science Fiction: Studies in Film*. New York: Ace, 1981.

Prior, Alton. *Bawdy House Girls: A Look at Brothels of the Old West*. Sacramento, CA: Stagecoach Publishing, 2006.

"The Rink." Directed by Charles Chaplin. Mutual Film, 1916. http://archive.org/details/ CC_1916_12_04_TheRink.

Robinson, David. *Chaplin: His Life and Art*. New York: McGraw-Hill, 1985. Reprint, London: Penguin, 2001.

———. *The History of World Cinema*. New York: Stein and Day, 1981.

Rugg, Linda Haverty. *Picturing Ourselves: Photography & Autobiography*. Chicago: University of Chicago Press, 1997.

Rutter, Michael. *Upstairs Girl: Prostitution in the American West.* Helena, MT: Farcountry Press, 2005.

Ryan, Michael. *Marxism and Deconstruction: A Critical Articulation*. Baltimore: Johns Hopkins University Press, 1982.

Rydell, Robert. *World of Fairs: The Century-of-Progress Expositions.* Chicago: University of Chicago Press, 1993.

Sampsell-Willmann, Kate. *Lewis Hine as Social Critic*. Jackson: University Press of Mississippi, 2009.

Sarris, Andrew. *The American Cinema: Directors and Directions, 1929–1968.* New York: Dutton, 1968.

Saussure, Ferdinand de. *Course on General Linguistics*. Edited by Charles Bally, Albert Sechehaye, and Albert Riedlinger. New York: McGraw Hill, 1966.

Schickel, Richard. *The Essential Chaplin: Perspectives on the Life and Art of the Great Comedian*. Chicago: Ivan R. Dee, 2006.

Sears, Joseph. "Foot-Ball: Sport and Training." *North American Review* 121 (1891): 750–53.

Sennett, Mack. *King of Comedy*. Garden City, NY: Doubleday, 1954.

The Seven Chances. Directed by Buster Keaton. Metro-Goldwyn, 1925. http:// www.fandor.com/films/seven_chances.

Shull, Michael S., and David E. Wilts. *Doing Their Bit: American Wartime Animated Shorts, 1939–1945.* Jefferson, NC: McFarland, 2004.

Shusterman, Richard. *Body Consciousness: A Philosophy of Mindfulness and Somaesthetics*. Cambridge: Cambridge University Press, 2008.

Sontag, Susan. *On Photography.* New York: Farrar, Straus and Giroux, 1977.

Stallybrass, Peter, and Allon White. *The Politics and Poetics of Transgression*. Ithaca, NY: Cornell University Press, 1986.

Steichen, Edward. *A Life in Photography.* Garden City, NY: Doubleday, 1963.

Stein, Lisa. "The Travel Narrative as Spin: Mitigating Charlie Chaplin's Public Persona in *My Trip Abroad* and 'A Comedian Sees the World.'" PhD diss., Ohio University, 2005.

Stewart, Garrett. "Modern Hard Times: Chaplin and the Cinema of Self-Reflection." *Critical Inquiry* 3, no. 2 (winter 1976): 295–314.

Telotte, J. P. "Lost in Space: Television as Science Fiction Icon." In *The Essential Science Fiction Television Reader*, edited by J. P. Telotte, 37–53. Lexington: University Press of Kentucky, 2008.

Terman, Lewis, and Catherine Cox Miles. *Sex and Personality.* New York: Russell and Russell, 1936.

Thompson, Kristin, and David Bordwell. *Film History: An Introduction.* New York: McGraw-Hill, 2003.

Trachtenberg, Alan. *Reading American Photographs: Images as History, Matthew Brady to Walker Evans.* New York: Hill and Wang, 1989.

Trahair, Lisa. "The Comedy of Philosophy: Bataille, Hegel, and Derrida." *Angelaki: Journal of the Theoretical Humanities* 6, no. 3 (2001): 155–69.

Truffaut, François. *The Films in My Life.* Translated by Leonard Mayhew. New York: Simon and Schuster, 1978.

Twain, Mark. *Adventures of Huckleberry Finn.* 1885. Reprint, Berkeley: University of California Press, 2003.

———. *A Connecticut Yankee in King Arthur's Court.* 1889. Reprint, Berkeley: University of California Press, 1979.

———. *Life on the Mississippi.* 1883. Reprint, New York: Oxford University Press, 1996.

Valery, Paul. "Poetry and Abstract Thought." Translated by Charles Guenther. *Kenyon Review* 16, no. 2 (spring 1954): 208–33.

Van Gelder, Robert. "Chaplin Draws a Keen Weapon." *New York Times*, 8 September 1940, n.p.

Van Riper, A. Bowdoin. "A Nation on Wheels: Films about Cars and Driving, 1948–1970." In *Learning from Mickey, Donald and Walt: Essays on Disney's Edutainment Films*, edited by A. Bowdoin Van Riper, 103–11. Jefferson, NC: McFarland, 2011.

Vance, Jeffrey. *Chaplin: Genius of the Cinema.* New York: Harry N. Abrams, 2003.

Veblen, Thorstein. *Theory of the Leisure Class: An Economic Study of Institutions.* New York: Macmillan, 1902.

Walker, Charles R., and Robert F. Guest. *The Man on the Assembly Line.* Cambridge, MA: Harvard University Press, 1952.

Ward, Lester. "Our Better Halves." *Forum* 7 (May 1888): 258–63.

———. *Pure Sociology: A Treatise on the Origin and Spontaneous Development of Society.* New York: Macmillan, 1903.

Watts, Steven. *The People's Tycoon: Henry Ford and the American Century.* New York: Random House, 2006.

Weber, Max. *The Protestant Ethic and the Spirit of Capitalism.* 1904. Reprint, New York: Scribners, 1958.

Weissman, Stephen. *Chaplin: A Life.* New York: Arcade, 2008.

———. "Charlie Chaplin's Film Heroines." *Film History* 8, no. 4 (1996): 439–45.

Whyte, William H. *Organization Man.* 1956. Reprint, Philadelphia: University of Pennsylvania Press, 2002.

A Woman of Paris. Directed by Charles Chaplin. United Artists, 1923. Burbank, CA: Warner Home Video, 2004. DVD.

Žižek, Slavoj. *Enjoy Your Symptom! Jacques Lacan in Hollywood and Out.* 2nd ed. New York: Routledge, 2001.

———. *Looking Awry: An Introduction to Jacques Lacan through Popular Culture.* Cambridge, MA: OCTOBER Books/MIT Press, 1992.

Zucker, Wolfgang M. "The Clown as the Lord of Disorder." In *Holy Laughter: Essays on Religion in the Comic Perspective*, edited by M. Conrad Hays, 75–88. New York: Seabury Press, 1969.

Index

About the Contributors

James E. Caron is professor of English at the University of Hawai'i at Mānoa. In addition to publishing articles on comic art and comic laughter, he coedited *Sut Lovingood's Nat'ral Born Yarnspinner: Essays on George Washington Harris* (1996) with M. Thomas Inge and published *Mark Twain, Unsanctified Newspaper Reporter* (2008). He is currently working on a book project exploring the concept of comic belles lettres in the antebellum United States.

Benjamin Click is professor of English at St. Mary's College of Maryland, chair of the English Department, and director of the Twain Lecture Series on American Humor Culture. He has lectured and published widely on Mark Twain and the teaching of writing and writing assessment. His current research explores the rhetorical effects of silence in the works of Mark Twain. He is also working on a book that examines humor as a rhetorical strategy in environmental writing, a genre that is sometimes seen as taking itself too seriously.

Randall L. Gann earned his Ph.D. from the University of New Mexico in 2011 and is an instructor of English at Northern Arizona University, specializing in film studies, nineteenth- and early-twentieth-century American literature, and critical theory. A film and television professional for more than twenty years, Gann owned and operated a production company that contracted with such outlets as the BBC, CNN, ESPN, and NBC, among others. He also produced a segment of the *Imus in the Morning* program for MSNBC from 1998 to 2008, and his media resume includes numerous credits as director of photography, assistant camera, lighting designer, and editor.

Marco Grosoli earned a Ph.D. in film studies from the University of Bologna. He is currently a British Academy postdoctoral fellow at the University of Kent (Canterbury). He has coedited (with Monica Dall'Asta) a volume about the cinema of Guy Debord and has published in several academic journals and edited collections, including *Fata Morgana, Il Mulino, Cinema & Cie*, and Zizekstudies.org. He collaborates with various movie journals and sites, such as *Film Comment, La Furia Umana, Sentieriselvaggi.it, Filmidee.it*, and *Spietati.it*.

Lisa Stein Haven is associate professor of English at Ohio University Zanesville, where she specializes in twentieth-century British and American literature and silent film comedy. In 2010, she organized and hosted the "Charlie in the Heartland: An International Charlie Chaplin Conference" in Zanesville, Ohio. She is the author of *Syd Chaplin: A Biography*. Her next book is a cultural analysis of Chaplin's Little Tramp during the years of his exile from the United States: 1953 to 1977.

Lawrence Howe is professor of English and film studies at Roosevelt University. He is the author of *Mark Twain and the Novel: The Double-Cross of Authority*. In addition to his work on Mark Twain, he has lectured and published articles on a wide array of American Studies topics, including the confluence of politics and grief in the AIDS Quilt and macaronic puns as clues in Poe's detective fiction. His scholarly work in film studies includes articles on the mythographic films of presidential library museums, Greyson's *Lilies*, and Hitchcock's *Rear Window*.

Rachel Joseph is assistant professor of theatre at Trinity University. She earned her PhD in drama from Stanford University and her MFA in creative writing from the University of Arizona. Her scholarly and creative work focuses on the intersections between mechanical reproducibility and presence. In addition to recently published articles, "Disappearing in Plain Sight: The Magic Trick and the Missed Event" and "Glittering Junk: Jack Smith and the Vast Landfill of Identity," her most recent play, *The Screen Dreams of Buster Keaton*, premiered at the Overtime Theatre in 2013. She is currently at work on a book project, *Screened Stages: Representations of Theatre within Cinema*.

Charles Maland is the J. Douglas Bruce Chair in the English Department at the University of Tennessee, where he chairs the cinema studies program. He is the author of *Chaplin and American Culture: The Evolution of a Star Image*, among others.

Cynthia J. Miller is a cultural anthropologist specializing in popular culture and visual media. Her writing and photography have appeared in edited volumes and journals across the disciplines. She is the editor of several collections, including *Too Bold for the Box Office: The Mockumentary from Big Screen to Small* (2012), *Undead in the West: Vampires, Zombies, Mummies and Ghosts on the Cinematic Frontier* (with A. Bowdoin Van Riper, 2012), and the award-winning *Steaming into a Victorian Future: A Steampunk Anthology* (with Julie Anne Taddeo, 2012). Cynthia serves as series editor for Scarecrow Press's *Film and History* series, as well as on the editorial board of the *Journal of Popular Television*.

Aner Preminger is associate professor at the Hebrew University, Jerusalem, and the head of film track in the Film and TV Department, Sapir Academic College. A film scholar and an independent filmmaker, he has been involved with production, directing, and screenwriting since 1986. He is the author of *François Truffaut—The Man Who Loved Films* and *Law, Ethics and Reflexivity in Krzysztof Kieslowski's Decalogue*, among others. His many films include *Present Continuous* (2012) and *One Eye Wide Open* (2009).

A. Bowdoin Van Riper is a historian who specializes in depictions of science and technology in popular culture and is currently Web coordinator for the Center for the Study of Film and History. His many publications include *Cadets, Rangers, and Junior Space Men: Televised "Rocketman" Series of the 1950s and Their Fans*, coedited with Cynthia J. Miller. He received the Popular Culture and American Culture Associations' Ray and Pat Browne Prize in 2012 for *Learning from Mickey, Donald and Walt: Essays on Disney Edutainment Films*. His current projects include *(Re)Locating the Frontier: The Western in International Perspective*, also coedited with Cynthia Miller.